Further Praise for *Teachers Have It Easy*

"We will have achieved a kind of Golden Age—enlightened, hopeful, and advanced—when teaching is treated as the preeminent, transcendent enterprise it really is, and children are recognized as the foremost members of society. This book maps the fault lines between that ideal and the hard, sometimes brutal realities we face in schools. It charts, as well, a hopeful path for the struggle ahead."

—WILLIAM AYERS, Distinguished Professor of Education, University of Illinois at Chicago, and author of *Teaching Toward Freedom*

"How can it be that those devoted souls who labor so long and hard to teach our children to be thoughtful citizens must work in embarrassingly shabby schools and get paid salaries that are almost at the bottom of the national pay scale? *Teachers Have It Easy* explores this shameful reality thoroughly and thoughtfully. Every public official with anything to do with education should read it, weep, and then get mad as hell and do something about the problem."

—ORVILLE SCHELL, dean, Graduate School of Journalism, University of California, Berkeley

"If American citizens truly believe in building a world-class public education system, we might consider paying our teachers more than third-world wages. Most of us lucky enough to have benefited from the attention and care of public school employees have no idea what these mentors go through—the early mornings, the late nights, paying for school supplies out of their own (already threadbare) pockets. This book is an argument for righting such appalling wrongs."

—SARAH VOWELL, *This American Life* commentator and author of *The Partly Cloudy Patriot*

TEACHERS HAVE IT EASY

THE BIG SACRIFICES
AND SMALL SALARIES
OF AMERICA'S TEACHERS

DANIEL MOULTHROP
NÍNIVE CLEMENTS CALEGARI
DAVE EGGERS

THE NEW PRESS

NEW YORK
LONDON

To our teachers
and all teachers

Requests for permission to reproduce selections from this book should be mailed to:
Permissions Department, The New Press, 38 Greene Street, New York, NY 10013

Published in the United States by The New Press, New York, 2005
Distributed by W. W. Norton & Company, Inc., New York

LIBRARY OF CONGRESS CATALOGING-IN-PUBLICATION DATA
Eggers, Dave.
  Teachers have it easy : the big sacrifices and small salaries of America's teachers /
Dave Eggers, Nínive Clements Calegari, Daniel Moulthrop.
    p.   cm.
  Includes index.
  ISBN 1-56584-955-8 (hc.)
    1. Teachers—Salaries, etc.—United States—Case studies.   2. Teachers—Workload—
United States—Case studies.   3. Teachers—Job stress—United States—Case studies.
4. Teachers—United States—Attitudes—Case studies.   I. Moulthrop, Daniel.
II. Calegari, Nínive.   III. Title.
LB2842.22.E44 2005
331.2'813711'00973—dc22   2004063155

The New Press was established in 1990 as a not-for-profit alternative to the large, commercial publishing
houses currently dominating the book publishing industry. The New Press operates in the public interest
rather than for private gain, and is committed to publishing, in innovative ways, works of educational,
cultural, and community value that are often deemed insufficiently profitable.

www.thenewpress.com

Printed in the United States of America

10 9 8 7 6 5 4 3 2 1

CONTENTS

ACKNOWLEDGMENTS

Journalists are always reliant on people who are willing to share their stories and open their lives. Countless people did that for us. In addition to those whose interviews appear, there were many others whose interviews and emails helped to inform our work. We owe all of them an enormous debt of gratitude.

We could not have produced this without Ellen Reeves, our incredibly gifted editor, and the incredibly helpful staffs of 826 Valencia, McSweeney's, and The New Press.

Very special thanks go to the following friends and family, without whom we never would have found the time, energy, and gumption to complete this: Jean-Claude Calegari, Nínive and Bruce Dohrmann, Nínive Carmen Calegari, Dorothy Russo, Jewel Moulthrop, Robert Moulthrop, and Vendela Vida

Additionally, the following people—teachers, advisors, mentors, volunteers, school district employees, friends, colleagues—

provided invaluable assistance in various ways, and we offer them our deepest thanks for all their help: Robert B. Gunnison, Katy Wright, Amy Rees, Elisa Dumesnil, Christina Henry de Tessan, Ryan Crawford, Lindsey Keenan, Linda Stansberry, Kate Nicolai, Melanie Mah, Rachel Richardson, Phil Roh, Jane St. John, Gavin Pherson, Kate Petty, Alvaro Villanueva, Tracy Barreiro, Dianne Neff, Jean Horne, Yosh Han, Susan Tu, Quressa Robinson, Virginia Apple, Brian Cronin, Frank Barnes, Mark Isero, Eve Gordon, Greg Peters, Julia White, Amie Nenninger, Devorah Lauter, Erin Neeley, Betsy Grady, Dominic Luxford, Eli Horowitz, Andrew Leland, Lizi Geballe, Jordan Bass, Ari de la Oliva, Angie Dungan, Jenny Bunshoft, Mac Barnett, Jamie Yen, Jonathan Dearman, Beck Dearman, Alyssa Schwartz, Lydia Chavez, Richard Ingersoll, David Card, Caroline Hoxby, Henry Louis Gates Jr., Matthew Miller, Allen Odden, the staffs of various school districts (most notably in Denver and Helena), and the media liaisons for the NEA and AFT and their affiliates, who were very helpful in connecting us with teachers to interview.

We hardly had any difficulty finding teachers willing to share their stories with us. Another book could be written with their stories alone. We extend our thanks to everyone who offered to be interviewed: Adam Sawyer, Alda Noronha-Nimmo, Alicia Meno, Alison Frydman, Alyssa Nantt, Amanda Deal, Amy Hufnagel, Andrew Cronk, Annie Holub, Annie McNally, April Niemela, April Sharpe, Barb Meiers, Barbara Gray, Barbara Rose-Loffredo, Beth Daly, Bill Coate, Bob Hilmer, Carmen Ledesman, Carrie Critton, Catherine Fisher, Chenta Laury, Chris Strunk, Christina Straight, Christopher McTamany, Christopher Wolfe, Cindi Swingen, Corrie Johnson, Dammian Tucker, Dan Beutner, Dan Silver, Dana Chavez, Dave Denning, Dave Evans, David Waite, Dawn A. Jaeger, Dean Schuba, Dennis McLain, Dierdre Shumate, Dina Beatty, Doug Hamilton, Duane Richards, Elizabeth

Grady, Ellen Wehrle Knowles, Emily Lewis, Eric Benner, Eric Colburn, Eric Fleming, Evan Milman, Evelyn Soltero, Felicia Sawyer, Frank Tempone, Gerardo Barrios, Gia Troung, Gloria Brown, Gloria Lawrence, Greg Worley, Guilan Sheykhzadeh, Heather Holberton, Heather Woodward, Holly Artz, Jason Heinz, Jean Taylor, Jeffrey McCabe, Jennifer Jenkins, Jeremy Glazer, Jill Bazar, Jill Cavan, Jimmy O'Karma, Jocelyn Morse, Joel Arquillos, John Etheridge, Joseph Perna, Judy Jones, Julianne Eckhardt, Julie Hamil, Karen Herzog, Kate Trainor, Katie Stein, Kelly Lane, Kim Meck, Kristin A. McKinney, Krzys Piekarski, Lara Lighthouse, Larry Schwarz, Laura O'Neal, Lauren Randolph, Linda Hamilton, Lisa Morehouse, Lizabeth Barnett, Lori Hickox-Monjaras, Majorie Garland, Margaret Griffith, Matt Cheeseman, Matt Huxley, Matthew Fox, Maureen Kay, Megan Chrisman, Megan Clark, Melissa Roderick, Merritt Zaichik, Michelle Hurley, Miles Wooley, Monica Goulart, Monique Laliberte, Nada Bizic-Teague, Nancy Gutmann, Nancy Pepper, Nathan Busse, Oscar Guerra, Patrick Logan, Patrick O'Rourke, Paul Callan, Paul Gard, Paul Story, Rachel Cross, Rachel Zindler, Richard Adelman, Richard Zapien, Ritsa Nichols, Ryan Kindstedt, Sam Mink, Sara Jattleson, Sarah Bent, Sarah Olson, Scott Roderick, Scott Clark, Shannon Ables, Shannon Kaisler, Shelby Grant, Shelley Szipszky, Shirley Hirano-Ralston, Simon Sanatana, Siri HHS Khalsa, Stacy Major, Stacy Markowitz, Stacy Robinson, Stephannie Peters, Teena Nash, Tera Fenixx, Tim Swihart, Tina Wong, Tom O'Malley, Tracy Ramberg, Val Haskell, Vickie Wood, Victoria Greenlee, William M. Grothus, Ximena Sarango, Zoe Diacou.

In any effort like this, there is the strong possibility we have overlooked somebody who contributed in a very important way. We hope that's not the case and that we may be forgiven if we have neglected anyone. Again, thank you.

IT'S TIME TO DO WHAT'S RIGHT

When I was growing up in Piedmont, West Virginia, in the 1950s and 60s, I wanted to be a doctor. More precisely, my mother wanted me to be a doctor, because a medical career for a black man at the time was the surest sign of success, a success rooted in smarts, discipline, and motivation, and bringing with it intellectual validation, social importance, and financial security. As a boy pursuing my mother's dream, I loved school, I loved reading, and I loved my teachers, who, I was convinced, loved me and my future. Their job was to give me the information and confidence I needed to be the best doctor my little corner of the world had produced.

I never gave one thought to becoming a teacher, despite the reverence and even adulation I felt for the many who had put me on Piedmont's path to success. It wasn't until my first year of college, at Potomac State, that I began to think about teaching as something I wanted to do and perhaps could do. A professor of English, the brilliantly named Duke Anthony Whitmore, was wholly responsible for teaching me that I could make a life out of what I loved most in all my years of school: discussing great stories and inventive ways of telling them with people who wanted to learn and understand the same kinds of things I did. I have no idea what Professor Whitmore earned when he redirected the course of my career—we talked about making a life, not making a living. In Keyser, West Virginia, it couldn't have been much. The public school teachers in this book have in common with my dear professor the potential to provide information and inspiration in equal and abundant measure. They hold our young people's lives in their hands.

For that, they deserve more than just the fond reminiscences of grateful adults (we agree, I'm sure, that so many have earned at least that). They also deserve the intellectual validation, social importance, and financial security that other trained, skilled, and responsible professionals enjoy.

Let's give it to them.

—Henry Louis Gates Jr.
JANUARY 2005

DO TEACHERS HAVE IT EASY?

CONFLICTING, CONFUSING, AND
MISGUIDED VIEWS OF THE PROFESSION

There are three lines of reasoning concerning teachers and their salaries. The first says that teachers are paid well—perhaps too well. Their workdays end at 3 p.m. and they have summers off, so they should be happy for what they get. The second school maintains that though their job is difficult, teachers are paid adequately, and the profession inherently involves a certain amount of sacrifice—much like, say, the clergy. The third school of thought says that teachers need to be paid more, sure—were there the money available to do so. But with education budgets already chronically squeezed, where would that money possibly come from?

This book's purpose is to convince members of the first two groups that we need to pay teachers more, and to offer to all three groups some ideas about how better teacher pay might be possible. In this book, we take the position that if communities find ways to pay their teachers better, the profession will attract the best and brightest, will retain these teachers, and will be able, within a generation, to build the best education system in the world.

Unless we fundamentally change not just the way we look at the system but the system itself, schools will continue to suffer from the three primary effects of low teacher pay:

Many who could enter the profession don't.

Every year, thousands of ambitious college students consider teaching as a career, only to abandon the idea once the reality of their potential earnings—and the attendant lifestyle choices—sets in. Students who seek a competitive and creative atmosphere—and the prospect of being paid well for succeeding and innovating—are put off by the future offered by most teaching positions. These capable people, perhaps some of the most qualified and brilliant, go into any number of fields with better pay and more freedom. Their opting out limits the talent pool from which teaching draws, and is in large part responsible for the constant teacher shortages with which the nation struggles.

Thousands of great young teachers leave early in their careers.

A recent study by University of Pennsylvania sociology professor Richard Ingersoll found that 33 percent of teachers leave within the first three years of beginning their careers, and 46 percent leave within the first five.[1] Though they enter the profession with high hopes and plans to stay, they find that with their limited earnings and the great pressures of the job, they simply can't afford to teach. Many leave once they start their own families and need more substantial income to support their children.

NEW TEACHER SALARIES LAG BEHIND
BEGINNING SALARIES IN OTHER OCCUPATIONS (2002)[2]

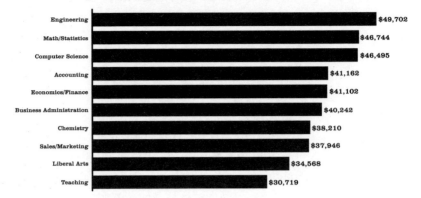

Engineering	$49,702
Math/Statistics	$46,744
Computer Science	$46,495
Accounting	$41,162
Economics/Finance	$41,102
Business Administration	$40,242
Chemistry	$38,210
Sales/Marketing	$37,946
Liberal Arts	$34,568
Teaching	$30,719

Low pay has a debilitating effect on morale.

Teachers are highly educated professionals, but they are often treated as a strange hybrid of babysitter and civil servant—and the salary scale reinforces this perception. The effect can be a slow grinding down of teachers' enthusiasm for their work. The corollary effects of low pay—when teachers cannot afford a decent home, a new car, or a college education for their own children—also weigh heavily on their shoulders. The traditional lockstep model for career earnings, without bonuses or incentives, was a response to an economic reality of another era. Today's college graduates are less likely to seek out a forty-year college-to-pension sort of position. They want to be rewarded for personal innovation, to be involved in the direction of a school and given chances to lead reform efforts. They want to be recognized and valued. They want to dedicate themselves to helping children learn and know their pursuit is worth a livable salary.

Fundamentally, we need to rethink not only wages for teachers, but also how we go about recruiting and keeping them. Right now, we pay teachers poorly, and when these poorly paid teachers fail to meet society's expectations, we blame *them*, ignoring systemic factors—and then impose new guidelines, budget restrictions, and tests upon them, making their jobs even less appealing.

This system, of course, is logically questionable. In any other work environment—corporate, civil, or creative—putting so many restrictions on one's staff would be anathema to attracting or keeping the best employees. In virtually any field, the brightest, most inventive professionals gravitate toward those companies and organizations that afford them the best working environment, the most creative latitude, the best pay, and the most potential for advancement. But in the educational arena, we expect teachers to attain advanced degrees, navigate an endless string of restrictions and requirements, and provide for the future and safety of our children, and for it all, to be paid less than longshoremen or bus drivers.

The fault for this lies in many places. As a whole, the country has a lingering attitude that assumes that teachers are not breadwinners. The long-standing belief has been that teaching is or should be the occupation of a young woman, or a woman married to a man charged with providing for the family. This is, of course, how the profession used to be—dominated by women who were often paid only with room and board.

Historically, there were only two professions available to well-educated women—nursing and teaching—and thus the profession could choose from the brightest women in the country. But now things are different. The same talent pool of well-educated women might choose to go into medicine, law, engineering, architecture, or a thousand other fields, and yet teachers' salaries aren't competitive with any of these professions, in large part because we still see teaching as essentially altruistic. Ask a teacher how many times they've had this conversational exchange:

"What do you do for a living?"

"I'm a teacher."

"You're a teacher? Oh, *good for you.*"

But rare is the teacher who wants to be pitied or spoken to like someone who has joined a nunnery. Most teachers want to be considered the peers of other highly educated professionals—scientists, doctors, lawyers, engineers—charged with shaping the future of the world. Though respect for the profession has grown over the last thirty years, the indignities suffered by teachers and accepted by communities are at odds with the esteem in which we hold them. Teachers with master's degrees and PhDs are often seen painting houses and cutting lawns over the summers, working extra jobs nights and weekends to make ends meet, and neglecting their own children so they can continue to teach ours. These and other subtle indignities—such as many teachers' inability to buy homes near the schools where they work—are tacitly accepted as part of the contract.

This is essentially where those espousing the second school of thought rest their argument. After all, they are fond of saying, nobody goes into teaching to get rich. It's this kind of circular logic—we don't need to pay teachers well because they don't expect to get paid well—that cripples efforts to improve our public schools. It's just one of the strange assumptions made by those content with the status quo. While we're at it, it's useful to examine some of the other assumptions people make about teacher pay and the lives of teachers.

Myth No. 1: Teachers have a great hourly wage.

Often, when people argue against an increase in teachers' salaries, they break down what teachers earn by the hours in their official contract. In the Hoover Institution's quarterly *Education Next,* Richard Vedder writes that a teacher's hourly wage comes to about $29 an hour, which turns out to be more than the hourly pay rate for civil engineers, architects, editors, and reporters, among other occupations.[3] It also turns out to be the kind of fuzzy math that doesn't take into account a number of realities.

• Most teachers work far beyond the hours stipulated in their contracts. A 2001 NEA study, "Status of the American Public Schoolteacher," found that teachers worked an average of ten extra hours per week.[4]

• The contract day does not include time spent at home planning lessons or grading student work, which can range from an hour in the evening (to plan the next day's lesson) to sixteen hours on the weekend (to grade dozens of essays).

• In order to maintain their certification, teachers are often required to attend university classes and professional development seminars in the evenings or on weekends. (And teachers are often required to pay for these classes—themselves—out of their already strained salaries.)

• Finally, a teacher's hour is not comparable to an architect's hour—or the work hours of nearly any other job. Public school teachers often are so busy—keeping forty students at a time safe and attentive—that they can go six hours at a stretch without a moment even to go to the bathroom. For this reason, teachers' hours should be compared to those of other high-stress jobs—like air-traffic controllers, firefighters, or pilots—that afford employees a good deal of time off in consideration of the high intensity of the hours worked.

Myth No. 2: Teachers get summers off.

It's a twelve-month salary for nine months of work, many people argue, or a nine-month salary paid over twelve months. Putting aside the fact that many districts across the country are extending the school year, many teachers find that summer vacations are often not really vacations at all—that they work most of those two months, in a number of ways:

• In order to maintain their credentials or move up the salary schedule, 23 percent of teachers must attend classes during the summer, an expense for which they are reimbursed meagerly, if at all.[5]

• As much as 42 percent of teachers teach summer school or work a different, non-teaching job.[6]

• Much harder to track are the hours teachers spend writing and revising curriculum for the upcoming year.

There's every reason to believe that changes in how we pay teachers could include higher pay in exchange for more summer work—integral to the best schools.

Myth No. 3: There is no relationship between higher-paid teachers and higher-achieving students.

The nonprofit research organization Education Trust compiled studies from around the country about the effects of high quality instruction on student performance. In these studies, researchers used a variety of measures—annual standardized tests, student performance in classes—to measure teacher effectiveness and the impact teachers have on their students. Turns out that good teaching means smarter students. This is what they found:

• On state assessments in Tennessee, formerly low-achieving students gained an average of 53 percentile points after one year with the most effective teachers; their peers gained only 14 points with less effective teachers.

• Over three years in Dallas, Texas, elementary students assigned to a succession of effective teachers saw their average reading scores rise from the 59th to the 76th percentile. Students who worked under three successive ineffective teachers went from the 60th percentile to the 42nd.

• In Boston, tenth graders with effective math teachers averaged 14-percentile-point gains. Those with ineffective teachers posted no gain.

These measurements are largely based on student performance on standardized tests called "value-added assessments," which measure student progress over multiple years and compare actual progress with the progress that might have been expected with an "average" teacher. If value-added assessments turn out to be accurate and useful measures of teacher effectiveness, they will be one of the most beneficial consequences of the recent push for more standardized testing. And if it helps to identify high quality teaching, there is every reason to believe we can pay a premium for that kind of teaching.

Economist Eric Hanushek writes, "The difference between a good teacher and a bad teacher can be a full level of achievement in a single school year." Studies using standardized tests in reading and math bear this out. In Dallas, students who had effective teachers in the third, fourth, and fifth grades tended to score close to or in the top quartile. Students who had a succession of ineffective teachers for the same years were more likely to find themselves in the bottom quartile.[7]

Myth No. 4: The unions are the problem.

Teachers' unions are often the scapegoats for teaching-reform failure. For example, the National Education Association remains a staunch advocate of a salary schedule based strictly on years of experience and educational credits rather than merit. Times do seem to be changing, however—unions have become part of, or instigators of, reform efforts.

• The United Federation of Teachers (UFT) and the American Federation of Teachers (AFT) support programs to identify the most effective teachers and give them more money and smaller class sizes in exchange for taking on the toughest teaching assignments.

• The Denver Classroom Teachers Association, an NEA affiliate, was a driving force behind the development of the Denver Public Schools' ProComp pay system, which links raises and bonuses to teacher performance, skills, knowledge, and results with students (see Chapter 12).

• Montana's Helena Education Association, affiliated with both the NEA and the AFT, worked hand in hand with the district to create their Professional Compensation Alternative, a program that provides incentives for teachers to take on responsibilities outside the classroom and focus their professional development on what will be best for their students (see Chapter 12).

PERCENTAGE OF WORKING WOMEN (AGE 25–34) WHO ARE TEACHERS[8]

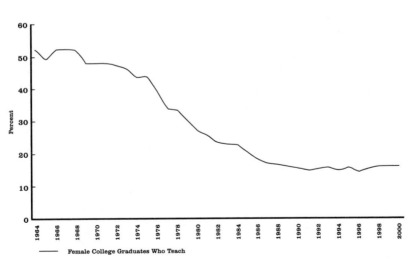

Female College Graduates Who Teach

Myth No. 5: Working conditions, not pay, need most improvement.

Without a doubt, teaching ought to be made a more manageable job. Classrooms should be comfortable places for teachers to work and children to learn. Teachers should have easy access to the tools of their trade—clean rooms, supplies, a phone line where parents can reach them or leave a message. So many basic necessities are frequently missing in our often-dilapidated schools, but equally or more important than fixing the plaster on the wall is putting the very best minds in these classrooms and making sure these teachers can remain on the job. Every time a great teacher has to leave the profession, a school suffers enormously—more so than if one of the computers in the writing lab needs new software. The mood of a school starts with its teachers. If teachers are content and can be proud of their work and compensation, their self-respect trickles down and is felt by every student.

Myth No. 6: Most teachers have a spouse with a second income, so they don't need to be paid more.

As strange as this sounds, it's still a commonly held opinion. Fifty years ago, this might have been a plausible argument. The situation now is simply different. Both employment in the United States and the social fabric of our communities have shifted dramatically in the last quarter century to the point where we can't continue to pay teachers as if their paychecks are some kind of supplement to their spouses'.

• Twenty-five percent of teachers who are married to employed spouses are married to other teachers.

• Mean household income for teachers is $77,739. According to the U.S. Census, the mean household income for other professionals who hold a master's degree is $96,240. The figure for those with a "professional" degree is $137,138.

Teachers are no longer the childless maidens of the nineteenth century, waiting to be married off, nor are they the providers of a paycheck made superfluous by their husbands' better-paying jobs. They are single mothers raising children. They are husbands. They are the fathers of families of four or more. They are single people who hope to settle down with someone and wonder if their pay will make that possible. They are, like all of us, people who need to make a living and who want to raise their families in a home in a decent neighborhood without having to ask their parents—or friends or relatives—to co-sign a loan.

Myth No. 7: The job is comparable to other professions with similar pay scales.

There is no job like teaching. There are virtually no other positions in which one person is responsible for not only the safety of, but the inspiration for, up to thirty-six individuals at once. The level of concentration required is extremely high, given that most occupations allow workers to drift off in thought, to surf the Web, to get coffee any time they wish—to control their own destinies on a minute-to-minute basis. Not so with teaching, a profession that holds its members legally responsible for the well-being of a roomful of children for up to seven hours at a time. Add to that the continuing education required of teachers and the myriad extracurricular responsibilities—from coaching the wrestling team to helping students with personal problems.

* * *

In fact, let's look for a moment at all of the traits a great teacher must simultaneously embody. Elsewhere in this book, we explore more thoroughly the many facets of good teaching; here we'll summarize.

- Teachers in an increasing number of districts are required to have a master's degree; many districts are using master's degrees to meet the teacher quality provisions of the federal government's No Child Left Behind act—and a large percentage of teachers have advanced beyond that degree. They must have a wide range of knowledge, such that they can answer innumerable questions about innumerable topics. In short, they must know a lot about a lot.

• They must be able to communicate that knowledge to a roomful of very different individuals. Teaching is not limited to reading lessons from a book; for thirty-two students there are thirty-two ways of teaching. Thus, a teacher must be endlessly flexible and creative, able to adjust any lesson plan to reach those students who require different strategies.

• A teacher is a moral force. This is often ignored, but teachers are among society's most indispensible elements. The expression "pillar of the community" has no more apt application. Gaea Leinhardt, a professor at the University of Pittsburgh's Graduate School of Education, put it this way in an interview:

"As parents, we entrust our most precious assets to this system. We leave our darling child with this person. That person has to be very worthy, and has to be deeply moral. I don't mean to be fuzzy about that; he or she has to have a real commitment to acting in a humane, honest way, intellectually and in a person-to-person fashion, all the time."

This is no easy task. Most adults resist the notion of being seen as a role model. How many times have we heard athletes and pop singers insist they're not role models? Few other professions require its members to act with courtesy, with ethical precision, with honor and patience—at all times, inside school or out. Because teachers are role models, there is no margin for error in their personal and public behavior.

• A teacher must inspire. It's not enough simply to drill facts and figures into the heads of students. The best teachers instill in their students a desire to do great things, to crave learning, to yearn to achieve. A teacher, therefore, must be a forward-looking—and likely happy—individual. As Leinhardt explains, "You have to have teachers who are prepared to keep offering an optimistic future vision so students can keep working towards that future vision."

Now, have we all had a teacher or two who was not so optimistic, whose ideas about the world were weatherbeaten? Of course. And is it possible that one of the factors in dampening a teacher's optimism is that they aren't earning enough to live a comfortable life?

* * *

Increasingly, government reformers—especially those on the conservative side of the political spectrum—seek lessons from the business world to improve conditions and performance in the public sector. Taking that cue, let's look at teaching and the distribution of funds in a typical school.

Let's work with an imaginary school, which we'll name after a twenty-first-century entrepreneur and call Jeff Bezos High School. JBHS is a large urban school that, according to test results, is not performing well. Its students' scores are under the state average, attendance is poor, dropout rates are high, and teacher retention is a problem. JBHS lost three of its best teachers last year and is having a hard time filling those slots. The remaining teachers are of varying levels of talent and inspiration. A few of the tenured instructors are just going through the motions, and some of the younger teachers are frustrated with the lack of mentorship they're getting from the more experienced faculty.

If we were to follow the current administration's education policy, we would deal with these issues by testing low-scoring students even more frequently. We would place more restrictions and requirements on teachers' curricula. To replace the three teachers who left, listings would be posted on the district Web site, with the standard salaries and pensions offered. Though we know that new policies or incentives would bring in a different quality of candidate, we might be unable, due to district policies, to change the job descriptions or compensation offered.

Now, applying applicable business models, what would a company do to turn this situation around? The first thing Bezos would do is find the very best educators available. "Surround yourself with the best people," Bezos and other successful businessmen say again and again. To that end, he would recruit the best college candidates, would try to poach great teachers from other schools, offering salaries to encourage the brightest teachers to join JBHS. The package Bezos would slide across the table would include freedom to innovate, and incentives built in for high student attendance and excellent results—however JBHS chose to calculate them. Treating his potential staff members as highly valuable professionals—who likely have dozens of choices for careers, and myriad firms vying for their services—would ensure that he'd get the best candidates available.

There is an experiment being repeated at many schools and districts in Los Angeles, California; Helena, Montana; Denver, Colorado; and elsewhere. The experiment usually follows a pattern: district administrators, frustrated with their students' test scores and teacher retention, seek a broad revamping of the system, including and sometimes starting with teacher pay. Though they expect resistance from some teachers, they find the teachers, too, share the same frustrations and want to help create change. They ask members of the community and find that that they, too, would like to see improvements and can see how teacher pay might be a way to solving the problem. So they restructure their teachers' pay. They put teeth into yearly evaluations and give teachers more leeway in creating their curriculum. Bonuses are offered for higher performance—for everything from test scores to attendance to peer review—and coupled with strong base salaries; the schools soon have the best-paid teachers in the region, and thus a highly motivated staff. Teachers unwilling to adjust to this system sometimes retreat, leaving behind the most innovative and ambitious. And because the teachers are inspired, the enthusiasm and pride grows within the school and is felt by the students. The students, studying under exceptional and creative teachers, learn more and perform better. This is actually happening at schools like the Vaughn New Century Learning Center in Los Angeles (see Chapter 12).

.   .   .

The first part of this book focuses on the lives of teachers, primarily as they describe them in their own words. They speak of the second and third jobs they take on in order to make ends meet; they tell of the difficulties they find in buying a home and raising a family in places where the cost of living seems far beyond the limits of their take-home pay; and they speak of vows of poverty they feel they took at the beginning of their careers and the subtle messages about their own social status they find in their interactions with children and adults. Last, current teachers speak about their ongoing internal debates about wanting to leave the profession, and former teachers speak about what prompted them to leave.

The second part of the book is a series of explorations into why a substantial raise for teachers is justifiable. We look at just how complex a teacher's job truly is, and attempt to compare it to other common professions. We hear from people who thought about teaching—who truly, passionately wanted to become teachers—as they discuss why they chose not to. We explore the interrelated issues of prestige and pay, the confusion characterizing how the public views teachers, and the extraordinary efforts communities undertake to avoid paying teachers more.

In the final part of the book we offer profiles of various districts and schools around the country attempting serious salary reform. More and more studies show that the most important factor in a student's success is the quality and aptitude of that student's teacher. Though at first, teacher quality may feel like a nebulous concept, more schools are defining exactly what high-quality teaching looks like and awarding higher pay for meeting those criteria. The effects in these places are far-reaching. There are ongoing, honest, and open conversations about the kind of teaching people want to see. There are hundreds of candidates applying for vacant positions at these schools. There are teachers motivated to both work harder and stay in their jobs. And, most important, there are higher-achieving students as a result. "I think it's a mind-shift," says Becky Wissink, president of the Denver teacher's union, "the realization that the teachers' working conditions are the students' learning conditions. Those are one and the same." We also include short profiles of some smaller or less successful salary-reform efforts that offer lessons for communities interested in beginning their own reforms.

The way our public education system is right now is not the way it has to be. These things can change, and that is the unabashedly earnest hope of this book. Teaching in public schools could be one of the most sought-after jobs, attracting the top candidates from the best schools. Teaching could be a profession that the most gifted college graduates routinely choose over practicing law, and the very best teachers could be choosing to teach in the toughest schools because those schools might be the best-paying employers. This is not an exercise in fantasy. Changes like these are beginning to happen in pockets throughout the country. They can happen everywhere.

But we need to act quickly. Every day, a great teacher leaves the profession because he or she can't afford to teach.

WHY JONATHAN DEARMAN, THE HEARTBEAT OF LEADERSHIP HIGH SCHOOL, LEFT TO SELL REAL ESTATE

WHAT HAPPENS WHEN THE BEST TEACHERS CAN'T AFFORD TO STAY

Greg Peters is finishing a bowl of lemongrass soup in a loud Thai restaurant on Valencia Street, and he's about to cry. Peters is the principal of San Francisco's Leadership High School, a public charter school that has just finished its seventh year. Peters has to hire new teachers for the fall—it's early July— and he's remembering a teacher he had to replace a year earlier, a thirty-six-year-old African American man named Jonathan Dearman.

"When he announced he was going to leave, I cried," Peters says. "I couldn't believe it. Jonathan was one of the best we had. I'm going to cry right now thinking about it. I think our kids are in desperate trouble."

Peters, who is white, has been in education since 1991, when a teacher's starting salary was $16,000, and he dresses young and stylish—like a musician who also happens to be a high school principal. He wipes his eyes and sits back.

"We don't have a single African American teacher on staff now. It's the end of the year, the kids are gone, the teachers are gone, we have about four or five teachers left to hire, and the reason that we still don't have those positions filled is that we've held out as long as we could. And now we're going to hire a bunch of white people, and it makes me crazy."

* * *

In the back corner of HSM Realty, Finance, and Management, Jonathan Dearman is eager to get out of the office. All six feet and 240 pounds of him is squeezed behind a desk that next to anyone else would appear normal-sized but for him looks Lilliputian. His calendar is light today. A visit to an apartment building he's trying to sell has been postponed, so instead, he will take phone calls and run a short staff meeting. It's still early, though, and the meeting won't happen until his oldest sister, Tracy, arrives. She does the property management part of the business. Dearman's other sister, Kelly, brokers loans. With Dearman selling houses, HSM is a one-stop shop for most real estate needs.

Dearman has an envelope to drop off at another realtor's office nearby, and he feels like a cup of tea. There's nothing pressing to do, so he gets up and walks out the door.

"That was one of the first things I realized when I got out of teaching," Dearman says, smiling and strolling—and he does stroll—down Steiner Street in San Francisco's Lower Haight district. "I can leave when I want to. I can go to the bathroom when I want, I can go get a cup of tea when I want, and I can eat when I want. I couldn't do that when I was a teacher."

It's a warm, white-blue day in the city, the kind of morning that highlights the advantages of having a flexible schedule.

"I went back to Leadership," Dearman says, "and I was talking to Elisa Dumesnil [a former school counselor there] and I said, 'How oppressive has my life been for five years, that I couldn't even go to the bathroom?' We didn't even have running hot water! The phones didn't really work. Everything was hodge-podge. There were mice and rats. It just got to be depressing."

When he left Leadership High School, Dearman, thirty-four years old and with a master's degree in education, was making just over $40,000. Two years later, he makes that much in two months.

Dearman's departure left a tangible void in the Leadership community. Jennifer Wofford, another former Leadership teacher who left because she couldn't pay her bills, says she and others on the staff were envious—"in a healthy way," she's quick to add—of Dearman's abilities to inspire students.

"He could get them to do work that none of the rest of us could. We could not motivate our kids the same way. Dearman had this presence at school because he was a great educator to begin with. Also, it was incredibly reassuring for kids to see a very powerful black man on campus, and now we don't have that. Sort of a double whammy."

Lydia Bell, one of his former students and now a sophomore at Gonzaga University in Washington State, takes pride in being the one student who was in every one of Dearman's classes.

"He could be intimidating in the beginning, like that first day of school," she says. "The first thing he said was, 'This is probably the hardest class you'll ever take in your life.' And it was."

For the minority boys at Leadership, he was the teacher who became, in many cases, a surrogate parent. During his last year, he set up an informal support group, a sort of Boys of Color Club. Loran Simon was one of these surrogate sons. Now a sophomore at San Francisco State, Simon plans to become the first African American president.

"The minority men in our class were underperforming academically and Dearman took the lead," Simon says. "Every Tuesday, he and [math teacher] Mr. Malloy would meet with us and talk to us about what was going on and how we were doing in each class, and then we'd strategize about ways we could do better. When we'd meet in those groups, it was like talking to a friend or a counselor, someone who's not going to judge you, who's not going to get upset with you, but someone who's going to try to help you. There weren't any other black men at the school who were doing that. Some of the young men came from Hunter's Point and the Fillmore area, and there's no way they're going to let a white man or a white lady tell them how to overcome their struggles."

Dearman's dedication to his students cost him. Since he'd begun teaching, he had accumulated almost $15,000 in credit card debt, some of which had been spent on classroom supplies. He was so focused on his classes that he often miscalculated the daily insulin injections he needed to regulate his diabetes and once landed himself in the emergency room overnight—only to return to the classroom at 7:30 the next morning. He says he routinely worked seventy- to eighty-hour weeks because that was the only way he could come close to feeling successful. Despite it all, he says, he never felt more than 70 percent effective.

"No matter what you do, no matter how hard you work—and I worked as hard as I could—there was this feeling that I couldn't be completely effective," he said. "I could only really reach 70 percent of the students, and that was working blood, sweat, and tears. That was if I was totally neglecting [my wife] Becky and the kids, in terms of not spending any time with them, and neglecting myself and my health. That's if I just gave all of myself over to it. But, at best, I could be 70 percent effective. That other 30 percent left school feeling like there's no hope. They had no plan, or they didn't feel right in the world. That was the awful thing about working in a school for me. Thirty percent of them, thirty out of one hundred, were going to feel hopeless. It's a setup."

Teaching was a job Dearman loved. Were it not for the pay, the time away from his family, and the pervasive sense of being less effective than he wanted to be, he says, he would have been happy teaching for the rest of his career. As it is, he left teaching with no immediate plans to return—and is so disenchanted with public education that he and his wife decided to homeschool their own children.

*   *   *

Greg Peters, Leadership's principal, sees little hope in attracting and keeping people like Dearman.

"I think, 'Why would people want to come into the profession and do what our school requires, which is to work their butts off?'" he says. "Not only are we a public school, but we're a charter public school. A poor charter public school in California in the Bay Area. We do not pay our teachers enough to survive or to have a family. To me, it's about survival."

The departure of great teachers is, of course, not unique to Leadership. As a charter school governed by its own board, Leadership can make adjustments to its hiring policy—even if such policies are not always successful. But in the San Francisco Unified School District (SFUSD), there are no affirmative action hiring incentives, and creating a teaching force reflective of the demographics of the city's student body—21.4 percent Latino, 14.5 percent African American, 40 percent Asian and Pacific Islander, 10 percent white, and 14 percent "other nonwhite" or declining to respond—continues to be a challenge for the district.

For San Francisco schools superintendent Arlene Ackerman, recruitment, retention, and compensation represent a nest of issues for which there are more questions than answers. In the four years she has headed the SFUSD, teachers have seen starting salaries rise from $32,000 to about $40,000. But she says she knows this is not enough for anyone who wants to live in an urban area, and it's "a far cry from what other beginning professionals make."

"How do you get people of color, people who are multilingual, people who can teach math and science?" she asks. "How do you get them into the school system when they can take jobs in industry and make double what a teacher makes? What do you do for a teacher who consistently gets results—who's willing to go above and beyond and do whatever it takes? It's going to require that we look at this issue of performance and incentives."

But then again, she says, the district has no plan to answer these questions or even to spend any time discussing them.

The problem, of course, is not limited to San Francisco. Linda Darling-Hammond, a professor of education at Stanford University, studies the trends in teacher quality and training.

"Right now the student population in the United States, particularly in public schools, is rapidly becoming a majority of students of color, from a wide range of racial, ethnic, linguistic backgrounds. It's very important to have the teaching workforce and the leadership workforce in education representing the families and the children who are going to school. We need more African American and Latino and Asian American and Native American education leaders so that we can build school environments that are responsive to the students they're going to serve."

There are nearly 3 million teachers in the United States, paid an average of $44,367. Starting salaries range from as low as $20,988 in North Dakota to as high as $36,294 in Alaska. In 2002, California had the highest average pay—$54,348—but adjusted for cost of living, the state actually ranked eleventh, below

Pennsylvania, Georgia, and Indiana, among others. In some regions, these pay levels seem substantial, but when compared to the salaries of those in fields requiring similar levels of education, the wages of American teachers are not competitive, reflecting centuries-old thinking about the profession.

*   *   *

Early educational efforts in the United States differed community to community, depending on the resources available. In some towns, churches doubled as schoolhouses, with local clergy teaching during the week and preaching on Sundays. In other areas, women taught out of their homes in exchange for pennies a day. Some communities with schoolhouses paid teachers with "boarding rounds"—teachers would move every few weeks from one family's house to another and be provided with room and board at each. Not until the early nineteenth century did education become a public institution; school districts were formed and run by local school boards. Then, as now, budgets were tight. Districts saved money by hiring female teachers, who were paid much less than their usually better educated male counterparts.

Teachers of either gender were poorly paid, however. Horace Mann, the school reformer, documented teachers' salaries in 1843 as compared to other professions. He found that the following workers earned significantly more than the teachers at the time: "journeymen, shoemakers, carpenters, blacksmiths, painters, carriage makers, wheelwrights, harness makers, cabinet and piano forte makers." Teachers' salaries were also a concern due to high teacher turnover. One study found that only one segment of teachers—male teachers working in an urban setting—made enough money to provide for their families.[9]

In the late nineteenth century, as the United States changed from an agrarian to an industrial economy, men were lured away from teaching by the prospect of greater earnings in other professions. The career prospects for women, however, continued to be limited to low-paying professions like education. The relative abundance of the female labor force kept the prevailing wages low.

Although teacher unions had existed as early as the 1850s, they did not begin to amass anything resembling their current clout until the beginning of the twentieth century. Around this time, the National Education Association began to advocate two ideas that quickly caught on. One was equal pay for female and minority teachers. The other was a "lockstep" salary schedule, which based pay on the level of education earned by a teacher and the number of years he or she had taught. This pay system is still the most widely used salary structure in public and private education, and it is still supported by the NEA. For its critics, however, it is a fabulously effective disincentive to improve teacher quality and an impediment to successful recruitment. It is also, they say, the reason why teachers like Jonathan Dearman leave.

Had he stayed in teaching, Dearman might have had one of the higher teacher salaries in the country. In terms of real dollars, however, his salary after thirty years would not even have doubled. San Francisco's current salary schedule starts at $40,388, goes up roughly $530 a year for fourteen years, then plateaus. A teacher feels a slight bump up in earnings when he accrues thirty or sixty units of graduate credit (in any subject, not just education or the teacher's speciality). In the second half of a hypothetical thirty-year career, a teacher gets roughly a $2,000 raise every three years. Had he stayed in teaching, at the end of his career—2030 or thereabouts—Jonathan Dearman would be making $70,407.

*　　*　　*

Dearman lives a few blocks from his office, in the Haight-Ashbury neighborhood. He's sitting on his deck, three stories up, while his six-year-old daughter, Anika, points a Super Soaker into the neighbor's yard to see how far its stream of tap water will shoot. The bright midday light reflects off Dearman's nerdishly square glasses, making it virtually impossible to see his eyes—the only remotely unreadable thing about him. His voice booms, his laughter filling any space he inhabits. He moves his large, meaty hands around as he talks, and between the expansiveness of his voice and gestures, he seems taller than his six feet, bigger than he actually is.

The question of how he got into teaching baffles him, as if he hasn't considered it and still can't explain it. He searches for an answer, his hands gesturing uncertainly, until he slaps them down on his thighs. "That's a good question," he says. He turns to his wife, but before she can respond, he launches into his academic and career history.

He grew up in San Francisco and graduated from St. Ignatius College Preparatory School, a Catholic school in the Sunset district. Although his grades were unpromising, he was admitted to San Francisco State University, where he planned to study music. He dropped out after three semesters, realizing he wasn't ready for college. After a quick string of uninspiring jobs, he began selling women's shoes at the Tanforan Shopping Mall in San Bruno, just south of San Francisco.

"Three months of selling women's shoes and I thought, I don't want to do this anymore," he says. "This woman came in with feet the size of this table, and she wanted a seven narrow. I thought—because I had just heard this line from a comedian—that the only way a seven narrow is going to fit on your foot is if I give you the box it came in. I thought, I don't want to sell anything. It just felt very"—and here he raises his hands to his throat, pretending to be unable to breathe—"unhealthy. I realized I didn't have many choices here in terms of what I could do with the educational background I had. That was it—shoes."

He went back to school at San Francisco's City College with plans to become a lawyer, like his sister Kelly, his uncle, and his father, a San Francisco judge. Dearman thought about becoming a teacher but didn't believe he was talented enough.

"I didn't think I could do it. I knew I couldn't cull that energy and inspire. I thought it was the greatest thing to do, literally, the most profound, greatest thing to do. I wasn't really thinking about the money. I just didn't think I could do it. There's all this stuff happening on emotional, spiritual, and intellectual levels where you have to connect with a group, and with the individual, and hold all this together. I felt I couldn't do that, but I'd love to be able to."

He eventually transferred to the University of San Francisco to finish his bachelor's degree. At USF, he began to see teaching in a different light. "I was totally inspired by my political science professors. You could tell they were into what they were teaching. That was the first time I realized you have to love what you're talking about if you're going to teach it. That was the first thing I got."

He got it, but after he graduated, he went into real estate. He took the broker's license exam and began working for his grandmother in the office of which he is now part owner. "I made some good money," he says. "It's hard not to make money in real estate, but I hated it. Completely hated it."

"I needed to make a life change, and my wife and mother-in-law were teachers I really respected," he says. "Becky had been teaching for five years and was brilliant. She would come home and we would talk about classroom management stuff. I was inspired by what she was doing and how good she was. I wanted to check it out, get my master's in education. But I didn't know if I wanted to teach."

He returned to USF on a scholarship, intending to get a master's in education. One of his professors was Herbert Kohl, an education reformer and author of *I Won't Learn from You* and *Should We Burn Babar?*

"I remember being struck by [Dearman's] intelligence and his perception," Kohl says now. "Clearly, he was deeply interested in urban education and transforming schools. But one of the things that was striking about him was that he had a larger view of things. He had not originally conceived of himself as a classroom teacher. He was much more interested in education per se. I remember we had conversations in which I was basically saying, It's one thing to be interested in education, but if you want to really develop your ideas and your commitment and get a fuller view of education, there's no harm in—and considerable delight in—teaching itself, and then comparing the practice and the work that you've experienced with your ideas."

That proved to be an influential conversation for Dearman. He began to refocus his studies toward classroom teaching, rather than only the broader issues of education.

"After being in Herb Kohl's class, I thought, yeah, I'm definitely going to teach," he says. "It wasn't just his class. It was him, hanging out with him. He was talking about all the brilliant things you could do in education, all the things a school could be."

After student teaching at Wallenberg High School in San Francisco, Dearman's first solo assignment was in the social studies department at Irvington High School in Fremont, about thirty miles southeast of San Francisco. At the time, Irvington was part of the Coalition of Essential Schools, a nationwide network of reform-minded schools geared toward improving learning conditions for all students. One of Irvington's central practices was called "outcome-based education," a way of structuring an entire school—courses and graduation requirements—around the set of skills students should have when they graduate. Outcome-based education is often defined in opposition to traditional schools and courses that structure themselves around time (the eighteen-week semester, for instance) or content (modern European history, or American literature).

Dearman's two years at Irvington were successful, he says, but it was a "100 percent blood, sweat, and tears experience." In the long term, working there was not possible. There was the hour-long commute in each direction, his baby daughter was in day care, and his grandmother was dying. "I wanted to be closer to the city," he says. "And I didn't want to work in just any school."

*   *   *

At thirty-two years old, Dearman set his sights on Leadership High School, well known as an incubator for innovative approaches to learning. Dearman marketed himself to the Leadership administration as the ninth-grade academic literacy teacher they were advertising for. Popular in northern California public schools, academic literacy teaches the basic skills that high school teachers assume ninth-graders already have—reading comprehension, library research, writing term papers, basic grammar, and spelling.

"I kind of lied," Dearman admits, "I said, 'Sure, I can do academic literacy, sure, basic skills.' I've never even seen those books where people learn by phonics, and this is what I was imagining they were requesting of me—to teach grammar."

His bluff worked. Dearman was hired, and his teaching assignment that first year—what he refers to as his "freshman year"—was to be the only academic literacy instructor for the entire freshman class of 120 students. Thanks to his training in "outcome-based instruction" at Irvington, Dearman started thinking about the class by raising some basic questions.

"I asked, What happens to the senior-class teacher who's

teaching an American government class, and he wants his kids to write a basic five-page essay on some amendment, and the kids have no idea where to start?" He was determined to give the freshmen not just the skills they would need make it to their sophomore year, but the skills they would need to succeed throughout their academic careers. He wanted them to have all the note-taking, research, composition, and editing skills out of the way.

"Then, they can get down and have some conversation and do some learning, without having to learn how to write an annotated bibliography or how to construct a paper or critically think their way through."

For Dearman, to "get down" in a classroom—and he uses this phrase more than any other when he describes learning—signifies complex thinking, intense and productive classroom dialogue, and expression uninhibited by the dearth of basic skills afflicting so many students in urban high schools.

* * *

Lydia Bell, Dearman's former student, is spending her summer working at a clothing store on Haight Street, and on her break sits in a café, recalling the standards he set. Bell, whose mother is black and father is white, has an easy smile and becomes effusive when she describes Dearman's class.

"His work was so hard that college work is easy in comparison," she says. "In his class, you start paying more attention to detail, and you can do things more thoroughly. Now, teachers are impressed with the work I turn in because when I do assignments, I find myself thinking, 'What would Dearman think of this?'"

When they speak of the challenges of his class, many of his students mention their first assignment, a geography project which started as a group-produced report about how the Leadership High School community divided itself. Freshman students interviewed students in other grades about cliques and where they were hanging out and why. Using their findings, they drafted a paper and a short oral presentation together.

In the next phase, Dearman asked students to map the downtown city block where Leadership was sited. The assignment grew in complexity and turned out to last the whole semester. By December, students had worked in groups to make a scale map of the block, complete with legends and annotations, explaining how each area was used and by whom. Students also wrote sociological research papers, using their interviews as primary source materials. At the end of the semester, each student group gave two presentations—one for the class and one for Dearman, in which they had to defend the thesis of their paper.

Despite the fact that Dearman had some specific ideas about the skills his students would learn through this project—how maps work, how to conduct interviews, how to write a research paper with a perfect annotated bibliography—the students were not always aware of all they were learning. One student says that one of the most important things he learned was how to speak up and tell a teacher that his expectations were unreasonable. Others say the challenge of the project brought them together. Dearman's expectations pushed them further than they'd been pushed before. Once they'd completed the assignment successfully, almost any project seemed within their grasp.

One unintended consequence of the project was 120 freshmen with the kind of esprit de corps usually found among Marine recruits in the midst of boot camp. "It broke the ice," Lydia Bell remembers. "It was intense, but everybody had something to complain about, so everyone had something in common. You would talk to people you wouldn't ordinarily talk to about this project that you hated. And then suddenly, you were getting along."

In the second semester, Dearman created a Model United Nations for the freshmen, a course he designed to build students' understanding of global politics. The next year, he followed his freshmen into their sophomore year and taught a class simply called Leadership. Required of all sophomores, the course focused on learning the interpersonal skills needed by people who lead different kinds of communities and groups—building consensus, for instance, or mediating conflict. In his last year, Dearman continued to teach the tenth-grade leadership class as well as a class he called The Creative Process, a year-long course in which students wrote and produced an original theatrical musical.

Dearman was widely recognized as being the toughest grader at Leadership High School, with a penchant for perfection that often earned him the ire of his students. He says he once handed a student's paper back because, on one line of the bibliography, there were two spaces where there should have been one. Though his rules were rigid—a paper turned in a day late always meant one grade dropped, A becoming B, and B becoming C—he offered students the kind of empathy they would more likely find in a peer than a teacher.

"What I would do is divest myself from the rule, even though I put the rule there," Dearman says, explaining his way of playing both bad cop and good. "I would say, 'You're going to fail if you don't all work together on this project.' Later I would sit down at the table with them and say, 'Man, yeah, that sucks, you might fail. How are we going to do this? How are we going to figure this out so you pass?'"

He smiles at the genius of his ploy, a pedagogical tool he learned watching his daughter's preschool teacher mediate a dispute over a tricycle. "Invariably," he says, "they would work it out."

*   *   *

Dearman is in his office, retrieving a copy of a CD from a file cabinet full of contracts and home listings. He's hesitant to play the song, composed and performed by his students the last spring he taught. "OK, I'll play it," he says, placing the CD in the portable stereo on the window sill.

Every year, Leadership suspends normal classes for a week, declaring it a "Week Without Walls." Teachers work with a group of students for five full days on whatever that teacher is interested in. Since Dearman was interested in the creative process, his classroom became a music studio in which fifteen students came together to collectively write and produce a song—three days for the writing, two for recording in a professional studio.

The piece on the CD starts with a spacey guitar riff, heavy on the wa-wa and reverb. It's soon joined by a horn, drum beat, bass guitar, and then, the surprisingly confident vocals of one of Dearman's students. Eventually, her classmates join her for the chorus:

We are

United

As one

He shakes his head in disbelief. "It was a great week," he says. "It was exceptional. All I had to do is play bass, and they wrote the song. They wrote the song and practiced it, did the arrangement, and everyone felt good about it. I didn't really teach. I just experienced this massive supernova."

That song—an eleven-minute cross-genre epic—was one of many supernovas (a word he uses often to describe his students and their work) inspired by Dearman. There was also the song a group of students wrote after their classmate Andrea Bastidas died of cancer.

"Writing music was something we had done all year," Dearman explains, "so a group of the kids, all juniors, started writing. We had a poem, and we just put it to music. We were trying to mourn, to sit with this and not escape it but to experience it in a really healthy, mindful way and to write this music. We wrote this song in two days, and played it at the funeral service. It sounded beautiful. The song had never sounded the way it did at the church. We did it at school, and it sounded awful. We did it at an assembly, and it sounded awful. But then, at the memorial, we started singing, and everyone was looking over and smiling. That was beautiful. Really beautiful."

Elisa Dumesnil was a counselor at Leadership then. Though she has since moved on to work at a school in San Mateo, south of San Francisco, she still remembers how important the process of writing and performing that music was for the community.

"This was one of those best-case scenarios. It was just so full of grace, such beautiful grieving," Dumesnil recalls. "It was transforming for so many kids who have been exposed to so much violence in their neighborhoods. These kids had experienced a lot of grief and were practiced in dealing with it by drinking or getting high or ripping off a store or something like that. Their first instinct was to slam their fist into a locker or run, and that almost happened, but it didn't because there was another opportunity for them. You never know when they face grief in the future, if they'll think, 'I have other things I can do.' What Jonathan and other teachers did was amazing and helpful. But what Jonathan did with the music was something only Jonathan was capable of doing."

Dearman was the teacher students loved to hate—the school's toughest grader—but, more important, he was the teacher the students were desperate to please. He was also the teacher who, in the middle of class, while students were working on visual aids for their Model UN presentation, might jump up on a table to sing along with the Earth, Wind and Fire song playing in the background. His classrooms were music-filled, and Dearman's simple love of life rubbed off on the students—they came to him for anything and everything. His classroom was almost always open at lunchtime, jammed with students listening to records or watching a movie. Dearman extended that openness to teachers as well. Eve Gordon, a four-year Leadership veteran, says Dearman was essential to the sanity and stability of the staff, providing support and a much-needed sense of humor.

"Jonathan was incredible," Gordon says. "He was a combination of this big, political, strong, righteous black man, and also this incredibly sensitive, tender, hippie-ish spirit. I remember our first year. He had a crystal, and when things got really intense, he would give us some comic relief by waving this crystal around. He would say, 'Take a dip in Lake You,' as if to say, 'Take a step back. Go inside. Take some time.' When he first did that, we were almost hysterical, and you never see that at a meeting of teachers."

* * *

February 2002 turned out to be the winter of Dearman's last year in teaching. A friend called to ask him to take over the sale of a house. He still had his real estate license and a mountain of debt, and he thought he could manage teaching and selling a house at the same time. It was harder than he expected. He was taking calls on his cell phone in the midst of helping students with their homework.

"I wasn't doing either job well," he says. "Some days, I was working twenty hours. I was getting four hours of sleep. I was working at Leadership until 4:30. I would go back to the office after school, and I would go and work there, meeting with clients until 10. After they left, I'd have to do school stuff or real estate stuff into the night. And then I had my family," he adds, laughing.

He sold the house. His commission check was $14,000,

enough to retire virtually all of his credit card debt. He realized then that if he could do that only three times a year, he would match his current teaching salary. Real estate had earning potential and a far less intense schedule. Teaching offered debt, ridiculous hours, and an abiding sense of being less effective than he wanted to be.

"At that time, it was clear I couldn't do both, so I had to make a decision," he remembers. He floated the idea of giving up teaching to his wife. "She was all for it. But it's funny—we didn't say, 'Oh, we'll make so much more money.' It was an embarrassing sort of hush-hush admission that I could make more in real estate. It was something that was part of the decision, but it was something I would never admit was part of the decision at the time. It was, though. It was."

Dearman talked his decision over with his principal, Greg Peters, and by March, he had decided that this would be his last year. The costs—lost time with his family, money he wasn't making—were too great. He decided to tell the students at Leadership by writing them a letter that teachers would read to students during the school's advisory period. He says he doesn't recall that reading the letter to his own advisory group was difficult, but his former students remember it differently.

"I was so sad, oh my gosh," Lydia Bell remembers. "I was crying. I felt like such a dork, but then I looked around, and everyone was fighting back tears. It's hard for me to open up to people, and I don't know if I ever opened up to anyone as much as I opened up to him. There was a lot of joking around, but he really was there for people."

Rachel Russell, a student representative on Leadership's board of directors, was hit hard. "I thought, who am I going to talk to? I would spend my whole afternoon or my lunchtime in his classroom. He broke me out of my shell, pushed me to start talking to other people. It was sad when he left. People kept trying to get him to stay a little longer, at least until we graduated. We all worked to help each other through it. He was the backbone of our class."

Dearman's departure was felt beyond the walls of the school. Lydia Bell's father, Gordon—a taxi dispatcher—shared his daughter's sentiments.

"His leaving was Leadership's loss," he says. "He didn't pay attention to molds. Instead, he made his own. That was one of the things I liked about him and about Leadership—there was always something different happening there. He was one of the jewels in their crown."

*   *   *

Patricia Gándara of the University of California at Davis has been studying race in the classroom for most of the past decade. She says that in addition to the important function teachers like Dearman provide as role models to both minority and white children, they also provide a conduit to parents in the community.

"There can be a lack of comfort and a lack of connection with parents, and that's a very, very important thing to consider," Gándara says. "When a black parent walks into the classroom and sees a black teacher, that buys a lot of trust. Oftentimes, that trust doesn't exist. In public schools we're working with kids whose parents don't really trust the schools to do the best thing for them or their kids. So the more we can have people who engender trust in the community and trust on the part of parents, the better."

Sylvia Jones is one of those parents. Her son, Stuart, was in Dearman's unofficial Boys of Color Club. "I was sorry to see Jonathan leave Leadership," she says. "He really helped teach the kids to be themselves. At most schools, kids don't learn about their own culture, but he made it seem like it was good to be black. He taught my son to be a man first and black second. My son looked forward to going to his class. He made school fun for the kids."

The void Dearman left was tangible. In her first three years, Rachel Russell, the student representative on Leadership's board, had a 3.7 grade point average. After Dearman left, she almost failed some of her classes, and her GPA plummeted.

"It didn't feel good," she says. "I took on too much and I didn't have the right resources. I didn't have the right person to talk to, to encourage me anymore. I was left on my own to become an adult. I had to encourage myself and learn that there's not always going to be someone for me to talk to. I was not ready for that."

Though they were angry and disappointed, Dearman's best students, surprisingly adept at spotting a silver lining, tended to put a positive spin on his leaving. As Russell puts it, "His leaving helped me. It grew me up. It made me an adult."

Loran Simon's reaction was similar. "His leaving was really something that spoke out to me because it showed that he was concerned about the well-being of his family, and that's also an important thing to learn as students. I was mad at him. Everyone was mad at him. But then, we understood what he had to do. He had to take care of his family."

For Simon, his role model's departure was not reason to let his grades slip. "If we were to drop out, or we were to let our grades fall, then that would be a slap in the face of what he taught us. Giving up was something we weren't allowed to do."

Teachers felt the loss as well. For some, the departure of a man who had been a mainstay and a founding force in the school brought into question their own ability to continue.

"It was incredibly demoralizing," says Eve Gordon, who, after considering leaving Leadership for three years, finally did so in May 2004. "I felt that way every time anybody who was deeply involved got to the point where they had to leave. How can we do this incredibly important work without these people, folks who seem so central to what we're doing? How can we do this work when it is not sustainable? What does it mean about doing such worthwhile, important, and critical work when we, collectively, cannot really stay in it?"

*   *   *

Almost 310,000 people teach in California public schools. The California Teachers Association estimates that one in five is in his or her first few years of teaching. Teachers like Dearman—in their first five years of their careers and making a significant impact on the lives of their students—leave every year, but the state has no hard figures on where they're going or why they're leaving.

Margaret Gaston runs the nonprofit Center for the Future of Teaching and Learning in Santa Cruz, which advocates an information system to track teachers throughout their careers. She says that despite media coverage declaring victory over the teacher shortage, the situation has not changed much for urban schools.

"We have a continuing and chronic shortage of teachers in certain school settings that hasn't abated much since 1989, when we started tracking the numbers for certain schools. When you look at suburban schools, it has abated. Just not in urban schools," Gaston says.

She describes efforts by the state legislature beginning in 2000 to create a "robust teacher pipeline" that would include recruitment centers across the state and financial support for teacher candidates working toward their credentials. There was one program geared toward keeping accomplished teachers in hard-to-staff schools: a set of bonuses providing up to $30,000 over four years for those teachers who became certified by the National Board for Professional Teaching Standards—a year-long process of documenting lessons and student work in an extensive portfolio—and who were committed to teaching in underperforming schools for four years.

"In 2003, that pipeline was dismantled," Gaston says. "You have expectations for student achievement spiking right now, but the support for teacher development is plummeting. It's not just losing the cost-of-living adjustment. These programs are wiped off the books—zeroed out. It's a train wreck three to five years out."

Little of the bonus program for National Board–certified teachers remains. It's still on the books, but the legislation funding it has been amended to make clear that awards will be granted "to the extent that funds have been appropriated for this purpose in the annual Budget Act." It is, effectively, a dead program. When it did exist, of course, a teacher like Dearman would have been hard-pressed to find additional time outside the classroom to meet the stringent requirements of National Board certification.

Regardless of current budget constraints, pro-education legislators in Sacramento have been eager to put together their wish list, which they did with California's Master Plan for Education. This master plan is an updated pre-kindergarten-to-college version of the master plan from the 1960s that led to California becoming the model American public higher education system. Among the many reforms in the plan—geared toward addressing learning barriers for all students, starting in early childhood—are a handful of recommendations dealing with changing the work of teachers.

How much would it have taken to retain Jonathan Dearman? About $100,000, he says. At this point, very few policy makers are willing to pay a teacher that kind of money. Beyond agreeing that teachers ought to be paid more, few are willing to put dollar figures on a teacher's worth. Instead, they talk about the need to improve the conditions of schools, about making the job generally more desirable, and pairing that with raises that don't provoke sticker shock.

"One of our goals is more appropriate compensation," says Stephen Blake, the legislative consultant who wrote much of the actual plan. "We all talk about how education's a priority. We all know it is, in fact, the basis of our future, yet we pay teachers like shit. [The legislature has] in mind a meaningful compensation scale and ramping it up over time."

Blake says the legislators on the master plan committee felt considerable urgency about "the true crisis brewing around teaching," but sheer numbers and current fiscal realities make the idea of salaries competitive enough to attract candidates from private industry impossible.

"Nobody believed that with 300,000 teachers it could be feasible to go into an $80,000 or $90,000 a year range, but certainly we needed to be doing better than starting salaries of $32,000— where we were a couple of years back," Blake says. "If somebody has a chance to start out at $50,000 [in private industry] versus starting out at $30,000 teaching, it's not a very tough choice. Whereas, if it's $50,000 versus $42,000, and you have a passion for the $42,000 job, that counts for something. If the circumstances are made better for you in that working environment, and there's the possibility of quick salary advancement—something better than today's salary structure—that might keep you moving forward in the teaching career path."

Apart from a higher starting salary, what Blake describes is entirely hypothetical. There is no money appropriated to ramp up teacher salaries. And outside of San Francisco, teachers don't start at $42,000. The average beginning salary in California in 2003 was $34,805. That beginning teachers are paid even that well is a legacy of the late nineties, when the state was flush with dot-com revenues. Then-governor Gray Davis routinely bestowed "governor's money" grants to schools to fulfill local wish lists, and the legislature was able to invest enough money to substantially raise the floor for teacher salaries, subsidizing the costs for the lowest-paying districts.

The current reality, says State Senator Dede Alpert of San Diego, who led the committee that wrote the master plan, is that "almost nothing is in place." Salaries are not likely to rise anytime soon, and other programs, such as tax credits and forgivable loans for teachers, have gone the way of the National Board certification bonuses.

"We're in dire fiscal straits right now," Alpert says. "We haven't had state money to do even the things we had done in the past few years to try to help incentivize people going into the teaching field. It's difficult, and it's not just California. It's a nationwide problem. It's been hard to do the extra things to help people get into and stay in the profession."

Alpert says she believes good teachers ought to be paid $100,000. She imagines the profession could be transformed, and teachers could advance in their careers and earnings without leaving the classroom for jobs in other fields or school administration. If she could design the future of teaching, the best educators would become master teachers, leading teams of apprentice-teachers, and would be earning top dollar for that.

"We all give lip service about how important teachers are," she says, "about what a difference they've made in our lives, how much we respect teachers, but we really don't step up to the plate to make the kind of public investment to show that's really true."

It turned out that the other two African American teachers at Leadership were leaving the same year as Dearman—one to pursue a graduate degree, the other to work at another school. Feeling this loss, Greg Peters wanted to make a change to the school's hiring policy to help attract a suitable replacement.

"I put a clause in saying the principal would be given discretion to give a hiring bonus for those teachers in great need. Any given year, it might be a math teacher, it might be a Spanish teacher, but it might also be a teacher of color. And the board went nuts. There were a significant number of people on the board who said they were all for [giving bonuses for] math and science or special ed, but it was people of color and parents of color of this board who said this was discriminatory. 'We don't need to pay them extra to come here,' they said."

Still, Peters pushed for it, and found his only support on the board in Rachel Russell. "It needed to be done," Russell said. "At the time, Leadership only had three African American teachers, and they were leaving. The school has a high percentage of African American students, and if they don't have someone to represent them, someone who has gone through the same type of struggles, it's harder for the students. My senior year, there weren't any African American teachers at Leadership. It was really weird. Suddenly a white woman is leading the black student club. You feel lost."

Generally, San Francisco offers $1,000 bonuses for teachers in high-need subjects such as math, science, and special education, and Superintendent Ackerman has tried to solve the retention problem by providing more instructional resources to beginning teachers—in the form of mentoring by veteran teachers and dedicated on-site substitute teachers (so teachers won't have to cover an absent teacher's classes during their own free periods). She acknowledges, however, that these kinds of solutions are much more inexpensive than providing raises to attract more higher quality candidates to the schools that need them the most.

At Leadership, Peters won this battle and was granted the discretion to offer "high need" bonuses to qualified African American candidates. But in two years, he hasn't yet been able to hire an African American teacher.

*　*　*

California's master plan is a twenty-year vision, contingent on funding that doesn't exist. For Jonathan Dearman and the students at Leadership High School, this doesn't change their reality. Back at Leadership, it's summer and the students are gone, as are the teachers and the administration. Dearman is standing in what's called the courtyard but is actually a parking lot flanked by two rows of dilapidated portable classrooms. On this gray, windy San Francisco summer day, California's master plan seems a great deal farther than twenty years or the eighty miles of highway between here and the state capital.

"It's this progressive, liberal guilt we put on ourselves as teachers," he says. "The media and the government, they feed on that. They totally do. They say, 'If you're a teacher, obviously it's not about money. I thought you were an angel, I thought you were a saint. You're a teacher, aren't you?' They use that. I felt like there was this outside pressure not to talk about the money. There was this huge green elephant in the room with a dollar sign on it that no one could talk about.

"You can't have a healthy, comfortable quality of life and care about children at the same time. You have to be poor to do that. This is all in my head. But culturally, that's the thing, and I bought into it."

He is asking questions about how a situation that pushed him out of teaching can change. He is talking about the type of school he could teach in if he were to come back to the profession, one with classes no larger than fifteen students, one in which he could "kick ass and get down" and still be able to spend time with his family. He is talking about wanting a PhD in education and to be a part of making systemic changes. And he's late for an appointment to meet a client who is selling a house. He has to go, but it's clear he would like to have been able to stay. He says Leadership is still one of the best places to teach in San Francisco.

"But to go back, there's got to be some changes around here," he says. He turns and walks to his car, a Mercedes-Benz with custom rims. He will probably work a total of fifty hours on this sale, and then he'll get a check for $15,000.

THE STRANGE AND INCREDIBLE LIVES OF YOUR CHILDREN'S TEACHERS

"LOOK DAD, MY BIOLOGY TEACHER IS SELLING STEREOS AT CIRCUIT CITY!"

WHEN ONE SALARY ISN'T ENOUGH, A STARTLING NUMBER OF TEACHERS MOONLIGHT IN A STARTLING ARRAY OF JOBS

At least 20 percent of public school teachers report having second jobs outside of the field of education.[1] Their reasons vary. Some younger teachers are supplementing their income to help pay off their student loans. More experienced teachers with families often need the extra income to pay for necessities as their families grow. Many teachers live paycheck to paycheck, the extra job providing them with cash they can actually save.

Resorting to second jobs during the summer is a popularly accepted custom for America's teachers. It has long been common for a student to see her English teacher working at a local restaurant, or her history instructor painting houses. No one, neither teachers nor parents, makes much of a fuss about it—though whether or not such moonlighting enhances or diminishes public

NEW TEACHERS FEEL UNDERPAID[2]
How much do you agree with the statement:
"I am seriously underpaid?"
(respondents: new teachers)

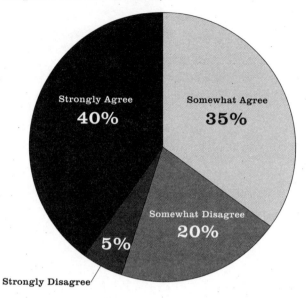

respect for the teaching profession is up for debate. And as wages stagnate, the problem seems to be getting worse.

A 2004 survey conducted by Sam Houston State University in Texas found that 35 percent of the teachers who responded had extra jobs, compared to 22 percent in 1980. Teachers worked an average of 9.9 hours per week outside of school during the school year. Seventy-six percent of those who held extra jobs felt it was detrimental to their performance. In addition to their hours in the classroom, these Texas teachers worked as counselors, farmers, antique shop clerks, office administrators, cabinet makers, church choir directors, newspaper delivery persons, service managers, ministers, waitresses, and cake designers.[3]

On the following pages, we will hear from a range of teachers, mostly men, who work at least two jobs. The strain these extra work hours put on their teaching and on their families is obvious. That teachers would have to take on these sorts of jobs is a troubling by-product of their poor pay, underscoring America's complex and somewhat incongruous attitude toward educators. There is no comparable occupation whose importance is acknowledged by society but which is not quite considered an actual, full-time job.

Erik Benner, 32, History—Cross Timbers Middle School, Grapevine, Texas
I've been teaching history for eight years now, and the whole time, I've been working nights and weekends at the local Circuit City. It pays decently, and it helps me make ends meet. We've got three-year-old twins and an eleven-year-old. Without the second job, it would be extremely difficult. The irony is that the extra job, which helps buy my kids nice things, takes me away from them on the weekends. I work at the store every weekend, and some weeknights. If I have a day off and I'm not at school or I'm not at the store, I go pick up the kids from day care. I'll have them home and have dinner ready for Mom when she gets home. I guess we make the best of what we do have. You have to.

I coach, too. Football season is pure chaos because I have games two or three nights a week, and then I work at Circuit City. During football, I can work as much as eighty to one hundred hours at both jobs combined. And then, right after football ends, because it's retail and Circuit City does well in December, I've got to get ready for the Christmas season. When I'm on vacation, I try to work a full-time pay period. My last paycheck will be for seventy hours. That covers Christmas break—I pulled fifty hours in one week.

I get to school at 6–6:30 in the morning, open the gym and locker room up for morning football practice, and then I go through my normal teaching day. We have practice until 4:30 or 5 in the afternoon. If there are games, I won't be home until 9:30 at night. Every Friday night we have to go scout other teams and film games and stuff like that. It's Texas. Football's big. It's a twelve-hour day if there are no games. And if there are no games, then I can work four and a half or five hours at the store. I also work Saturday and Sunday. Normally, right now, I'd be at work, but I've got a cushy schedule this weekend. I'm working the nights both days.

I have a buddy who started at Circuit City the same time I did. He's actually a store manager now—he has his own store. I think he just has an associate's degree, but he's making the same as I do working two jobs. Here I am with a degree. It's a little disheartening. I know if I went that route, I could be a manager at Circuit City, but I wouldn't enjoy it.

Working my second job, I'm making more money than somebody with a master's and twenty-plus years of experience, which is sad. But I wonder: Will I ever be able to stop working two jobs? I guess if you want nice things, you've got to work extra.

It doesn't bother me. It bothers my wife more than it bothers me, because I've done it for ten years. I'm used to it. But, being newlyweds, she'd like me to have weekends off. She doesn't like having to go to church by herself.

Daniel Beutner, 38, Fifth Grade—Kyrene del Sureño Middle School, Chandler, Arizona

In college, I remember thinking teachers don't get paid very much, but that's okay. My first teaching contract was in 1988 and I made $19,500. As a college student, that's a lot of money when you're used to making $4,000 a year. I thought, I could do that; I could make it work because I'm not materialistic. As time went on, I got married, had two kids, and realized, wow, bills add up. We were having all kinds of problems, because my wife was a teacher, too. So I started taking on part-time jobs.

When I was twenty-one years old and working as a teacher, summer came around and I thought, What am I gonna do? A parent approached me and gave me a job with his landscaping company. I was one of the guys, making five bucks an hour pushing a lawnmower. They had contracts with local strip malls, and they were making a lot of money.

The next school year, I figured that rather than working for five bucks an hour, I could start my own business. So I started doing it on my own, cutting residential lawns. Every weekend for ten years, I would go out, cut people's grass and install sprinklers, that kind of thing. I reached the point where I realized I could do this and make more money as a landscaper than I could as a teacher. I didn't want to do that; I wanted to teach. So I started my own little business: DB's Lawn Service.

When I cut lawns, the kids would come out and say, "Mr. Beutner's here!" It was a big exciting thing. And I just said, "Hey! How's it going?" I figured I was showing them a good work ethic. I was never embarrassed about it. More often than not, I would cut grass for other teachers, female teachers whose husbands made money. That didn't bother me. I think it was just the lack of free time. I wanted to make it work but I wasn't home much. That didn't make me real happy. At a certain point I figured if I ever was going to make money, it was going to have to be outside the profession of teaching.

At one point I was working three jobs. I was a teacher, I had my own landscaping company, and I delivered newspapers early in the morning. I did that for a solid year. I would get up at three in the morning, get in my car and go down to the local high school where the newspaper truck would be. I'd pick up 250 papers or so, bag them in the middle of the night, and deliver them.

Then I would get home, take a shower, go to school, and teach all day. After I'd done my planning for the next day, I'd go home, make dinner, spend a little time with the family, and go to bed.

In the morning, if the truck with the newspapers was late, I would sit there in the parking lot. It would be about four in the morning and I'd just keep my car running and grade papers while I waited for the newspaper truck to come.

Matthew Cheeseman, 38, Science—East Nicolaus High School, Nicolaus, California

When I first started teaching, I'd look in the newspaper and see if someone needed a mover for the day. I'd show up and just be part of a team that would move furniture and stuff. I think I got $20 an hour. I'd take anything where I could just grab some extra cash to pay off a bill, that kind of thing.

It was really hard for me this past year because I couldn't find a summer job. At East Nicolaus High, with only 280 students, we don't have a summer school. We don't have any K through 8 schools in our district—just the high school. So, technically, I'm the only science teacher in the district. I applied to several places to teach summer school, and for whatever reason, I wasn't even interviewed. Washington Unified openly told me at the door, when I turned in the application, that they were going to offer summer school positions to all of their own district people—especially anybody they had laid off. So I applied to Home Depot and Lowe's for a part-time summer job, but was declined because I could only work four weeks.

*   *   *

This second-job survival strategy is not always sustainable for teachers who want to raise a family. It's one thing to be young and running from your classroom to the restaurant where you bar-tend, but it's a different scenario altogether to be missing time with your family in order to pay for basic expenses. These situations are familiar to many lower-middle-class families, but it's hard to blame professionals with master's degrees for expecting a single paycheck that might suffice. After all, how many of their similarly educated peers who work in other professions also spend their nights bussing tables or cleaning other people's homes?

Rachel Cross, 30, History and Algebra—Oneida Middle School, Oneida, Tennessee

I'm a single mom, and I did everything at school I could do, as far as tutoring and summer school. But it's gotten so bad that for almost a year, I cleaned houses. I'd just take my son with me and go clean houses. It's not that I think I'm too good for that. It didn't bother me to sweep, and it didn't bother me to mop. But every time I would scrub a toilet, I would think, "I went to school for four years and did very well, and I'm doing this."

I was doing it two to three times a week at night and on Saturdays, probably four to five hours, and making about $30 to $40— about $100 a week total. I would get off work and go clean houses and then get home at ten.

I have cried several times, and it's like, you're on your knees in front of this toilet, and you're almost praying, praying that it'll get better, that you won't have to do this forever. But at the same time, you've got to be thankful, because this'll be thirty extra dollars. It's a tank of gas, or it may be part of your co-pay if your child gets sick.

There's always something. That's the nature of having a child. One afternoon, he was riding home with my mother and she gave him a couple of dollars because we were going to go to the movies or something, and he said, "I'm going to give this to my mommy, because even though she doesn't tell me, I know she doesn't have a lot of money." That just broke my heart. He was probably four at the time.

Skip Lovelady, 42, Science—Redwood High School, Larkspur, California

Outside of school, I'm a waiter at Plumpjack Café in San Francisco. I've been there since the restaurant opened. I also do a fair amount of independent computer support work for some small companies and individuals, doctors and so on. I do graphics and digital work and digital video editing, but I also do troubleshooting and help with hardware and software and things like that. I've taught summer school here for eight summers in a row now, which is fairly grueling—it's another five weeks of teaching.

I've been married twenty-three years. I'm trying to stay married, but my wife and I never go out on Saturday nights. I never take a day off at Plumpjack. I work every Saturday night, all year long. I'll be off this Saturday because of the science fair—and I've had to save a bunch of money to compensate for that. But yeah, it's just tough. We had made a commitment not to leave our son anywhere except with his parents. No day care, none of that. So I started taking on extra jobs—tutoring, and the restaurant—and everything else I could get my hands on.

I tutor one to three nights a week. One hour per kid, which turns out to be an hour and a half, two hours by the time I drive there and drive back. I miss storytelling time for my kid, bedtime, you know, stuff like that. I'm out of the house two or more evenings per week.

Ultimately, I do all of those things for the money. All those jobs, except for the restaurant work, have an academic component to them, which I love. I'm glad I could find extra work in that field. I support my family with that. If it really was just about the money, then I could find other work that pays more, outside of school. But the truth is, if I didn't need the money I really

wouldn't take on all those evening jobs, even if they were academically related.

* * *

On average, teachers nationwide earn an additional $3,250 a year
from moonlighting. The bitter irony is that a good deal of the
teachers earning extra money end up putting it right back into the
classroom. In 2001, the National Education Association asked
teachers to calculate how much of their own money they had spent
during the past school year to meet the needs of their students.
The average was $443, a 9 percent increase over the 1994–1995
average of $408.

Steven Herraiz, 40, Kindergarten—John Muir Elementary School, San Francisco, California

Now, nine months out of the year, I work sixteen hours a week at
a bar. I spend about fifty hours a week teaching. On the weekends,
on Friday nights and Sunday mornings, I work at the bar. Fridays
I come home after teaching and take a nap. And then I go to work
at nine on Friday night and come home at four in the morning.
By the time I come home on Saturday morning, it's this huge
marathon of work and I'm exhausted, so I sleep most of Saturday.
Then on Sunday morning, I go back to the bar from seven in the
morning until two in the afternoon.

What's really tragic is that when I first started teaching, I was
making the same amount of money bartending two days a week as
I was teaching five days a week.

I spent $3,900 of my own money last year on my classroom.
That's a lot of money. And it's not anything extravagant. It's stuff
like paper clips and art supplies and paint and the things you
would assume that the district provides and they don't. It's horri-
bly demeaning and I try not to focus on it. I was active in union

work a couple of years ago, but I didn't get anywhere with it. I didn't feel like we were being heard. There are so many obstacles to being a good teacher that I just said, What can I control myself? I can have a second job and not have to worry about supplies.

I kept thinking that the second job was going to give me the extra money I need to be an effective teacher. In other words, I can buy snacks for my kids. For the last eight years, I've been buying the food that gets them through the morning. A typical day has me stopping at the market because the school doesn't provide any sort of nutritious snack for the kids. And the kindergartners need to eat every few hours to get through the day.

* * *

Many teachers are surprisingly good-natured about this job juggling, especially when they can look back on it after their earnings allow them to concentrate on teaching full-time. But it's apparent that these years of strain take a permanent toll on one's psyche.

Richard Adelman, 52, English—John Bartram High School, Philadelphia, Pennsylvania

There was a time in my life when I worked four jobs. I worked as a teacher, and then in the summer I worked all kinds of jobs—as a restaurant manager in Atlantic City, in an auction house, as a photographer, and as an SAT tutor.

I generally worked the summer until I was about thirty-five years old. For a while I worked on the boardwalk in Atlantic City during the summer. They were always glad to have me because before casinos, there wasn't much doing before the summer started. Once the season started, they needed a lot of people, but they were anxious also to get rid of people once the summer ended. So a teacher is perfect. That summer job was murder. Some of those jobs I had as restaurant manager were fourteen, sixteen hours a day.

On the weekends, according to the season, I would do two, three, even four photography jobs. If I did four weddings in a weekend, that would be basically from 8:30 in the morning on Saturday until late on Saturday night, 12 o'clock. And then on Sunday morning, maybe from twelve to ten at night. If I had one wedding job, it was an easy weekend, just a Saturday night. It depended on the season. There are a lot of bar mitzvahs and weddings in the autumn and the spring. I did children's portraits. I would teach at school, and then I would have, let's say, a children's portrait at 4:30, in New Jersey. So I'd have to run out of school and run over and photograph a kid.

I was trying to make ends meet. I don't think I ever really shirked my fatherly responsibilities. I don't remember ever feeling guilty about that. What I didn't have a lot of time for, as I recall, was fun. I lost all my friends, because when you work on the weekends and you can't keep track of your friends, when you have a lot of responsibilities and a lot of work to do, your friends end up being the people you know at work. I had friends I had made at college but I lost them. That part of my life is the one I . . . regret losing touch with all the friends I had throughout the course of my life.

It's almost as though I was traumatized by all the work I did— a kind of post-traumatic stress syndrome.

·   ·   ·

The effects of teacher moonlighting are obvious and varied. Teachers who run themselves ragged working two jobs—while juggling their family lives besides—are unlikely to be functioning at the highest levels. Thus, low teacher pay makes the most ambitious teachers—those who want to teach so badly that they're willing to sell stereos on the weekends—less effective educators.

The teachers most inclined toward excellence are the first to be spun out of the teaching profession, because they realize that they cannot succeed at a level that's acceptable to their sense of achievement. The strain of the two-job lifestyle prevents them from teaching at a satisfactorily high level, and prevents them from being adequately present for their families. Their students suffer, their families suffer, and so these teachers are much more likely to burn out. And even working two or more jobs, most teachers cannot afford to live in the communities in which they teach.

THE TEACHERS LIVE
IN ANOTHER TOWN

WHY A TEN-YEAR TEACHING VETERAN
WITH TWO MASTER'S DEGREES STILL NEEDS
HER FATHER TO CO-SIGN A HOME LOAN

Back in 2002, the average price of an existing single-family home in the United States passed the $200,000 mark. In Boston and Los Angeles, that figure was around $250,000. In the San Francisco area, median home prices ranged from Oakland's comparatively low end at $350,000 to the real estate absurdity across the water, in San Francisco, where you can spend half a million on your first home.

Real estate prices in many markets have climbed, and teacher salaries have not kept pace. For teachers new to the profession—especially in many urban areas—the prospect of being able to buy a home on one's own is the longest of long shots. Take the example of New Jersey, where housing prices are close to the national average. There, the average starting salary for teachers is $35,311 in the first year. Typical home financing might be 20 percent down, with a thirty-year fixed mortgage at 6 percent. With taxes and insurance, the monthly housing cost is probably over $1,500. Compare this to a beginning teacher's monthly take-home pay, which is about $2,000. Of course, new teachers are more likely to start their careers with hefty student loans than with enough savings for a down payment. The average debt of graduates with master's degrees is over $30,000.

According to the Center for Housing Policy, schoolteachers are priced out of homeownership in thirty-two metropolitan markets. They estimate that in order to qualify for a loan on a median-priced home ($156,000), workers need a yearly salary of at least $49,000.[1]

So what does the average teacher do? Some keep renting or living with roommates. Some live far away from the schools at which they teach. Whatever they do, they make sacrifices.

Jeffrey McCabe, 34, Algebra—Wootton High School, Montgomery County, Maryland

I originally lived in the community where I worked: Frederick County. But in order to do that, I was coaching soccer, I was coaching swimming, I was coaching a club team, I was teaching night school, I was proctoring SAT tests and tutoring on the side. Even then we weren't making ends meet. So I had to transfer to Montgomery County, about thirty minutes away. I went from an eight-minute to a thirty-minute commute. Then we found that we couldn't even afford that. We had to move further out, to Carol County. Currently I commute forty-two miles because I can't afford to take a job in the county where I live. I pass about five high schools on the commute before I even get to the highway that takes me to the school where I teach.

Matt Huxley, 38, Vice Principal—Berkeley High School,
Berkeley, California

I was able to survive as a teacher, but not to save money for a house. That was the hardest part. The fact that I could not buy a house made me angry and sad because I loved teaching, and while I knew it was not a high-paying profession, I still thought I would be able to save for a home. In fact, I remember having conversations with an assemblywoman who was interested in education issues; I talked to the superintendent, to other teachers and administrators. I felt it was ridiculous that the low salaries prevented people from coming into the profession and buying homes. That obviously made me angry because I wanted to live and work in the same community, so I thought about getting out of the profession. And I have to say that one of the reasons that drove me to administration was so that I could make more money and buy a house. I didn't know when I'd be able to afford a house on a teacher's salary.

Joel Arquillos, 32, Social Studies—Galileo Academy of Science and
Technology, San Francisco, California

Without help from my wife and her family, we'd have to live somewhere else and I'd have to commute or live in a different community altogether. Luckily, my wife's grandmother had put aside some money for her—about ten grand. That and about $7,000 we saved up on our own was enough to make the minimal down payment on a place.

When interest rates were low, we found a place on the ends of San Francisco that we could actually afford. We didn't think it was going to be possible, but things worked out. We almost didn't get a loan due to how little we had, but we were able to edge it out with a little bit of help. We are unique. I've seen some other teachers who have started buying places, but it's usually in Oakland or somewhere farther out, and they have to commute. It's a shame that you can't live near your school. It's a crime.

*   *   *

Part of putting down roots and integrating into a community involves home ownership. In most urban centers, home ownership is a serious financial challenge for teachers. In affluent areas, it's impossible on their salaries. Those who teach the children of the wealthy are expected to commute half an hour to an hour from less expensive suburbs—underlining teachers' status as de facto second-class citizens.

Alyssa Nannt, 37, Special Education—Easton High School, Easton, Maryland

I had been renting for years and years and I thought to myself, Well, I really do want to own a house and feel like I'm part of the community instead of moving every year.

But I didn't have anything saved in the bank. My parents were willing to give me about $1,000 for a down payment. I had debt of about $15,000 left on my student loans, and I had approximately $20,000 of credit card debt—just accumulated over the years of trying to survive and go to school and work and that sort of thing. I had those debts when I went in to the real estate agent.

The only thing I could afford was a $60,000 townhouse. Talbot County, where I teach, is a very affluent county. There's a ton of waterfront. It's a very beautiful place to live. There are just not any affordable places to live. They keep building new houses all the time, but they start at $200,000. I remember the list of possibilities, as far as realistic homes I could get—there were maybe five or six on the list and that was pretty much it. That was really kind of a downer.

I remember I was angry. I was angry because I felt like I had given so much to the community to educate the children—and being a special ed teacher to boot. You work with the neediest kids. Easton High School is the largest high school in the county, and some kids have rough backgrounds. I felt like I deserved more because I had put so much time and energy and love—and money, even—helping out these kids, buying them notebooks, buying them folders, buying them other school supplies. To have just that tiny list of viable housing options was heartbreaking to me. It really was.

One of the agents I talked to said, "Well, you could get married, and then you'd have more combined income." And I said, "Why should I?" It's almost like you're being punished for the choices you make. Being a teacher really limits you in the property that you can own, having a place you can call your own and be proud of.

The townhouse community I live in is pretty much Section 8 government-subsidized low-income housing. When you enter my part of the townhouse community, there's a dumpster on the left-hand side that's always overflowing with garbage. A lot of the houses around here are missing screen doors, the paint is coming off, some of the outside lights are damaged. I know in the past there have been shootings here and there. When I told my parents I was buying a townhouse in this community, they were appalled that I couldn't afford anything better. They said, "Look, you know, you're working full time. You've got experience and it's ridiculous that you have to live like this." I wouldn't say it's the worst part of Talbot County, but it's definitely down there. So I've got two big dogs, and they keep me company.

Mark Isero, 30, Social Studies and English—Leadership High School, San Francisco, California

The initial salary was okay with me because I was a little bit younger. I wasn't looking into what it means to have a life, what it means to have a house, what it means to be more comfortable in my thirties. Now I'm a little bit more ill at ease. I don't feel like I'm going to get out of teaching, but it's very strange to look down the road and know where I'm going to be. I can see what my raises are every single year. And if it's difficult now to get a house, there's a possibility that I'll never get one, unless I change my job. But that's not what I want. I specifically made the choice to come to the city to teach. A lot of people are suggesting that I leave teaching entirely, but I like what I do.

* * *

If you're a teacher or married to one, chances are you're struggling, and where you live might not be what you imagined when you dreamed of a life as an educator. Linda and Doug Hamilton met when they were both teachers. Though a successful teacher, Linda left the profession years ago, first to pursue writing, then corporate work. It was her career change that enabled the couple to live a better life.

Linda Hamilton, 38, Senior Project Manager, WorldRes.com; Doug Hamilton, 40, World History—San Lorenzo High School, San Lorenzo, California

Linda: If I wasn't with Doug, I wouldn't be living in this neighborhood. It's too scary for me, honestly. But with Doug here, it's fine. It was important for him to live in a neighborhood that was somewhat reflective of the population he taught.

Doug: I grew up in Oakland; this is my home. But, oh no, we live here strictly because of our income. Linda's painting a nice face on it. It's not because she's with me that she lives here, it's because it's what we can afford. And she's agreed that because I stay in the house and protect her, we'll live here. But otherwise we would definitely live in an upscale neighborhood with safe streets so we wouldn't have to worry and have an alarm on the house and stuff like that. That's a direct result of our income. The only reason we were able to buy this is because she works for a company. If it was just up to me and my income? We wouldn't have bought a damn thing. Ever.

.   .   .

In most cities, teachers who own comfortable homes fall into one of two categories: those who have bought recently (likely with high-earning spouses, or some other source of income), and those who bought years ago, when home prices were within reach. In 2004, however, homeowning prospects are ever-diminishing.

Nancy Gutmann, 61, English—Brookline High School, Brookline, Massachusetts

In 1978, I was making $15,000. I remember this very clearly because my husband is a college professor. We were each making $15,000. Our salaries have been pretty much parallel. After I started teaching, we were looking for a house to buy. We finally found a house, made an offer, and it was accepted. My husband said to the realtor, "Now I just hope we can get a mortgage."

She said, "Oh, no problem."

He said, "Well, I'm not so sure." These were the days where you didn't get preapproved. "I talked to a bank about the numbers and they thought they looked pretty shaky."

She said, "But you're two professionals."

And I said, "Our combined salary is $30,000 a year," and her jaw dropped open.

It's one of the few times I've actually seen someone's jaw drop open. It was clear that this realtor thought she was dealing with a sure thing because we were two professionals, and then when she heard the actual amount of money we made, she was shocked and thought that the sale had gone down the tubes.

My son Eric is teaching at Brookline, at my school. Our house was $127,000 in 1978. I don't remember exactly the calculations, but recently we were figuring what my salary was, in relation to home-purchasing power. I made $15,000 and could afford a $127,000 house, whereas my son's salary is in the low $40,000s, and this house is probably worth almost a million dollars now. It's clear that the proportions have skyrocketed, so that it was much easier to buy a house then for a teacher than it is now. Salaries are simply not keeping up.

I forget what the law is called, but you have to have a certain number of low-income apartments in your town. I don't know if this is a federal law or a state law. Every time a developer builds a building, a certain number of apartments have to be left for low-income people. So the town is very interested in getting low-income professionals, particularly town employees, because they'd like to have town employees in town. This means you can buy a two-bedroom condo for maybe $200,000, which is below market rate, especially in a brand-new building, if your family income is less than $50,000. That would be for a teacher without a spouse who worked, or a single teacher. It's possible to live in Brookline now, but only under those special programs.

.   .   .

Most parents would agree that having their children's teachers living nearby is desirable, recognizing that this can only strengthen the overall sense of community, and students' sense of being cared for, watched over, and guided by an interlocking network of adults who know them and have a vested interest in their well-being. Imagine a community in which all of the local schools' teachers were able to live. Students would see their former and future teachers at religious services, at restaurants, at fairs and parades, at the car wash. Because teachers are among the most influential adults in students' lives, their presence would seem to be an essential component in any community's planning. But this is not generally the case, and until efforts are made to welcome teachers into the cities and towns where they teach—to facilitate their proximity—communities will be weakened, and the latticework that gives young people a sense of security will be that much less effective.

THREE

IT'S NOT A BAD SALARY
IF YOU'RE SINGLE

BUT TRY RAISING A FAMILY ON IT

As noted in the previous chapter, many teachers will tell you that teaching was financially feasible when they were single. It provides a modest income, certainly enough for one person to live on in most areas, and it's a meaningful job to which they can happily dedicate twelve-hour days and even weekends. When they marry and start contemplating starting a family, however, the numbers no longer add up.

The expenses are not all that surprising. Child care is the biggest line item. Then consider health insurance, food, diapers, clothes, and a future where all these costs will continue to grow. The U.S. Department of Agriculture estimates that families with a child born in 2000 will spend over $178,590 over eighteen years raising that child.[1] That's almost $10,000 a year. How is that possible when your salary is only $35,000?

These figures lead vast numbers of teachers to leave the profes-

71

sion. Much like missionary work or a stint in the Peace Corps, teaching is seen by thousands of the best young people as a two- or three-year assignment before they have to get serious about settling down and creating a proper economic nest for their families. Those who try to build families around teachers' salaries must be exceedingly resourceful—or independently wealthy.

Amanda Deal, 35, Fourth Grade—Mineral Springs Elementary School, Winston-Salem, North Carolina

My husband is self-employed, so when he started his own business, I had to start carrying my whole family on the insurance provided through the school system. That meant about $450 a month coming out of my paycheck, which means that my take-home pay is now $1,260 per month. My husband was married before, and two of his three children live with us. One is a sophomore at community college, getting ready to transfer to Appalachia State University in the fall, and the other is a sophomore in high school. They take music lessons. It's very hard for us to come up with money for that.

My salary and my husband's salary are roughly the same at this point because he just started his business. With a $950 mortgage payment per month, utility bills, and paying for community college tuition, plus my tuition to get my teaching certificate, plus books, plus music lessons—every week, we sit down and say, okay, we have $40 until we get paid again. That is very stressful, especially when teaching is the kind of job where you don't really have a break at all during the day, so you always have to bring work home at night. You need to look at what the kids have done that day so you know what you need to focus on the next day. You've always got to be planning for the next week. It's very, very hard.

We had to acknowledge that we can't afford to go out to dinner very often. For fun, it ends up being the same thing over and over: let's rent a movie because that's the most economical thing. For a family of four to go out to a movie, by the time you buy tickets and popcorn, you're talking fifty bucks, and we just can't afford that.

Matt Huxley, 38, Vice Principal—Berkeley High School, Berkeley, California

As I was thinking about getting married, I thought it would be best if my wife had the opportunity to stay at home. But that was not going to be possible on my salary, so that was another reason I explored other professions. It was another source of anger because I felt that I worked really hard and gave everything to the profession, and yet I could not find a house and I could not provide for my wife to stay home with our child, which is really important to us.

Greg Worley, 37, Fifth Grade—Parmelee Elementary, Oklahoma City, Oklahoma

My first year was ten years ago. I made close to $25,000. My wife had been teaching for ten years, and she was making less than $30,000. Now, I just did our taxes, and combined we made $67,000 last year. That's not all just from school. My wife teaches Sunday school and gets paid for that. We both have summer jobs to supplement our incomes. So, over the year, she holds three jobs, and I hold two. In the summer, I tutor Native American kids to get them ready to take the GED, and my wife still works at the summer program where we met.

When our son was born, it wasn't too bad. We struggled a little bit to keep up with the bills. We had to call the electric company and ask them to give us an extension on making our payments. We tried to buy a car, but we didn't qualify for a loan because of our income. Same thing with our house. We had to rent a house because our income wasn't enough to get a loan. We had our son, Scotty, and we struggled to make day care expenses. That's what killed us the most. Putting him on our insurance was a pretty hefty amount. For Scotty alone, it was running us about $350 a month for full-time day care, and then on top of that, the insurance was $225. When we had our daughter, all of that doubled. Our day care expenses went to $700, and our medical insurance, just for the kids, went to over $400 a month. That was the roughest time for us, before they both started school.

I still don't know how we did it. We were late on everything. There were times when we came home and our electricity had been turned off. You know, we're talking about two college graduates. My wife had a master's degree in early childhood education, and I had graduated from college, and our electricity was getting turned off. We were borrowing money from our parents, and we were draining them dry. They were very helpful—I don't know what we would have done without them.

Things are a lot better now. This last summer, after twelve years of marriage, we qualified for a home loan. Our debt ratio wasn't as high, so we were able to buy a home, and we bought a home in August—in Norman, about twenty-five miles south of Oklahoma City. It's where the University of Oklahoma is. It's growing fast, but it's a nice little town. We bought a 2,000-square-foot house for $150,000. There are months when we still struggle. We don't pay bills in December so we can buy presents for our family, and then it's a struggle to catch back up.

August is always tough, when we go back to school and have back-to-school expenses to prepare our classrooms. We spend about $1,000 a year on our classrooms.

I don't want to sound bitter, because we both love our jobs. I recently finished my master's degree in administration, so I'm looking for a higher-paying job. I love teaching, but both of us can't remain as teachers and do what we want to do as a family. I want to travel with them, I want them to see things. So I got my degree in administration and I'm looking for a job. I have mixed emotions about that because I love teaching. I wish we were able to stay in the classroom. But it's impossible.

Joel Arquillos, 32, Social Studies—Galileo Academy of Science and Technology, San Francisco, California

I don't know what we'll do. We can't live where we live right now. We live in a one-bedroom condo, about eight hundred square feet. There's no way we could raise a child in a place like this. We'd have to get something that has two bedrooms. Depending on what my wife is doing, I don't know how we could afford to live in this town. Or even buy another place that has more room. I hope it happens, but I don't know.

We'd have to move. We might go to a different area—we've talked about that, too. We might move upstate, up to Oregon or Washington or somewhere else. But I like the city. I'm a city guy, so it's hard to leave this. And the kids who are coming to Galileo, they're really interesting kids. They're a lot like I was and I like that, I like that about them.

* * *

Mothers have a variety of strategies for balancing motherhood and a teaching career. Supported by high-earning husbands, many can take maternity leave or even leave teaching for a few years to care for children. This is simply not the case for single mothers, or for teachers who happen to have married other teachers.

Cindi Swingen, 37, Fourth and Fifth Grade—Sexton Mountain Elementary, Beaverton, Oregon

I have two kids. Matthew is six and Laura is three. I got divorced and I still wanted to be a parent. It's just the three of us here. I have a great little family. I love my life, but it's really expensive. Some months, my child care alone is $1,400.

When I started teaching, I started saving in advance, knowing my salary was going to prohibit having kids. I figured I would never make enough to cover my expenses if I didn't save. So I saved a few thousand dollars. One person living on a teacher's salary is a fine living. You're not wealthy, but I bought a home and a car, and it was fine. I went to college and got my master's.

My first home was $98,000. I had a roommate, so that made it easier. When I decided I had to move, I was already pregnant with my second child.

I have three sisters, and one of them is very wealthy and very generous. I said I need my house payment to be as low as possible, like $800 a month, and I don't have enough money to put down. She said how much do you need? I said I need $17,000 and she gave me $17,000. My mom gave me $12,000, so then I had a nice big down payment.

I moved into this little house for $159,000 and my payment is about $900 a month. I pay $1,200 a month for child care, $60 a day. It's really good day care—$30 a day, per kid. It's expensive, but it's not outrageous compared to what other people pay. Until recently, I was bringing home $2,400 a month, so I guess that's half—$1,200 to child care. And then another $1,000 for the mortgage. So I've been taking out of savings for the last two years.

I have an okay house. It's not a nice neighborhood. It has people with refrigerators on their front lawns, couches on their porches, that kind of thing, which doesn't really fit with my image of how professional I feel, and how educated I am. It's not where I thought I'd be at thirty-seven years old.

We don't go on vacations unless somebody else pays for it. My mom has us go to the beach for a weekend every summer, and she pays for that. Last summer, we went to a resort with a friend who invited us to go, so it didn't cost anything. But we don't usually go anywhere. I don't belong to a health club. I just got a cell phone because my car is so old. We went to two restaurants and one movie last year. I cut my own hair. I do my own nails. You just make do.

Michelle Hurley, 33, First Grade—Center Street School, El Segundo, California

I've been teaching for six years and took this year off for maternity leave. I had twins last April. Before that, I had been teaching first grade in El Segundo. We moved here because we knew we were having the twins and I wanted to be closer to work. Cost-wise, it's a little cheaper here than in West L.A. We were looking around for two-bedrooms there, and we couldn't have done that. As it turns out, we were able to get a bigger place here, but my mother came with us as well. I would have had to work if my mother had not come with us and helped pay the rent.

We live paycheck to paycheck. We don't have the freedom or the flexibility to save the way we would like to. When we were both working, before we had kids, I was able to contribute part of my salary to a savings account so we'd have a little money for a down payment. But once I went on leave, I didn't have any income. And my husband doesn't have any expendable income at the end of each month at all. It's hard with twins. Diapers alone are enough to kill you—about $80 a month.

It is difficult. We know I'll have to go back to work, because we're not going to be able to afford to live on one income. We have child care to consider, too. I'd like to go back part time, but I'd have to use my entire salary just to pay for child care. One child alone can cost upwards of $400–$500 a month, and if I'm talking about trying to put two kids in day care, that's a lot of money. That's not even having someone in my home, which I would love to do. If I had my choice, I'd get someone to be here, in the house, and not have to schlep them someplace else. But I don't know whether that will work out.

. . .

A man could be working any job and, if he's the sole breadwinner in a household, the burden is enormous. But if he works long hours, as teachers do, he misses out, to varying degrees, on raising his own children. This is the case for many professionals, but the irony for teachers, of course, is twofold: first, he's not being paid as well as others with his level of education, and second, while he's missing out on time with his own children, he's spending all his time raising other people's children.

Christopher McTamany, 30, AP Economics, Government— Thomas S. Wootton High School, Rockville, Maryland

When I come home now, my daughter says "Go away," because she never sees me. She only warms up if I'm off for a few days, and then she loves seeing me. But I get up at 4 a.m., and I don't come home until 4:30 or 5 p.m. That's when wrestling's not happening. When wrestling is happening, I don't come home until 6:30 or 7, and that's on nights when we don't have meets. On nights when we have meets, I'm not home until 9 or 10. Then we have tournaments every weekend, so I'm away Saturdays, too.

I also proctor the SATs, to make an extra hundred bucks.

That's decent money for a Saturday, but it's all morning. Between the tournaments and the proctoring, I've been missing my daughter's sports events.

It's put a lot of strain on us. Even when I come home, I've got work to do. I've got a bag full of papers to grade right here that I haven't graded because basically, I've taken a little break today to wallpaper, read the paper, and play with my daughter. But generally, I would have been grading papers as well.

My wife is pregnant, and the one good thing I can say is that I'll be able to take six weeks paid vacation when the baby comes. They let you use your sick leave. I feel pretty bad for the students, though. That's the one place where I can actually say I have put my family first. In all other instances—and you can ask my wife—I have not done that when I wanted to. But for that first six weeks, I'm there.

*   *   *

South Dakota has the dubious honor of being among the lowest-paying states in the country. It has the lowest average teacher salary: $31,383—that's $13,000 below the national average. Anyone who imagines South Dakota must be a cheap place to live is misinformed. In terms of how far a teacher's monthly paycheck can go, teachers have as difficult a time in South Dakota as they do in Hawaii, where the average salary is $44,306 but still doesn't begin to cover a family's living expenses.[2]

Dawn Jaeger, 51, Social Studies and German—Deuel High School, Clear Lake, South Dakota

I started teaching in Minnesota in 1974. I taught there for three years, and I ended up in South Dakota. I took a $4,000 cut in pay, and when you adjust for inflation, I'm still making less than when I started teaching. I was making $10,000. When you consider the cost of living increase, my $35,000 has less purchasing power than my $10,000 did in Minnesota.

Three years after I got here, I married a local farmer. The farming is not much better than teaching, economically. We have two children. Our son's a law student at South Dakota State University, and our daughter is a high school senior.

We were doing pretty well until about five years ago. Between reversals on the farm and the fact that we had some vehicle problems, we ended up getting into credit card debt, because we didn't have the cash on hand to make the repairs. For five or six years, things have gotten really tight.

The first two years, it wasn't so bad. People think kids are going to get cheaper as they get older, but they don't—they get more expensive. You have to have more vehicles. People don't think about that. They say things are cheaper in South Dakota, but they're not, because so many things are nationally priced, like automobiles. Things have to be hauled farther distances because we're remote. Our gas is cheaper than in California, but for the Midwest, it's actually fairly high.

We've cut back on some things, but probably not as much as we should. We stay home more. We can get into school events free, so we got to those as our primary activity. We have cable TV rather than going to the movies—that kind of stuff.

We're having to pay for things on credit because we don't have enough salary to cover things we're not expecting. Everyone in our family wears glasses, for example. My glasses and my son's glasses are extremely expensive because we have very poor eyesight, so we have a $500 bill for glasses and no insurance to cover it. We just get farther and farther behind. The farm has always been able to pay for our utilities and property taxes. But there hasn't been money left over to pay us a wage.

Compared to some people, our debt's not real high. It's about $11,000. We're hacking away at it. We pay off about $300 a month. It'll take awhile.

*   *   *

A teaching career guarantees a life of subsistence earning—month to month and hand to mouth—for the teacher and her own children. Cindi Swingen says, "You just make do," and that's true for most teachers. They often don't have choices to make, just sacrifices. Maybe, like Greg Worley, they let the bills slide in December to pay for Christmas. Or they go without the big things—vacations, say, or eyeglasses.

Some people argue these are sacrifices teachers willingly make. As we wrote in the introduction, teaching has never been a well-compensated profession, and those in favor of the profession's status quo argue that no one goes into it to get rich. Nevertheless, there was a time when a teaching salary could still firmly guarantee a spot in the middle class. That was more than forty years ago. Today, reality has changed. Though there are economically depressed pockets in the country where a teaching gig might be among the best career options currently available, a teacher's salary is no longer the key to a dependable paycheck and a middle-class living. It's more like sentencing your family to a future of scraping by, which, on bad days, feels a lot like holding them hostage to your ideals about worthwhile employment.

If teachers go into the profession with their eyes open, aware of their future sacrifices, they are also expecting a certain amount of prestige. They expect to feel that esteem in which so many people profess to hold educators. The reality they find is often quite different.

FOUR

DRIVING THE
RUSTBUCKET

THE SOCIAL COSTS
OF CHOOSING TO TEACH

P rofessionals who choose to work in public education are, to
some extent, choosing a relatively spartan existence, or are
acknowledging, as San Lorenzo, California, history teacher
Doug Hamilton has, that "money will always be an immediate
concern in my life." Furthermore, they're choosing to live with so-
cietal attitudes toward the profession that are conflicted at best.

Though the teaching profession enjoys a fair amount of prestige, as measured in polls (a Harris Poll reported in 2003 that 73
percent of Americans would say that teaching, at any grade level,
is a profession with "very great" or "considerable prestige")[1] a majority of teachers say they feel underrespected in their communities, and almost every teacher can speak about being seen, despite
the purported esteem of their occupation, as a second-class citi-
zen. They are expected to drive the most dilapidated car in the
parking lot; they are expected—or at the very least, people are not

RELATIVE STANDARD OF LIVING FOR TEACHERS
IS LOWEST IN 40 YEARS[2]

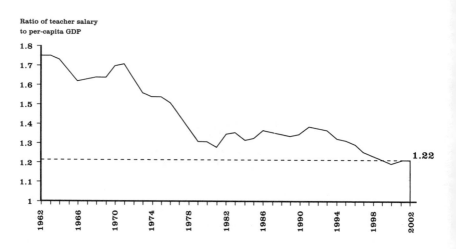

Ratio of teacher salary
to per-capita GDP

surprised if they need—to get help from their parents to buy homes or take vacations.

It's this subtle condescension—"Teachers are great, but it's acceptable that they're poor"—that many educators find grating, and it takes some of the joy out of the job. In the chapters to come, teachers allude to attitudinal problems they experience and to the social costs of teaching; here, they speak to these subjects directly.

Dave Denning, 28, History—Cross Timbers Middle School, Grapevine, Texas

There was a girl I dated for a long time, through high school and into college. In my senior year, I said, "I wouldn't mind maybe going into teaching," and she said, "Don't waste your talent on that."

You think about things like that. Am I wasting my talent doing this? My wife is in the business world, and you go to dinners and you wonder what they're thinking: "Good for him, he's teaching," but you also wonder, what are they really thinking?

Doug Hamilton, 40, History—San Lorenzo High School, San Lorenzo, California

I remember when I met my future father-in-law. I intended to marry his daughter, and every time I saw him, he said something like, "You know, Doug, you're a talented guy. You're a likable guy. Why can't you be a salesman? Why don't you get into another profession? One that's going to pay you?"

I said, "Well, you know, Bob, I like to teach. It's my thing. It's my passion."

He would say, "But you can be passionate about other stuff. Teaching isn't going to pay you. You're not going to be able to buy the big house." Because I was a teacher, her parents didn't consider me a very good breadwinner.

April Sharpe, 31, Art Teacher—Homestead High School, Homestead, Florida

When I started as a teacher, I knew that my parents were disappointed. They were shocked. Their initial response was, "You don't need a $100,000 education to do this." They expected me to be an attorney or a veterinarian. They looked at teaching as something temporary. They expected me to continue with my higher education and move on. They would come right out and say it: "You should have been a lawyer." My mom thinks I settled for what was comfortable and what she thinks was easy. At this point, though, they're proud of what I do. When they come to school events or something makes it into the paper, they are so proud. Last year I was Teacher of the Year, and they were ecstatic. So it yo-yos back and forth.

Brian Mock, 31, Social Studies—Catalina Foothills High School, Tucson, Arizona

I teach in a very affluent area. It's frustrating seeing kids drive up in a Mercedes or BMW or SUV. With all that stuff in the back of my mind about paying bills, it's definitely jaded me. Luckily not that much. But I'm single. I live alone. I have cheap rent. I get some assistance from my family.

There's a class thing going on, and everyone knows it. It's frustrating because you've chosen this profession. It is a profession, but kids will joke, "Oh, my garbage man probably makes more than you." That's only some of them. Just as many have shown support for what I do.

The kids in this district are, overall, used to getting what they want, and they get frustrated when they don't. They want results when they hand something in. I'm sure a lot of them think, "Oh, he's jealous of me or of my dad or my family because he doesn't make much." Those vibes are always around. So much of it is just under the surface.

Every once in a while, a kid will bring up my salary and how it's not enough to buy a house or a nice car. For ten years, I drove an old Honda Civic, and kids said, "Oh, that's the teacher car." A teacher car is a '91 hatchback, with lots of papers all over the place. Kids would always joke, "So when are you going to get a new car?" And I said, "What do you mean? Why is that important?" and get them thinking about economic and class issues. It's a tool I use to get them to better understand where they are in the whole system—on top.

My grandmother helped me out a few years ago and bought me a new car. I guess I fit in with the kids now in that regard.

Kathryn Wright, 33, Second Grade—Hawthorne Elementary School, Helena, Montana

It's a contradiction. Due to a teacher's lack of pay, there's a certain stigma. People say, "Oh, you're so wonderful, you're a teacher, what a giver." But at the same time, there's a contradiction, a lack of respect. It goes along with not being able to lead a certain type of lifestyle. I had one parent in my neighborhood say to me, "Oh yeah, I went in for my daughter's preschool conference and I walked in thinking, 'I have so much more education than this woman—what can she tell me?'"

* * *

Teachers spend a good deal of money on their own education, and their earnings often do little to make up for those expenses. As in the case of April Sharpe's parents, it's not unusual for teachers to be concerned that they are "wasting" their $100,000 educations on a field that will not advance them financially.

Eric Lehman, 33, Fourth Grade—Hawthorne Elementary School, Helena, Montana

It's hard for me when I see the folks that I graduated with, with different majors—not that anyone is filthy rich—to see their salaries and the things they are able to do with their families. It bothers me. We do live paycheck to paycheck, and after ten years it feels like there should be a little more security. We save what we can. I love what I do enough that I've come to realize that there is more to life than money, but that is a pretty big choice to make.

My school is in the Upper West Mansion district—old money. Some of my kids—I'm not making this up—go to Tahiti for Christmas. One year I had a girl who was going diving off the coast of Tuscany. As a teacher, you're watching these young kids, and you think, those are experiences I'll never be able to provide for my kids. It tears at you. At the same time I can live vicariously through them.

We went home for Christmas to our friends' house and there was a new car in the driveway and a new addition. My wife and I live in a fixer-upper that we cannot afford to fix up. We do little things when we can, but as far as any major renovations, we don't have the money. It's not that I have any illusions about buying a mansion on the hill. It's that it's five days before the paycheck comes and my wife and I are squabbling over money.

Greg Worley, 37, Fifth Grade—Parmelee Elementary, Oklahoma City, Oklahoma

Thirty-five years old, and I'm calling Dad asking him to sign a loan for me. I'm a thirty-five-year-old college graduate, that's the worst thing. I should be proud of what I've done, and I don't mean to sound ungrateful for what I have. I know there are so many more who don't have as much. But we teachers have worked hard to get where we are, and it's just frustrating.

Elizabeth Grady, 57, K–12 Coordinator for History and Social Sciences— Cambridge Massachusetts Public Schools, Cambridge, Massachusetts

I was in the first generation of women who graduated from Radcliffe, in the late sixties, early seventies, as the glass ceiling was beginning to lift for women in nontraditional careers, but I was right in that last cohort, where, if you were a bright girl, there were only two career tracks open to you: to become a teacher or to become a nurse. I had not planned to be a teacher. I went to college to get my master's in anthropology, but the Vietnam War just totally destroyed any type of research in the social sciences. I defaulted into the old career mode and said, Okay, I'll become a teacher. But in terms of social costs, yeah, I've had kids say to my face, "You're so smart, why are you a teacher?" My response is, "Well, you want someone stupid to teach you?" I mean, what's the message?

I found that the more educated I got, the higher the social costs were. People would say, "You went to Harvard and you're a teacher? You have a doctorate and you're a teacher?" There was always that, and I think in my family it was tough, because I had a brother who was a multimillionaire, and the attitude of my parents was, "Well, you're as smart as he is, why did you choose this path?" But for me, on the other hand, the social costs aren't always all negative. Sometimes you do get a certain amount of grudging admiration for sticking it out.

I have a friend who graduated from Radcliffe in '77. That was the last year women were in a separate class from the men at Harvard, and at the twenty-fifth class reunion she was singled out as having an extraordinary career because she was a teacher. It was very sad, in some ways, because she was the only teacher who came out of that elite school. That's the tension.

For the longest time, I refused to sign in when I came to work. I said, "I'm a teacher here; if I'm not going to be here I'll let you know." I'm not going to punch the clock; I refuse to do it. I saw it as a form of civil disobedience. With teachers, there's this schizophrenia: Are you some sort of worker, or are you a professional? I don't think that's ever been ironed out. The unions tend to protect the worst teachers, and we're having a real fall-off in union membership in Cambridge because people say, "I don't want to be in this anymore. I don't want to pay the fees and I don't want to be in a union because I don't want that tag." I think that's an issue, that schizophrenia: Are you a professional or are you not?

*   *   *

The conversation about teacher pay does not have easily definable boundaries. When we think we are talking about the simple economics of not earning enough to raise a family, we eventually find ourselves talking about this nebulous set of social costs—not just failing to impress your future father-in-law, but the unsettling sensation of being lionized for your saintliness while simultaneously believing your friends think your profession isn't really a profession and that you're a rube anyway for working so hard in exchange for so little.

Teachers also seem to exist in a strange realm with regard to the status of their profession, somewhere between a union-protected workforce and a college faculty. We expect them to be brilliant and capable, and yet we treat them in a way that leaves them feeling untrusted, like Betsy Grady, who holds a PhD, mentions above—she'll let the school know if she won't be arriving at work, but she refuses to punch in like a person serving meals at a fast-food restaurant. It's the rare professional who can live with the seeming contradictions built into the field of public education.

Much of the tension around the status of teaching seems to derive from the feeling that teaching isn't actually that challenging, that even people with little or no training could do the work as well as the person in the classroom. It turns out to be much more complicated than many of us realize.

UNDERSTANDING— TRULY UNDERSTANDING —WHAT GOES INTO EFFECTIVE TEACHING

TO BE A TEACHER

EXPERTS TALK ABOUT WHAT IT TAKES
TO BE A GREAT EDUCATOR

B ased on our own experiences as students, we all have a sense of what happens in the classroom. We understand the basic processes and structures: students come in, teacher takes attendance, lesson begins. But when education and cognition experts speak about effective teaching, they paint a deeper and more detailed picture. From lesson planning to delivering instructions, from greeting children at the beginning of a class to introducing a new concept, effective teachers make decisions constantly—often very rapidly and sometimes even unconsciously—to create the best learning conditions for their students.

If every student came to school ready to learn and schools were the perfect environments for encouraging learning, a teacher's job would likely be significantly easier. But students at all levels do not always arrive in class ready to learn, and schools are sometimes so large they are not able make the individual needs of students the highest priority. Good teachers are always thinking in terms of large-scale, overarching goals, such as creating a positive classroom culture and fostering students' critical-thinking abilities. They are simultaneously moving students toward short-term, immediate goals—ensuring all students understand the instructions for that evening's Spanish homework, successfully transitioning from a lab experiment involving crickets to quiet reading time in a second-grade classroom, or making sure Anthony, who seems upset and might become disruptive, knows that his teacher cares about him and expects him to focus.

Here, a variety of experts—sociologists, cognitive scientists, education-policy thinkers—speak about the elements of effective teaching. The point of this chapter is not simply to take a detour into the world of pedagogy, but to explain why teaching is not just something anybody with a bachelor's degree can do. Good teaching is extremely complex, subtle, and nuanced, and it's well worth everything we can afford to spend on it.

Linda Darling-Hammond, Charles E. Docommun Professor of Education at Stanford University; Faculty Sponsor for Stanford's Teacher Education Program (STEP)

Darling-Hammond is the author or editor of nine books, including the award-winning The Right to Learn: A Blueprint for Creating Schools That Work, *and more than 200 journal articles that deal with educational reform, policy, and practice. She has served on the White House Advisory Panel's Resource Group for the National Educational Goals.*

First of all, good teachers know how to understand students' thinking: where they are, what they know, what they understand, and how they learn and perceive. They're able to plan a curriculum that starts from where kids are and gets them to where they need to go in any particular subject matter. They understand how the structure of the discipline works, and that allows them to figure out what the ideas are, the scope and sequence of what students need to encounter in order to build their knowledge so that it adds up to deeper understanding and proficiency within a discipline. That's a lot different than having an idea for a particular lesson on a particular day.

They know a lot about group dynamics, and know how to organize a large number of students, twenty or thirty students, so that they can work productively together, can learn from each other, can be presented with tasks that are interesting, engaging, and doable for them, and can accomplish those and achieve success and then build on what they know to achieve more success.

Anyone who has ever spent even two hours overseeing a child's birthday party gets a tiny glimpse of what a teacher needs to know. Most people would find it challenging even to keep kids busy and not in crisis for a couple of hours. They don't even have to ensure that the students learn anything or master new skills and proficiencies or become more socially adept or more responsible citizens. So think about what a teacher needs to know to do that. You have to think about not only being able to keep the students busy, but being able to organize them so that they get a lot of learning accomplished.

A teacher needs to know how to assess what students know and what they don't know, and what they're learning and how they're learning, so that they can use that assessment to solve problems in learning and to plan their curriculum.

Teachers need to know how people learn to read. Even a high school teacher needs to know how to help kids master both elementary and sophisticated skills in reading. Even if that teacher is a math teacher, she needs to know about literacy, because what kids can do has a great deal to do with how they can make meaning out of texts. And as many teachers find out, even some high school kids have not mastered those skills.

A teacher needs to know how students who have neurobiological differences and disabilities process information and learn, so that she can work with the 10 to 20 percent of students who have specific kinds of learning disabilities and special education needs. That may mean adapting the curriculum in a variety of ways for those students so that they can make progress. It's not enough to say, "You get it or you don't," or, "I got you the book." You have to figure out how to help everyone learn. A teacher needs to know today how to make content accessible to students who don't speak English as a first language and who may not speak English at all when they come into your classroom, how people acquire language and how you help them do that within a subject matter or field (with its own specialized language).

A teacher needs to know how to manage interpersonal relationships and dynamics among kids. For example, in any given classroom there are some students who are high-status students and other students who often get bullied or ignored by their peers, and the teacher needs to know how to help those students find a niche and a foothold so that they can be respected and become contributing members of the classroom. The teacher needs to know how to teach other kids how to consider one another respectfully, and get along and work together in productive ways.

And I'm just getting started! So much! A teacher needs to know how to collaborate with other professionals in order to build a school environment that meets all of the students' needs and allows them to have a coherent experience as they go from grade to grade and classroom to classroom and are helped by a variety of professionals.

A teacher needs to know how to work with parents and families, needs to understand different family norms and expectations and cultures and backgrounds and how to find common ground in working together on behalf of the child. A teacher needs to know how to get from parents what they know about the child, so they can be partners together. A teacher needs to know a lot about cultural context for learning because everyone's learning is shaped by their cultural expectations and experiences, and they need to know how to enquire into that because it's going to be a different set of beliefs and understanding and expectations and experiences that kids bring to classrooms in every different community.

Dan Lortie, Sociologist, Former Professor of Sociology at University of Chicago

Lortie is most famous for his book Schoolteacher: A Sociological Study, *which, though published in 1975, continues to be widely read by students of sociology and education. His current work focuses on elementary school administrators.*

The basic condition that makes the job of teachers difficult is that teachers—as persons, as individuals, and particularly in the lower grades—are trained to think that they're dealing with individual kids. But in fact they're dealing with twenty-five individual kids in each class. Somewhere in there, it is so emotionally trying that it's very hard for teachers to feel successful. There's always a sense that somehow or other, they could have done a better job.

The irony in this is that the smarter and more sensitive the teacher is, the more likely they are to feel that way. The [teachers who aren't as sensitive] think everything's great. In teaching, you have to learn to live with less than you want. Here they are, knocking themselves out for the good of these kids, and yet, somehow or other, not getting a sense of satisfaction. This is what I mean by uncertainty; it's built in. I don't think schools of education have done a good enough job preparing students for that tension of the one against the many, to develop better techniques for assessing what they have achieved. Standardized tests don't do it because teachers care about a lot of things standardized tests don't measure—cognitive things, not just affective things. Standardized tests are narrow. They differ in their utility in terms of what's being taught. It's much easier to test immediate comprehension in math than it is in social studies and art. Somewhere in there lies a difficult question to sort out.

Another complexity is the attitude of families. Willard Waller, a sociologist of education, first wrote in 1928 about this. There are several aspects of this as a problem. One is that when kids leave home for school, they move into a situation which is ordered in a universal way. It's their first experience in having to do what everyone else does. That's partly a function of schooling, to teach people how to live in an ordered world, where there are tasks that have to be done and standards you have to meet. They've got thirty kids from different families. Those families emphasize different things at home, and they've got to somehow combine and unite these kids into a working thing called a classroom, and it ain't the most natural thing in the world. It takes time, as kids go through the system, to get them grooved into the idea that, okay, I'm in Miss Jones's class, and in Miss Jones's class, you've got to do this, you can't do that—to learn the rules and obey the rules.

Deborah Stipek, Dean, Graduate School of Education at Stanford University

Stipek studies the motivation of children, early childhood and elementary education, and school reform. She served for five years on the Board on Children, Youth and Families at the National Research Council.

One of the various difficulties is the context in which teachers teach. Especially if you're teaching in low-income schools, you have, in some states more than others and in some communities more than others, a dearth of resources, and you're trying to meet the needs of children who have very complicated teaching needs—kids who need special services, kids for whom English is a second language. They need a lot of extra help in being able to master curricula when they're getting their teaching in a language in which they're not completely proficient. Many teachers are doing that with very, very thin resources.

There are scandalous contexts in which some teachers work. You have situations where there may be one phone that teachers have available to them, down the hall, and yet we know how important it is for teachers to maintain contact with families. I've seen schools where [during their breaks] teachers are lined up to be able to make a call home to talk to a parent of a child who is having some difficulties.

Often in schools there is no place for teachers to go when they have fifteen minutes to take a breath. There's either no planning time or very little planning time. We expect teachers to individualize instruction, to develop interesting, engaging units, curriculum units, but they're front and center with a group of twenty to thirty-five kids all day long, so when are they going to develop these units? They do it on their own time, they do it on Saturdays, and weekends, and until ten, eleven, twelve o'clock at night. If you're an English teacher, or a teacher in almost any subject, being able to review students' work—to give detailed feedback to students about what they are understanding and what they are not understanding, is a critical variable in being a good teacher and acknowledged to have important implications for how well students learn. So when are teachers going to do that if they're with kids all day long?

*　*　*

Those who study teaching and learning are aware of this fast pace and, in different ways than those who experience it, recognize the effects this pace has on teachers and the students they teach. Researchers like Gaea Leinhardt are keenly aware of the characteristics of good teachers, and are adept at articulating even the most intangible elements of the job.

Gaea Leinhardt, Professor, Graduate School of Education at the University of Pittsburgh

Leinhardt teaches courses on how teachers and students build a common understanding in the classroom. She coordinates the University of Pittsburgh's Cognitive Sciences in Education Program and is a senior scientist in the Learning Research and Development Center.

There are two things that make teaching extraordinarily hard. One is the intensity of being "on" for the six and a half hours that you're on, in ways that almost no other profession requires. You can't drop down and not pay attention, except for very slotted times, and that comes with a specific contract arrangement. When you're with the kids, you cannot *not* be there. That kind of intensity is quite hard. Because of the risks of not being available—the physical risks, the psychological risks, the emotional risks—you must constantly just be there.

For me, it's a sense of changing direction all the time. We're starting a lesson, and even if nothing is interrupting the lesson, I need to constantly remember where we were, where we're going, and where people are with me. How are we, as a group, evolving this understanding, and is everybody at about the same place? It's extraordinarily intense.

Go anywhere else and compare. Go down to a courthouse and look at judges and other professionals. All of them have breaks. Certainly, academics have breaks all the time. There are other professions where you need to be "all there," but the duration of being "all there" is usually a little shorter. In surgery, they don't always go back and do it the next day. They have one operation, and they know they're going to have a long one, and they prepare for it, and everybody around them, these huge crews, are there to literally mop their brow.

The other thing is that most of us who work with our minds are allowed to control the trajectory of a time period, whether that's a day or a week or a month. We decide, "This is what I'm going to do today." But teachers have a set of obligations—it could be state standards, local standards—and they have a vision of how they're going to get there. They're barraged with interruptions—nonstop interruptions and immediate demands. Those can come from the hierarchy of the school, where the loudspeaker is blaring every twenty minutes to tell you to come to such and such and fill out this form and be somewhere else, or it can be very local: Johnny's dog dies and Suzie's grandmother has cancer and Emily had nightmares all night. It doesn't matter. The immediate psychological environment is in front of you, and you have to cope with it. On a daily basis, it's very wearing.

As parents, we entrust our most precious assets to this system. Think about it: we're taking a little kid, and we're plunking him in a place that we don't know—we haven't examined the physical building—with a human being we haven't examined. We leave our darling child with this person. That person has to be very worthy, and has to be deeply moral. I don't mean to be fuzzy about that; they have to have a real commitment to acting in a humane, honest way, intellectually and in a person-to-person fashion, all the time. They can't be cranky. They can't lose it. Of course, they do, but we're really asking them not to. We're asking them to be above the fray, to be able to care in honest ways with these children, and to administer justice constantly—and in the meantime, to get something taught. It's the juggling, the interruption, the compromise with your own sense of control, that make it more complex than being an engineer who knew a lot of math and now wants to come back and stand in front of a class and teach arithmetic. It's much more complex that that.

It is being detached in the right way so you can make good, just judgment calls and so you can offer a constant optimistic vision toward the future. One of the challenges teachers of adolescents deal with is that one of the safest routes for adolescents is to withdraw, and in the kind of culture that we have now, that's actually a possibility. Someone can withdraw and still be functional. In other times and other places, withdrawing like that meant death. That's not what it means now, and you have to have teachers who are prepared to keep offering an optimistic future vision so students can keep working toward that future vision. That doesn't mean "get good grades in algebra so you can get into the calculus class so you can get into college." It means always imagining the future in all of its complexity, while having a social contract with the parents and the community that today, we're trying to get through these ideas of algebra.

David Klahr, Professor, Department of Psychology at Carnegie Mellon University

Klahr's primary goals in his research in cognitive development are to discover what children know and to explain how they come to know it. His work focuses primarily on science education.

Students often come in with misconceptions about how things work. Everyday language and scientific language have a lot of similarities. They seem similar, but they mean quite different things. A good teacher has to be sensitive, to try to figure out where the child is with respect to what they know, and not just whether they know it or not, but what do they know about this concept that's probably right, and what do they know about it that's probably wrong, and how can I build on what they know that's right, and how can I show them the parts that are wrong. That's the real difficulty.

Here's an example. You're trying to teach kids about electric circuits. When a circuit is open, no current is flowing; when it's closed, the current flows. The students are confused, because open usually refers to a situation when a door is open, and you can go through it. Closed usually means things are stopped. But in electric circuits, a closed circuit means the circuit is closed and electrons can move around that circuit. So there's a word that means almost the opposite in that context of what it means in everyday life. Kids get confused. Then you say, let's use the analogy of water flowing. That's a good one, because water flows, and electrons flow, so you think you have a nice analogy. But again, when you open the faucet, it flows, and when you close it, it doesn't flow, and this is the opposite of what happens when you open the switch and when you close the switch. That's a concept in which the terminology can drive you crazy. If a teacher isn't sensitive to that, the teacher's going to think this kid just doesn't get it. It has to be addressed directly. You have to say to the child, the reason you're confused is you're thinking of what happens in everyday language.

A lot of good teachers know their domain, and they know that kids have misconceptions. They walk around the classroom and they can look at Suzie and say she's got misconception x, and I know how to deal with that; and Joe has misconception y, and I can deal with that. It's not that formal, but that's what a really good teacher can do. That's why it's so important for teachers to know their subject matter. With twenty-five students, it can be twenty-five times as hard.

Assessment is also an important part. Teachers have to be able to figure out what kids know on a continual basis, and they need to have good, clear measures of the things they're trying to teach. Teachers face this conflict between state standards and high-stakes tests. They have to decide how to allocate their time—either to getting ready for some kind of high-stakes assessment or continuing with the unit they're trying to teach.

Steve Seidel, Director, Project Zero, Graduate School of Education, Harvard University

Project Zero supports a variety of ongoing research dedicated to "the development of new approaches to help individuals, groups, and institutions learn to the best of their capacities."

One of the big ironies is that schools are the primary institutions set up for the explicit purpose of teaching and learning, and they're very hard places to do that work. Even though that's their purpose, they're institutions, and teaching and learning are profoundly human enterprises. In so many ways, institutions don't adequately take into account the humanness of learning, of teaching, and of the significance of the relationships between people. I don't just mean between teachers and students but among students and among the adults as a community. There are a lot of human relationships in teaching and learning, and that's not always facilitated so well by the school setting. That's one of the tensions people in the profession of teaching in public schools struggle with. Often the whole time they're in their profession, they find ways to be there by negotiating between the human dimensions of real learning and real teaching and the institutional constraints of the school.

In schools, we as teachers tend to see a phenomenon like Shakespeare's sonnets and we think, this is probably a stretch for this group of thirty-five middle school students, so I'm going to simplify it in some way. Instead of twenty sonnets, I'm going to give them one. Instead of letting them really work with that one, I'm going to paraphrase it for them, or I'm going to do something that simplifies it. The intent generally comes from an understandable place, but in doing that we strip the phenomenon of its real interest and, in a sense, disrespect the complexity of the phenomenon. We also disrespect the potential capacity of these young people's minds to grasp this phenomenon and make sense of it.

So the nature of the task is to create a problem that's within—not immediately within, but potentially within—the capacity of these students to grasp and provide the support that gets them to the place where they can do that and totally respects the complexity of the phenomenon.

Making this happen in public schools takes an absolute clarity about, commitment to, and interest in the minds of your students. You have to believe that they have capable minds. It's a mind that's capable both of reason and of influence, of deep emotion and of struggling with deep emotion.

I think that's another thing that's very inhumane—schools are not particularly comfortable with emotion. A lot of teachers are not particularly comfortable with emotion because when you've got thirty-five kids coming through every hour, and you've got five, six classes a day and three to five classes to prepare for, it becomes very hard to say we're going to deal with everybody's feelings about everything. Part of what happens is that we then even strip the emotional content out of the subject matter that we're studying. Why should anybody be interested? We don't watch movies or TV that are endlessly stripped of emotion. Emotion is one of the absolutely key entry points for all of us to anything that has to do with complex human life—in history, in the arts, and so on.

Take a forty-three-minute class period. People need to come in, get settled, and talk to each other because they haven't been together, right? Some of them might have been, but a lot of them are encountering each other for the first time. There's a lot of social need. There's a need to say hello, if they've got any social relationship at all. If they don't, they need help saying hello because they're going to work together and try to identify long-term, large, project-based ideas, or this set of ideas or this material. Then, teachers need to find the discrete pieces that people can actually feel a sense of progress on, because by that time, it's really thirty to thirty-five minutes. It's basically an insane structure. But, in the real world of work, we do take time to say hello in the morning and ease in. You need to respect that.

*   *   *

The ability to teach specific knowledge about a certain content area—science, math, social studies—is one important skill, but just as important, or maybe even more important, is teaching children *how* to learn. We know teachers help students learn how to read, for instance, but we don't always recognize they must also teach how to *understand* what is read—a skill that becomes increasingly important for students in high school and college. The best teachers make this explicit and juggle dozens of teaching strategies simultaneously, adjusting them to the ever-shifting needs of their students.

Tom Sherman, Professor of Education and Adolescent Psychology at Virginia Polytechnic State University

Sherman is an educational psychologist who studies how children learn and how teachers can teach children to learn. He is a former public school teacher who now teaches in Virginia Tech's teacher training program, helping to train about 120 teachers a year.

One of the problems with thinking, and thinking well, is that it's not like watching Tiger Woods swing a golf club. You may not be able to do it like he does it, but at least you can see how he does it. On the other hand, if you have a student who is particularly good, you can see the outcome, but you can't see what's going on in that student's head. If you have two students, one who is a good thinker and one who is not a good thinker, the one who is not a good thinker really has no access to what the good thinker does. It looks like it's magic, or more likely, it looks like they've got something I don't have, so the student thinks, "They're smart, and I'm not."

It turns out that a lot of kids do develop that kind of a concept: You're a smart guy and I'm not. If I can figure out what you do when you solve a problem and I do those same things, most of the time, I can solve that problem, too. So the question then becomes, How do you get inside an individual's head to show how that thinking takes place? As I've said, you can model what you do, and think out loud. Instead of writing down the answer, you think through, out loud, how you got that answer. You do that in a variety of situations.

The second way is to teach the individual skills specifically. One of the key elements of sophisticated thinking is checking your work. When you think about it, if you don't know how well you've done, you really have no idea what you've done or whether you've done it well. A lot of times in school, kids are taught to wait for the teacher to tell them. It's not taught explicitly, it's just the way it works: Teachers tell you if you got it right or wrong. One of the things that teachers do that makes a big difference is asking kids, "You tell me what you got right or you tell me what you got wrong, because you really can't fix things if you don't know they're wrong." It's best to know this beforehand. That is, it's best if I know this is wrong before I submit it to my editor, or before I put an article in and it gets rejected because I didn't do it right or I didn't have the right information. The same thing is true with kids.

It turns out children who tend not to be high achievers rarely do that kind of self-checking. They look to the teacher. If you ask them, "Well, how did you do on the test?" they say, "Well, I don't know, I haven't gotten it back yet." Of course, we find that very often in higher education, where you ask students how they did on the test and they say, "How would I know? You haven't handed it back yet." You want students to say, "I think I got it," or "There was an issue, but I think I handled it." You want them to have a sense that they know how to handle the material. But that's got to be taught.

An effective teacher not only needs to be a sophisticated thinker him- or herself, but also needs to be able to model that thinking process. You have to make it transparent. Not only that, but you have to get the children to do it. In addition to that, you want children to have a variety of strategies to solve problems and address issues. A defining difference between children who are high achievers and children who are low achievers is that the low achievers have only one way of doing things. The high achievers will have several ways. If one doesn't work, they'll try another, and another. One of the things good teachers do is teach multiple strategies for addressing issues.

One of the best-known examples is this: Children who are good readers have multiple strategies for reading. They tend to read and know when they are understanding. When they are reading, they also know when they are not understanding. When they are not understanding, they have things they can do to help them understand. They may re-read. They may think, How does this relate to me? They may go back and find some material they may have read that will help them understand so they achieve comprehension. On the other hand, poor readers tend to keep on going. Oftentimes they know they don't understand. But they don't have any strategies for correcting their lack of understanding.

So the teacher's job is to teach other ways to read, other strategies for correcting a failure to comprehend. One of the most simple and effective strategies for dealing with comprehension failure is to re-read. A lot of kids think it's supposed to happen the first time. If you don't know, you don't know, and you're never going to get it—that's what they think. But if they use good reading skills, then they will understand when they read.

Another thing good teachers do is to focus on the core issues of the discipline. This helps students not just to understand the information but also to master the intellectual strategies of the discipline. Think about teaching history. In my day, if you went though history, it meant memorizing a lot of names, dates and places and thinking about the temporal relationship between them, and doing a lot of memory work—but now, sophisticated teachers are teaching students to do history. That is, to think through the interpretation of information and what the standards are for interpreting and judging information, rather than just accepting what's there. It means asking questions like, Where does this come from? What was that person thinking? Why would they have interpreted it this way? What are other ways of interpreting it? That's pretty sophisticated stuff, but it is the kind of thing that even very young kids can do, not like a PhD would, but asking the same sort of questions and dealing with the same sort of issues.

It illustrates that great teachers go beyond simply saying, "Think about it, think about it. Just sit there and think about it a minute." Well, hell, if I knew what to do, I wouldn't be sitting here not getting the answer. What does it mean to "Think about it"? So what these teachers are doing is focusing on the components of what we mean when we say "think about it" or "reflect." It might mean "Make some comparisons, create some criteria for making judgments and then apply those criteria, then determine whether you are satisfied or not satisfied," and you build those kinds of skills across time. No matter how old we get, we are still able to become better thinkers.

*　*　*

It's not just that a teacher's day is stressful and virtually devoid of downtime. Every moment of the teaching day, good teachers are doing a number of crucial tasks simultaneously: delivering instruction, keeping all students focused on the task at hand, assessing how well students are understanding, identifying why students are having trouble, modifying explanations and activities, making personal connections to suit the needs of different students, teaching skills that build on what students already know, and preparing them for future learning. In order to fulfill those curricular needs, a teacher must first address the immediate emotional and psychological needs of his students, which often requires that the teacher himself function as the model of moral behavior. Many teachers do this in schools that are sometimes difficult places to do that work.

Given the complexity of the job, it seems imperative to convince the most exceptional people to become teachers. Bringing the very best people to the job is a challenge, and all the recruiting tools in education won't make a real difference until one of them is competitive pay.

TEACHING BELL TO BELL

THERE ARE FEW JOBS AS DEMANDING AS TEACHING; MINUTE TO MINUTE, HOUR TO HOUR—AT ALL TIMES, A TEACHER HAS TO BE "ON"

Teachers live in a strange professional world, unique in that they don't have the freedom to set their own appointments with colleagues, to use the restroom when they want, to ease into their day or go and grab a cup of coffee when they're feeling foggy. Like their students, they live according to the bell.

When you ask a teacher to describe his workday, he often doesn't know where to begin, unsure whether to start with when the bell rings and the students arrive, or when he opens the locker room for morning football practice. There is often a sense of running or, as Anchorage, Alaska, middle-school teacher Julia Normand says, of riding a fast train without brakes.

There's also a sense that the actual workday of a teacher extends long past the official hours in the contract. In the 2001 "Status of the American Public Schoolteacher," the NEA reported that when they considered all the school-related work they did, teachers worked an average of fifty hours every week.[1] Obviously, many are routinely putting in much longer hours. In this chapter, several teachers describe, in the simplest terms, what their jobs look like and how they do what they do.

Doug Hamilton, 40, World History—San Lorenzo High School, San Lorenzo, California

Normally I'll get into work between 6:30 and 7 a.m. That leaves me an hour or hour and a half to assemble the day. Usually I run off my copies the day before, but I'll arrive in time to do the small things like change the board, put up the agenda, think about how I want to teach that day's lesson. If there's a lecture that day, I want to go through it a couple of times. I might draw things off the Internet as enrichment. Sometimes I'll make different charts or I'll change an assignment I've been thinking about the night before. So I come in and usually need all that time. Then the day starts, and it's a mad dash to the end.

Joseph S. Center, 26, English—Payson Middle School, Payson, Utah

Our school has seven periods. You're running at wit's end and stressing out. You have one prep period, normally. Last year, I needed more money, so I was teaching all seven periods, six periods of English and one period of percussion. If I teach a seventh period, I get another 15 percent added to my salary.

I would usually leave home at five in the morning so I could get to school at 5:30, in time to prepare for the day, because I didn't have a prep period. So I'd get grading done, get grades entered into the computer. Then I'd figure out what I was going to do my lesson on, make photocopies, and prepare lectures.

The kids come in at about 7:30, and school starts at 7:50. So I was usually still running and trying to get things ready until just after the Pledge of Allegiance and the announcements were over. I would teach seven periods, and usually I didn't get much of a lunch, again because I was trying to keep up with things.

You have to be on from 7:30 in the morning until 3:30 in the afternoon, and that's just the teaching part. After that, I was with the marching band two hours after school, three days a week. It's just nonstop work, exhausting. Last year was actually only my second year, and I was pretty burned out. If I wanted to keep teaching and if I wanted to maintain my effectiveness as a teacher, I couldn't keep doing that. So this year, I taught the standard six periods and didn't teach a music class, but I'm barely making enough money to get by.

Jeffrey McCabe, 34, Algebra—Wootton High School, Montgomery County, Maryland

I teach Algebra I, which is a double-period algebra class with over half the class mainstreamed special-education students [students with disabilities who take classes with their nondisabled peers, as opposed to those who take distinct special education classes]. It's me and another teacher, and we really have to spend the entire ninety minutes hand-holding the kids, going over the topics in many different ways just so we make sure that they can understand it, and then the hardest part is getting them to perform. We try to teach exactly what other teachers teach in forty-five minutes, but we do it over ninety minutes, over two periods.

A normal class structure is like this: the first ten minutes is a warm-up where I go around and check their homework. Then typically I try to do some type of hands-on activity. To do a traditional "Okay, now we're going to take notes on section 7.2" doesn't work with this group. You have to break it up in ten-minute chunks. You can't spend more than fifteen minutes on one activity; you've got to be changing things constantly. They know what is going to happen the last ten minutes: a cool-down. Very similar to a warm-up but it's actually almost an open-note, open-help, open-book, open-partner quiz that has them put everything they learned that day together and tries to answer questions they would be asked on a test or a quiz.

In the middle there could be a cooperative activity where I give them a worksheet that they try to work through together, and it's a problem-solving thing. Or it'll be teacher-directed. Or, depending on the topic, sometimes I have kids come up to the board and review the topic from the day before.

We do a lot of spiraling [reviewing material] in double-period algebra because I can teach the kids how to, let's say, complete the square to solve a quadratic equation on Monday, and Tuesday they'll come in and they won't know what the heck I'm talking about. But during the cool-down on Monday, 90 percent of the class would get at least a 90 percent on it. They do really well; it's just that the retention is not there. So we're constantly spiraling back. We're constantly doing stuff that we did three weeks ago, three months ago. Unlike a lot of kids, who can say, "Oh, I remember how to do that," these kids need to be re-taught it. So, you do have to build in a lot of time there to say, "Okay, remember when we looked at linear equations?" You even show them one of the problems they actually did, weeks or months ago.

Julia Normand, 65, English—Goldenview Middle School, Anchorage, Alaska

When I was working at a law firm as a computer-support person, my typical day amounted to coming to my desk with a cup of coffee and a roll. I'd sit down and go through messages, drinking my coffee. I'd greet my co-workers when they came in; I'd make a phone call to set up a meeting and plan my day. If I had to go to the bathroom, I just got up and went. I was in charge of my own body, my own life, and my own schedule. I had certain things to get done, and if it took longer than a day, I got paid overtime for it. It was a high-pressure job in many ways, but not in terms of having thirty people needing your attention immediately and knowing that legally, I'm required to be in the room. As a teacher, if I step out of the room to go to the bathroom and something happens, legally, I'm responsible.

It's just such a different thing. You feel like a person when you're working at another job, and you don't feel like a person when you're teaching. It feels like being a train. Somebody switches it on, and it's moving and you had better keep running. You don't have the option to make a personal choice like "I think I'll put this off until tomorrow." There are thirty people, and they need things. You go with it all day.

I guess the equivalent might be if thirty people called me at the same time to tell me their computers crashed. But that's just impossible. The network could go down and thirty people could call, but there'd be five or six of us in the IT department who would go troubleshoot it and one person would man the phones and say to people, "This is probably what we think is happening, it'll probably be about fifteen minutes, we'll let you know." You work at high speed on it, but it's not thirty people standing over you wanting immediate attention.

•　•　•

Teachers are required by law to stay within their classrooms. They are responsible for anything that happens when a student is in their charge. This is a reasonable requirement, yet because there aren't reasonable breaks in school schedules, teachers often lack the basic liberties most occupations take for granted.

Few other professionals see thirty or more clients at once, all with different needs, some of whom may be determined to work counter to your goals. The combination of these factors can be stressful, to say the least—especially when there is no possibility, for hours on end, of respite.

Nancy Gutmann, 61, English—Brookline High School, Brookline, Massachusetts

When you're on, you're on. If I have three classes in a row, there it is, fifty minutes, five-minute break, fifty minutes, five minute break, fifty minutes. I don't get any downtime. The intensity of it, that's one thing. When I come back after vacation, I sometimes feel like I've been assaulted because I've talked to about a hundred people before 9:30 in the morning.

The second thing is the huge variety of people you have to deal with. The fact that in any class of twenty-five, you've got the slow learners and the fast learners, the talkers and the nontalkers, and the kids who have a good sense of humor and the kids you can't make a joke with because they don't like that or they don't get it. It's like juggling—you have to keep all the balls in the air.

The third thing is the incredible amount of work outside of school. It's particularly true as an English teacher, but I have a friend who's a math teacher who spends almost as much time as I do. It's at least two hours every day and usually a good six hours on the weekends. I'm good at preparing, so I don't have to spend as much time on that as I used to, but grading papers still takes an inordinate amount of time. I collect fifty essays every Friday, and I grade those fifty essays on the weekend. That takes a long time on a Saturday. I do six or seven an hour. That's eight hours. I'm a fast reader, but I read them, think about them, and make comments on them. There's no way you can do it in less time than that.

Catherine Travelute, 29, English 9–11—Cross Keys High School, Atlanta

The going to the bathroom thing is a huge thing for me. I actually had to get a note from my doctor saying that I needed to be excused to use the restroom during the day. There were times I had to go six or eight hours without having a chance to leave my classroom.

Dan Beutner, 38, Fifth Grade—Kyrene del Sureño Middle School, Chandler, Arizona

There are needs in your personal life. Recently, we were told via e-mail that our cell phones must be off during the day. I'm divorced and remarried, and I've got four kids, two of whom are older and will be in high school next year. I have a cell phone so my children can get ahold of me if something's going on, and I've basically been told by my employer, "No, that's not okay." If I was working at my old office job and my kid wanted to get ahold of me, it'd be no problem. If I was in the middle of a meeting and my cell phone rang and I was with my boss and I said, "I've got to take this," he'd say, "Yeah, that's fine," knowing that it would take forty-five seconds and I'd be right back. But as a teacher, I'm not supposed to do that. That's another instance where you have to deny yourself.

When I left teaching, one of the benefits that I found working in an office with other adults was that you had the convenience of being able to use the restroom when you needed to, or if you just needed a break, you could get up and walk out onto the balcony, get three minutes of fresh air, and mentally refresh yourself. In the classroom, you don't have that opportunity. You're with students, and you're on the whole time. There is no "Give me a second." In a class, you have between twenty-three and thirty-seven kids, and they're all looking at you, asking "What do we do next? What do we do next? What do we do next?"

Good teachers train their kids how to answer that question, but one of the skills you have to have as a teacher is to be able to dictate what each person is doing every second of the entire school day. What if this kid finishes early or the other kid doesn't have time to finish? You have to adjust for that, and you have to provide something else that is of value, not just a time waster, not just "go watch videos" or "go play a game." The game has to be educationally valid and related to something you've recently taught and they've recently learned.

**Chris McCarty, 26, Former Eighth Grade U.S. History Teacher—
Seymour Middle School, Seymour, Tennessee**
My first teacher-mentor said to me, "You know you're a teacher if you can't think because you don't have time to." That's really how it feels. It seems crazy, but time flies when you're teaching because there's so much going on. Johnny's got a runny nose, and he needs to blow his nose, and he's got his hand up because he wants to go out. A girl might have a problem with a boyfriend, somebody's crying and she needs the girls to help her and console her. You've got to let them have time or otherwise it upsets the whole class. Or Johnny and Bobby like the same girl and they sit next to each other. They're giving each other dirty looks, and every time I turn my back something happens. Little things like that end up being hard to deal with because there's so much of it. You're trying to teach a lesson on George Washington, and at the same time, you've got to make an announcement about the school fair because you're doing a fund-raiser for the forty-third time that year. There are always a million things. It's the ultimate multitasking occupation.

A lot of times, you don't teach, not in terms of the subject matter. A lot of your job as a teacher is dealing with the everyday lives of the students, getting them through life, and trying to be more of a moral and ethical example than you are a curricular example. Kids would e-mail me about things going on at home, like "My dad doesn't understand why I dress this way." Part of your job as a teacher is to explain to them why it's important to listen to their parents and at the same time, explain to them what's going on through their parents' eyes, and explain it in their language. That's hard to do, because those are two different languages.

It's a proving ground. Everything they do is important. Middle school can be the hardest age. You have kids with the maturity level of a small child and the hormones of a teenager, and their bodies are changing. The difference between a seventh grader and an eighth grader is sometimes six to eight inches in height. They have massive changes on a daily basis, whether it's puberty or menstruation. These things are brand-new to them. Combine that with the fact that class structures start coming out. You have kids who are really popular for whatever reason, whether because they're the best athlete or because they don't have as much acne as the next kid, or maybe they wear better clothes.

The teacher's job is to remind kids that what really matters, and I hate to sound like *Chicken Soup for the Soul* here, but what really matters is just being themselves. Whenever you hear the kids say something they shouldn't, you have to be honest, and you have to tell them when they're treating people badly. I would tell kids, Yeah, I remember feeling that all this stuff mattered a lot, but really, when you get older, you're going to realize that it doesn't, and all those things you thought were a big deal really aren't. In the long run, you have two choices—you can do what everyone else wants you to do, or you can be yourself. The people who are happier when they get older are the ones who stuck to their guns and were themselves. It's hard for them to understand.

．　．　．

Teaching is a deeply human endeavor. Steve Seidel of Harvard's Graduate School of Education says, "One of the big ironies is that schools are the primary institutions set up for the explicit purpose of teaching and learning, and they're very hard places to do that work. Even though that's their purpose, they're institutions, and teaching and learning, are profoundly human enterprises. There are a lot of human relationships in teaching and learning, and that's not always facilitated so well by the school setting." The rapid classes, short breaks and running around are not conducive to building human relationships, which are critical to learning and understanding. Still, teachers do their best.

But few of us will ever understand what it's like to teach, how teachers' days compare to ours. In the next chapter, we make the case that a teacher's day is unlike any other.

SEVEN

A DAY IN THE LIFE

COMPARING YOUR DAY TO A TEACHER'S DAY

O n the following pages, we illustrate the difference between two typical workdays. On the right is the schedule of a typical pharmaceutical sales representative, whose job essentially is to get physicians to think about prescribing a certain medication more often. The day is based on the workday of an actual employee of a pharmaceutical company, but he asked that we not use his name or the name of his company. (A fictitious name has been used instead.) On the left is the schedule of high school math teacher Jeffrey McCabe. He chairs a department of eighteen teachers and sees more than ninety students every day.

The pharmaceutical salesman is paid $391.30 for his day. The teacher is paid $256.

JEFFREY McCABE SCHOOLTEACHER	PETER O'NEILL PHARMACEUTICAL SALES
4:00 AM	4:00 AM
Wakes up and works out in basement. Showers and gets ready.	
5:30 AM	5:30 AM
Commutes to work.	
6:00 AM	6:00 AM
• Arrives at school. • Goes to mailbox to pick up notes, receives concerns about class placements, book orders, lost calculators, and grades. • Goes to his office, skims e-mail.	
6:30 AM	6:30 AM
In his office. • Student comes in to make up a quiz. • Two more students who need help from the night's assignment arrive. They ask about one of the later problems that stumped them. They each have a question on a different problem. • Two teachers arrive, interrupting tutoring. One asks about a textbook order, another asks about the quiz to be given that week in Algebra 2.	

JEFFREY McCABE SCHOOLTEACHER	PETER O'NEILL PHARMACEUTICAL SALES
7:00 AM	7:00 AM
• Finds out that a math teacher is absent. Searches for that teacher's lesson plan and attendance sheets. • Meets substitute in absent teacher's room. • Provides orientation to substitute.	• Wakes up. • Turns on computer in home office. • Checks e-mail. • Checks office locations for day's sample dropoffs. • Synchronizes PDA. • Loads drug samples into car.
7:25 AM	7:30 AM
[First period] • Arrives in main office for Instructional Council (administrators and department heads) meeting. Topics covered: summer reading assignments, the awards assembly, and the new county grading and reporting policy. • Takes notes and leaves with a to-do list of items for follow-up.	Showers, gets dressed.
8:10 AM	8:00 AM
• Listens to student announcements on the loudspeaker. • Returns to office to pick up teaching cart. Pushes cart to room 290 for second- and third-period algebra with mainstreamed	Leaves the house in new Jeep Liberty—a company car for which insurance and gas are fully paid.

JEFFREY McCABE SCHOOLTEACHER	PETER O'NEILL PHARMACEUTICAL SALES
special education students, co-taught with a team teacher. • Quickly writes the agenda and evening's homework on the board as students are streaming in. • Greets team teacher. Quickly discusses the lesson they designed together the previous week. • Greets entering students. Overhears students complain about weekend and can tell that one student in particular is in a bad mood and will not focus well.	
8:25–9:10 AM	8:30 AM
[Second period] • Twenty-three students—three students more than the county-mandated limit for these kinds of special education classes—spend ten minutes doing practice problems. These are written on an overhead transparency prepared the previous night. • Takes attendance and enters attendance data into computer. Tries to make eye contact and chat with student he knows is in a bad mood.	• Stops at Starbucks for white chocolate mocha (nonexpensable today because he is not training new sales rep nor meeting physician for sales pitch). • Heads to first appointment, checks voice mail. • Calls girlfriend to say hi.

JEFFREY McCABE SCHOOLTEACHER	PETER O'NEILL PHARMACEUTICAL SALES
• Checks homework.	

• Talks with a student who has not done previous two assignments. Makes a mental note to call that student's home.

8:37 AM

• Explains next activity to students.

• Starts students on hands-on activity. This lesson is about factoring quadratic equations. Visits each student to discuss lesson, answer questions, and troubleshoot stumbling blocks and reinforce concepts from previous lessons that some students still do not understand. Several hands are often raised at once. Co-teacher also responds to students.

• Wraps up activity. Collects algebra tiles. Classwork is not collected, but will be checked in notebook check next week.

8:52 AM

• Hands out markers and one-foot by one-foot whiteboards to teams of four in the class. Makes sure to separate two students unable to work productively

JEFFREY McCABE SCHOOLTEACHER	PETER O'NEILL PHARMACEUTICAL SALES
together. Teams begin to work on different problems they will explain to the class. • Students talk through problems and record work on the white-boards. Student groups decide who will present. Co-teacher and McCabe go to the groups to facilitate where necessary and refocus groups that veer off the subject.	
9:10 AM	9:10 AM
• Five-minute break (second and third periods are together for both periods, so they don't travel; other students in school are traveling from period two to period three). • Students use restroom, get water, and come and talk to McCabe and team teacher about their concerns. Four students are in line to talk with him. Five minutes are up. • McCabe asks three of them to come to his office after school to handle individual concerns because they run out of time.	• Arrives at first appointment, at a family medical practice center. • Updates sales visit record in PDA while waiting ten minutes for doctor. Enters name of new physician in office (new possible customer). • Talks to Dr. A about product. Suggests possible future lunch meeting. Leaves samples and business card.

JEFFREY McCABE SCHOOLTEACHER	PETER O'NEILL PHARMACEUTICAL SALES
9:15–10:00 AM	9:17 AM
[Third period]	• Asks secretary if it's possible to see Dr. B.
• Same twenty-three students remain because Special Education Algebra is two periods long. Students return to their groups and prepare for rest of lesson.	• Updates PDA while waiting to see Dr. B.
	9:25 AM
• Students present group work. McCabe and team teacher point out errors in the first two groups' work. Co-teacher highlights exemplary work from one group for the class to see. The culture in the class is one of risk taking and one where mistakes are okay. No student feels embarrassed, but one is happy to have found a "common error" that may be shared. These problems are later used for review games.	Talks to Dr. B about product. Leaves samples.
	9:35 AM
	• Drives to next appointment.
	• Checks voice mail while en route. Returns call to mom, who lives nearby.
	9:47 AM
• McCabe and team teacher organize cool-down for the last ten minutes. This involves an open-note, open-help, open-book quiz that reinforces what students learned that day. It is made up of the same questions they will be asked on a test so that they can practice.	Stops by Best Buy to use gift certificate manager gave him for last week's successful lunch program. Buys new Xbox game and a CD. Listens to favorite song on new CD.
	9:57 AM
• McCabe and team teacher check in with students, answer questions and roam the room.	Waits in parking lot of next appointment until song ends.

JEFFREY McCABE SCHOOLTEACHER	PETER O'NEILL PHARMACEUTICAL SALES
10:00 AM	**10:00 AM**
• Third-period class over. Students gather up their things and head off to the next class.	• Goes inside, waits five minutes, updates PDA.
• Wheels cart back to the office. A student trails behind him asking about a low grade on an assignment.	• Meets with doctors. Leaves samples.
10:05 AM	
• Back in his office.	
• Lunch. Eats leftovers from last night's dinner.	
• Reads e-mails and listens to voice mail. Ten e-mails from administrators, guidance counselors, and other teachers, and three phone calls from parents, administrators, and other teachers. These have arrived since the school day started.	
• Receives a parent concern about a new teacher—has to respond immediately to make sure the situation does not escalate. All parent complaints about any teacher in his department come to him.	
• Learns that he needs to be at meeting with a student and her	

JEFFREY McCABE SCHOOLTEACHER	PETER O'NEILL PHARMACEUTICAL SALES
family the following morning. At this meeting McCabe will learn that he will be expected to further personalize the lessons so that this student can be successful in math class.	
• Reads and responds to an e-mail from a member of one of the geometry and calculus curricular committees that asks for input on a framework document that will standardize the curriculum in the eighth grade in the two feeder schools.	
• Reads two e-mails from parents whose students were not placed in honors and who wish them to be. These are among the 230 written appeals to change math placements McCabe will handle this semester.	
• Leaves several e-mails and all phone calls for later. Runs out the door to be on time for tutoring session.	
10:30 AM	**10:30 AM**
[Fourth period]	• Leaves appointment.
• Lunchtime tutoring for math students. There are four students	• Stops at post office on the way to next appointment to mail best

JEFFREY McCABE SCHOOLTEACHER	PETER O'NEILL PHARMACEUTICAL SALES
waiting with questions about different tests. Another three are working on various projects and want McCabe's feedback. Tutoring session requires understanding all levels of math and how to teach to all student ability levels.	friend's birthday gift and buy stamps.
10:50 AM	10:45 AM
• Runs back to office to pick up cart and overhead projector for his next class. • Writes agenda, evening's assignment, and warm-up problem on the board as students are entering. • Greets students. A junior asks a question about the upcoming SAT as he is settling in at his desk. McCabe answers the inquiry and resumes his work on the board.	• Arrives at next appointment, at a hospital. Chats with clinic secretary. • Spends five minutes with Doctor C. Leaves product samples.
11:00 AM	11:00 AM
[Fifth period] • Welcomes thirty-two students to pre-calculus. McCabe is concerned about an absent student; asks another student to call him at home to make sure he gets the assignment.	Feeling hungry, picks up muffin at deli. 11:10 AM Back on the road. Calls district manager regarding next weeklong sales seminar in Vegas,

132

JEFFREY McCABE
SCHOOLTEACHER

- Checks students' homework as students are doing a warm-up problem.

- Teaches lesson on vectors using overhead projector. Students take notes and ask questions. Uses the overhead transparencies he prepared the week before.

- Reminds students that they have an exam in a week. Students ask questions about content of the exam.

- Wraps up and reminds students to copy down their homework assignment. Student reminds him what time class is over.

- Takes his cart back to office.

11:45 AM

[Sixth period]

- Runs to main office, checks mailbox for memos and homework.

- Financial secretary stops him to ask about a bill for the math department.

PETER O'NEILL
PHARMACEUTICAL SALES

where he will be staying at MGM Grand. Can expect tour of Hoover Dam, UNLV basketball game, and three meals a day on company's tab.

11:20 AM

- Arrives at office of group of physicians. Waits ten minutes.

- Speaks to Dr. D for ten minutes. Convinces him product really is the best for patients. Leaves product samples.

11:45 AM

On the road to lunch meeting with Dr. E.

JEFFREY McCABE
SCHOOLTEACHER

PETER O'NEILL
PHARMACEUTICAL SALES

• Administrator stops to ask about the class schedule next year. He wants to raise the class size cap of Honors Geometry from thirty-two to thirty-three. McCabe disagrees and argues his point.

• Guidance counselor stops him to see if Tim Jones has been placed in the higher-level class yet. Counselor has also heard from the parents who e-mailed McCabe.

• Makes copies of agenda for department meeting that afternoon.

• Does not get a chance to get back to his office during this time. Realizes this and rushes to next class.

12:10 PM

12:10 PM

[AP Calculus tutoring]

• Six students are waiting with questions in AP Calculus. The AP exam is coming up and the students are anxious.

• Tutors students on functions, integrals, and derivatives.

• Leaves and returns to his office.

• Arrives at restaurant. Reads newspaper and drinks iced tea while waiting for Doctor E.

• Dr. E arrives. Sits down, chats about his kids, orders strawberry lemonade and crab cakes to start. Decides on salad with organic baby greens and barbecued Copper River salmon.

JEFFREY McCABE SCHOOLTEACHER	PETER O'NEILL PHARMACEUTICAL SALES
12:30 PM	
[Seventh period, office]	
• Eats a protein bar and shake.	
• Gets three calls while in office from other teachers and parents. Looks at sixty-four pre-calculus quizzes that need grading. Remembers three parents waiting to hear from him today.	
• Plans pre-calculus lesson plan. Doesn't finish lesson plan. Hasn't responded to principal yet on issue about a textbook decision for next year.	
1:20 PM	1:20 PM
• Takes cart to room 287 where he writes agenda, warm-up problem, and assignment on board.	Lunch check arrives: $62.10, with tax and tip. Bills it to expense account.
• Moves desks around to accommodate overhead projector and cart.	
1:25 PM	1:30 PM
[Eighth period]	• On the road, stops to pick up dry cleaning. Calls fly-fishing shop to check the fishing report for his favorite stream.
• Starts by checking homework as thirty-two pre-calculus students are doing a warm-up problem	• Ducks into bookstore to pick

JEFFREY McCABE SCHOOLTEACHER	PETER O'NEILL PHARMACEUTICAL SALES
they are getting from his over- head projector. • Teaches same lesson plan about vectors as fifth period. While teaching, thinks about how concerned he is for three of the students and feels that they will be better off not joining AP Calculus the following year. • Finishes up lesson; discusses upcoming exam with students. 2:10 PM	up a copy of *Moneyball* by Michael Lewis. 2:10 PM
• Runs back to office to get agendas for afternoon meeting he is leading. Students greet him at his office with questions and concerns. He asks them to come in the morning because he is running late for a meeting. Two of them are students who didn't get a chance to talk with him during an earlier break. 2:15 PM	• Checks voice mail. • Calls sales manager back. Talks about exceeding quota to the tune of 127 percent. His regional ranking is No. 1 and is in the top 10 percent nationally. If he gets into the top 5 percent, he will win an extra week of vacation and a first-class trip for two to the Cayman Islands—worth about $8,000. He is told what a great job he's doing. He decides, given that he did sixteen sales visits the previous day, he can probably get away with just one more sales visit today.
Skims his agenda on way to department meeting. Knows that there will be some tension about class assignments from some of the faculty next year. Starts to feel hungry but has forgotten his snack in his office.	

JEFFREY McCABE SCHOOLTEACHER	PETER O'NEILL PHARMACEUTICAL SALES
	2:35 PM
	After completing last sales call, heads home.
3:15 PM	3:15 PM
Finishes up meeting on time. Chats with several teachers as they leave the meeting.	• Gets home. • Checks e-mail, reconciles samples, inputs call notes.
3:30 PM	3:30 PM
[Back in the office] • Tutors two students who have waited for him. • Orders textbooks for the geometry team. • Finally gets to e-mails—answers two to upset parents supporting the math teacher's choice to place their children in the appropriate class the upcoming year. Knows that the e-mails will be printed out and showed to principal—writes delicately about students' skills. • Grades some homework, projects, and exams. Does not finish.	Plays new video game.

JEFFREY McCABE SCHOOLTEACHER	PETER O'NEILL PHARMACEUTICAL SALES
4:30 PM	4:30 PM
Leaves to go home with his algebra I book.	Does laundry and dishes.
6:00 PM	6:00–7:30 PM
• Arrives home, helps put dinner on table. • Cleans kitchen.	• Plays in softball game. • Goes out with team afterward.
6:30 PM	
Helps with baths and pajamas with his three children under six years old.	
7:00 PM	
Reads the sports section.	
7:30 PM	
Reads stories to children.	
8:00 PM	8:00 PM
Puts children to sleep. 8:30 PM • Plans algebra I lessons. • Begins grading quizzes.	Talks to girlfriend about taking tomorrow off to go fishing; will take company car and use subsidized gas.

JEFFREY McCABE SCHOOLTEACHER	PETER O'NEILL PHARMACEUTICAL SALES
9:15 PM	9:15 PM
Falls asleep in front of the TV while grading papers.	Watches TV, has a beer.

SO WHY DO THEY BOTHER?

TEACHERS TALK ABOUT THE COUNTLESS THINGS THAT MAKE IT ALL WORTHWHILE

Given the hours and the stress, and despite the numbers of teachers who do leave, the majority of educators tough it out and stay. Why? Of the nearly 200 teachers polled for this book, only one said that money was a positive motivating factor. He was a middle-school music teacher from Kentucky who explained that teaching "pays me more than I made in three years of bass playing. Now I make easily twice what any other jobbing musician in town makes."

In surveys for its "Status of the American Schoolteacher" report, the NEA asked teachers why they stay in the business of education. Not surprisingly, the top three reasons turned out to be (a) teachers enjoy working with young people; (b) they feel education is important; and (c) they have a deep interest in their subject matter.[1] This is a very dry way of saying that teachers love their jobs because teaching can be the most emotionally rewarding, intellectually invigorating, and soul-satisfying job on earth.

In this chapter, we let teachers tell those stories. These teachers are at all stages in their careers. Some are just starting out, some are many years in. Some will stay. Some, like Jonathan Dearman, will find other jobs.

Kim Meck, 35, Second Grade—Fire Lake Elementary, Eagle River, Alaska

I absolutely love teaching. I love to work with kids and bring the "ah-ha!" to them, and help them develop a love for learning. For my first experience with fifth grade, I got a class that decided they did not want to be at school. They thought it was the stupidest place in the world, and so my only goal was to instill a love of learning. By the end of the year, I had. This is a very important thing, especially at the grade-school level. We are all lifelong learners. We have to enjoy learning. It's a part of everyday life, no matter what you do.

I'm currently teaching second grade, and I've looped up from first grade with them, so this is my second year with more than half the class. It gives me a good relationship with the kids and with the families. Over the summer, I'll do things like send out postcards that say, "Ms. Meck is going to be at such and such campground, and you're welcome to join her for a picnic and a bike ride," and invite the families to come out and do things over the summer. We can keep the connections, so the transition in the fall is easy. When we get to school, we hit the pavement running, which is absolutely awesome because on the first day of school I can pass out assignments. I know where they are, I know what level they're reading at.

I'm teaching a lot of reading right now. They're starting to move into chapter books. When they're becoming more fluent readers, when they're talking about how you can see the pictures in your mind, you start that whole process of explaining, "You know, when I am reading, this is what it looks like in my mind."

You introduce that whole concept, and then all of a sudden, a couple of them start getting it. "Ms. Meck! Ms. Meck! The video! It's running in my head! It's great!" You can never get a book out of their hands. It's just that kind of excitement when they first discover it. That's the ah-ha!

That's why I'm teaching: because I can give that to somebody else and make them excited about it. There's such a huge world of reading, and when you give them such a gift, it's amazing. Now, that happened within the first three weeks of school, and I still can't take books out of some of their hands. Now we're at the end of the year, the last six weeks. It's those kinds of things, watching what happens.

I'll do strange things, like have them stand on their chairs if they're done with their math problem so that I'll know they're ready to give me an answer. Or I'll have them give me a silent signal instead of raising their hand, like sticking their tongue out. It helps them to develop a joy, really, of being there and making those connections, which are so important. If we don't build those connections, a lot of things in life end up being a lot more difficult than necessary.

The school is setting up my class for next year, and I always ask them, give me your toughest kids. By the end of the year, they're eating out of my hand. And I'm saying, why did you call this child a bad kid?

Elizabeth Grady, 57, K–12 Coordinator for History and Social Sciences— Cambridge Massachusetts Public Schools, Cambridge, Massachusetts
When the "teaching for understanding" curriculum model was first getting off the ground, [researchers] went around and plucked a bunch of teachers considered to be exemplary. They met with us, and picked our brains: How do you know what you're doing? How do you know what the kids are doing? Then

the researchers came in and talked to our kids. I was teaching a course in world history, and it was organized around ideas.

They yanked a kid out of my class and asked if they could talk to him about what we'd learned that day. I still remember him— Manuel Davis. He was about up to my knee—a small, skinny little kid, and the researchers carried him off, and they said, "Now, Manny, what did you learn in class today?"

Manny looked them in the eye and said, "I learned all about ethical monotheism."

They nearly fell out of their chairs.

That's what we were doing! Then they grilled him, and this kid held his own in front of all these Harvard researchers—he knew what he was talking about. That's when I knew it was sticking. I could take a pretty complicated idea and make it accessible to kids, and the kid was able to hold his own against the forces of maybe six or seven Harvard researchers trying to find out how he understood it and how he learned it. I knew it would stick, and it stuck.

It's hard, because we all know that when you're a teacher, the returns are not immediate. Every so often you find little notes, or a kid will send you a postcard. I always joke because now I'll meet some middle-aged fat guy in the street and he'll say, "Oh, you were my favorite teacher!"

Jeffrey Taylor Bauer, 31, Third Grade—Lincoln School, Englewood, New Jersey

I wasn't crazy about my childhood. Somewhere in high school, I got the idea that I would be a teacher so I could be there for some child where someone wasn't there for me. That's how I decided to be a teacher.

I ended up teaching in North Philadelphia. My school was a Title I school [a school where over 35 percent of the students live in poverty]. Ninety-eight percent were considered at poverty level back then. The population was about 98 percent African American, a few Latino. I taught kindergarten there for three years. Somewhere along the line, I started to realize I had a lot of misperceptions. I went to schools in Philly, so in high school I had mostly black friends, but I had misjudged things. I always thought that I was going to bring something like the Great White Hope to these poor little black kids. Then, somewhere along the way, I realized that my life was being enriched via another culture. There were things *I* was learning.

Simply put, I got a rough class this year. I got it because I know the principal figured that if anyone could take care of these kids this year, I could whip them into shape. I have, but it's been horrible. At times, I'll come right home from school and go straight to bed, sleeping until the next morning. I'm getting more gray hairs, and sometimes I want to pull my hair out. This morning, I was looking forward to seeing my kids. I was surprised. I missed them. I really did.

Every year, I feel like the culture of the classroom develops into a family. Even though there are children who obviously hate each other and there are kids who drive me crazy and want to test me, each one of them has got something. I have a little boy who is an excellent dancer and loves music, with a smile that lights up. He's so silly at times, and he's often lazy, but he sparks something in me that makes me feel alive. I have a little girl who's the perfect student. I just did report cards and she got straight As, but she's also got a good sense of humor. Kids are funny. I laugh. I have to tell you, I've never experienced joy in my life like I have with teaching.

There's joy in quiet moments. Every day after lunch, the kids have a chance to select books and read whatever they want. I have a large library in the class because I think choice is important.

There are times when I look out at the class and everyone's reading, silently. I'll look at them. I'll watch their little eyes moving left to right, and I'll think, that's awesome.

April Sharpe, 31, Studio Art and AP Art History— Homestead Senior High School, Homestead, Florida

Just this week, one of my students won a national poster contest. To see them succeed, or see them do something they thought they weren't capable of, to have them nationally recognized, is pretty good. The theme was "Coming together to build a better world." It's great to get to tell him his effort paid off and he is going to get to do things he didn't think he was going to get to do. He'll take a trip and make some money and have his work published.

It makes you very proud to be an instrumental part in making that happen. When my kids pass their AP art history exam and I know that they've gotten college credit, when they come to you and tell you, "I watched Jeopardy last night and I knew the answer and I felt so smart. My parents were impressed," that's a real boost. Anytime you make a difference, it's worth it.

Sam Stecher, 29, American History, Eighth Grade— Horizon Middle School, Kearney, Nebraska

I was a typical college student—searching. I started off in broadcast journalism, then moved to physical therapy. I'm not sure why. I wasn't happy with that, and I became a history major. My father said, "You're a history major, and you're either going to end up going into law, religion, or teaching." Halfheartedly, honestly, I chose the teaching route.

In Nebraska, we have Boys Town at Grand Island, which is about an hour's drive from where I live. [Boys Town provides residential and counseling services to abused, neglected, and abandoned children. Founded in Nebraska, the charity has been known as Girls and Boys Town since 2000.] I had an opportunity to do volunteer work at an emergency shelter. After my first night, I knew working with kids was where I was supposed to be. I was going through the intake process with a young man, just the paperwork, just the standard questions that legally you have to ask to have that person be in attendance at your facility. I was hit by that interaction, by looking at what that young man had been through, looking at how he handled the situation. He said, "You know, you're somebody who's paying attention to me, and that doesn't happen very often." Right there, I was sold. I knew I needed to be in this field. I knew I was supposed to work with kids. This is what I want to do. And from there, I've been committed.

For me, teaching is all about building relationships. If you don't establish a relationship with your students, you're wasting your time. A lot of teachers don't realize that because they're still of the old-school mentality—I'm going to teach, and you're going to learn. That worked for my father's generation, and that worked for a lot of people. The teaching techniques of thirty years ago were fine for thirty years ago. If you want to continue to use them, that's fine, but we're not teaching the children of thirty years ago. We're teaching today's students. It's a different generation, and they've got different needs. You can argue about what those needs are, you can argue about whether those needs are justified. You can argue about who should be taking care of those needs, at home or through society, or through whatever events, but what it comes down to is they're coming into your classroom with those needs. You can either address them and be successful, or you can use the old way and not address them and be miserable.

That's the best part of my job, going through and establishing that relationship. It sounds tough—I've got 100, 200 kids that I see—but if I'm making a concerted effort to make sure a student knows that I'm here, and to make sure that this student knows that I'm glad that he's here, the relationship building is the best part. It's the one part you're going to reap the most benefit from in your classroom.

It's just little stuff. You need to be at your door when the kids come in, and when the kids come in, you need to see them and shake everybody's hand, smile at everyone when they come in, talk to them by name, tell them you're glad they're there. It's too easy for you just to sit behind your desk, typing out your lesson plans, and then when thirty kids file into your classroom, you stand up and start to teach. Then you have no investment in the child and the child has no investment in you.

You need to make it apparent that you have an investment in the child, and you know what? It doesn't hurt to watch fifteen minutes of MTV every day. You have to know what they're watching, what their vernacular is, what their fads are. Whether you agree with it or not, you have to make them aware that you know those things, too. I look at teaching as an investment, and learning is the return that you get out of it. If I make those small investments through my teaching, the learning they get out of it is much greater.

My relationships differ with each student, just like they differ with each friend you have. I'm not friends with 150 different students, but something's working when I see them in the hallway and they make an effort to say hi to me. When I see them in the hallway and they turn around and walk back and say, "Hey, how's it going?"; or when everybody shows up to my class on time and I don't have to hassle anybody about coming in, that tells me they want to be there. I know it's working when I can say, "I know you don't want to do this homework, I know this seems pointless right now, but I'm letting you know I think this is probably going to work out for you in the long run." And they say, "Yeah, you're probably right."

It's great. It's the best thing in the world. I'm very lucky in that I can honestly say I love who I teach, I love what I teach, I love who I work for, I love who I work with. The money issue irks me. However, I always tell people, if money was the most important thing to me, I wouldn't have gotten into education to begin with. I had other options, and this is what I chose. I love what I do too much to stop doing it. The students are too important to me.

Scott Arnold, 42, History—Boise High School, Boise, Idaho

I came to teaching relatively late. I had been a college administrator. I have a master's degree in international relations and a bachelor's degree in history, and while I was working at a small college here in Idaho, I came to the conclusion that I missed the academic side. I was disenchanted with the college and university setting, and, in terms of instilling a passion for the study of history and the social sciences, I realized that one could have greater impact with younger students. So I came to the conclusion that going back to school to get a teaching certificate and giving this a try was something I needed to do. Quite frankly, I haven't looked back since. I find every day a joy, and it's one of the best decisions I've made over the course of my life. It's an eminently satisfying business to be in.

I teach Western civilization for sophomores here at Boise High School, and then I have advanced placement European history for seniors. I'm also the student council advisor, and I have a course on leadership. I thoroughly enjoy all of them. One of the things I was told by my mentor when I started in this business was that you need to reinvent yourself on a regular basis. You need to find those things that excite you about the next lesson—not just the lesson you're doing and not just the lesson you taught last week. Part of success for me comes from making the choice to create a teaching environment where I'm excited to be there, and I have something I'm looking forward to doing with the kids. I think they read us as well, and if they sense excitement and enthusiasm, that's going to affect them. It's like a musician and an audience. The musician can't perform well if the audience is sitting on their hands. It's a symbiotic relationship, and that's important in the classroom.

I'm challenged by the students. Most of them are smarter than I am, and I find that they sometimes take me in directions I hadn't anticipated. They force me to constantly reevaluate my understanding of historical events, my perception and bias, as much as I'm trying to challenge them in terms of their perception and bias.

It's not just for the kids who go to Harvard. I remember one young man in my American government class, a mixture of kids who were and weren't college bound. This young gentleman was one of those fellows who was giving every outward appearance that he was not interested in school, but, as a senior, he was still here, so ultimately, the diploma meant something to him. He didn't like to use his last name. He just went by the name of Rico. One of my greatest experiences, one of the moments I'm proudest of, was late in that first semester, when Rico brought in some tortillas his mother had made for me. At that moment, he was showing me that somewhere along the line, we had connected.

He was never my strongest student, but when I had a substitute, I would list a go-to kid in case there were any problems, and Rico became that kid. I've run into him once or twice. He's been working in restaurants, and he wants to open up his own business. I feel as much pride in terms of my working with him and preparing him for graduation as with any kid.

Paul Callan, 55, Electrical Technology—Ohio County Area Vocational Education Center, Hartford, Kentucky

The neatest thing happened to me in my first year. Actually, it happened in both my first and second year. There is this club called VICA (Vocational Industrial Clubs of America), and they have what's called a Skills Olympics. This organization represents a whole variety of different trades, from plumbers, electricians, carpenters, cabinet builders, bakers—trades taught in a vocational or technical school. The members have competitions once a year. In my first year, I had coached two students, one to enter the residential electrician contest and the other one to enter the industrial electrician contest. Both of those won at the school level, and then they won at the district level, and then they won at the regional level, and then they won at the state level—my first year of teaching! All I was doing was providing support. I was not telling them, listen, you need to do it this way, you need to do it that way. What I was doing was saying, "Listen, if someone's going to look at this, they're going to ask: Are you complying with the national electrical code, is your wiring neat and organized, are you practicing good safety measures as you perform in this competition?" I said, "That's what I'm going to judge you on."

So, these guys came out state winners and went on to a national competition. They didn't place in the nationals, but for a first-year teacher, I couldn't express to you how rewarding it was to have these two guys make it. That was a first for that school and that program. The following year, I had another student who did the same thing and went all the way to the state level. These were very rewarding things.

One of the students stayed after school one day. He said, "Can I practice?" I said, "Yeah." He said, "But I'm going to miss my bus.

I don't know how I'm going to get home." I said, "I'll take you home." This guy was an A student in my class, paid attention, and was involved in the coursework. You would have thought he came from an upper-middle-class home. But this guy came from a small little house: the living room was maybe twelve feet by ten feet. There was enough room for a TV, a coffee table, and a sofa, and there were maybe five rooms in the whole house. One bathroom, one living room, one kitchen, and two bedrooms. It was a little cracker-box place.

By anybody's expectations, driving along the side of the road, you would have said, "Oh, there's another dump." But this guy had self-esteem. I'm sure many of those students had self-esteem. They recognized they were from Kentucky, from a poverty-stricken area, that doing this program through the high school was going to afford them an opportunity to better themselves that wasn't ever offered to their families. So, they were hopping on that boat.

The boy who won the contest the previous year was a senior, and then the next year, he graduated. The high school was being renovated—the administrative offices, a whole new front and a tech library were being added. The contractor happened to be on my advisory committee, and he came down to the classroom one day, and asked, "Paul, do you have anybody who may be graduating this year or has graduated in the past, who wants to have some summer work?" I said, "Yeah, I've got about five of them here."

They had been carrying books in the hallway, and now they were wearing hard hats and had an electrician's tool pouch on their belts. They were making money. They were walking the same hallways, passing the same friends they were walking through school with and playing ball with, but they were employed. I tell you what, you couldn't have seen a prouder instructor anywhere to know that his guys were over there, building that structure, and they had the competencies to do this, after two years or three years of training in the electrical field. That was the icing on the cake for me then. I was in heaven.

One time I was teaching at the college level, and I was in the classroom teaching, and the phone rang. This guy said, "Mr. Callan? You may not remember me, this is Brian Hoheimer." I said, "Oh, I remember you, Brian." And he said, "I've been thinking about you for a while. You remember those couple of years we were in high school, and I was in your class? Remember I got that job with King Electric, working on the school?" And I said, "Yeah." He said, "Well, after that job, I applied for a position at a convent, out in the country, just two or three miles outside the city of Owensboro. I applied as an electrician, maintenance and electrician, and after about two years or so, the guy who ran the place retired, and the sisters thought I had done such a good job they decided not to post the position—they gave me the job. I really owe it all to you." I said, "Brian, you don't owe it to me, you owe it to yourself, because you worked hard for that grade. You worked hard for those life experiences." He was one of those guys who came from the poor side of the tracks.

Those are the rewards you get as a teacher, when you know you've made an impact on somebody's life. I know that I must be doing something right. But sometimes I felt, how come I'm not being acknowledged or rewarded or being given any kudos?

*   *   *

Paul Callan is representative of a large group of teachers who are inspired and who actually rejoice in their students' success. But when teachers this good don't feel appreciated, there's something systemically wrong. In the next section, we hear from teachers who are either struggling with or could no longer live with the inequities of their jobs.

BUYING IN, SELLING OUT, LOSING FAITH

NINE

CRISIS OF FAITH

WHY GOOD TEACHERS CONSIDER LEAVING

Even given the intangible but powerful rewards teachers discussed in the previous chapter, in the middle of their careers—or sometimes quite early on—teachers often experience a crisis of faith. Though most go into teaching wanting to affect the lives of their students and to "make a difference," many begin to feel that the sacrifices that come with the job are intolerable.

Of course, wanting to leave one's job isn't unique to teaching. People in any occupation have moments when they doubt what they're doing, their ability to do it well, whether the effort they put in is worth what they get out of it. But having a crisis of faith in the private sector doesn't carry the same weight as it does for a public school teacher. When teachers begin to doubt their desire to continue in the profession, they often feel they're letting down not only themselves but the students at their school, the parents, and the community as a whole.

The number of people thinking about leaving teaching dwarfs the number who think about leaving other white-collar professions. In a Texas study conducted in the mid-1990s, 44 percent of teachers interviewed were seriously considering leaving teaching.[1] The Society for Human Resources Management reports that across the U.S. workforce, only 8 percent of white-collar workers claim dissatisfaction with their jobs.[2]

Teachers think about leaving for a variety of reasons. The traditional assumption is that the majority of those who quit teaching are women who get married and quit to raise children, no longer needing the income. While this is true for a small number of teachers, there's another group of potential career teachers—both men and women—who give serious thought to the idea of leaving due to the profession's limited earning potential in relation to the myriad challenges and frustrations inherent in the job. The most heartbreaking scenario is when a teacher loves his job, wants to stay at his school, but simply can't afford to.

Outside of some areas of medicine or perhaps relief work, there is perhaps no profession in which so many want so badly to stay but conditions conspire to force them out.

Amanda Deal, 35, Fourth Grade—Mineral Springs Elementary School, Winston-Salem, North Carolina

I love teaching. I really love it. But the low salary, combined with the testing pressures we have in our state, make it hard. With the No Child Left Behind law, Texas and North Carolina were used as models because we're both big testing states. When you combine that sort of pressure and stress with the population I'm teaching, with not being able to make ends meet for my own family, you do have to sit down and ask, Are my priorities in the right place? Should I be sacrificing what I can do for my own family, for these other kids? That sounds cold, but the salaries are so low they force teachers to ask those kinds of questions.

No other profession I know requires as much continuing education for so little pay. I graduated Phi Beta Kappa with an undergraduate business degree from UNC Chapel Hill, a top-ranked business school at both the graduate and undergraduate levels. In spite of this education, as well as my experience having managing 150 people and an annual budget of over $3 million, the state didn't consider me "qualified" to teach fourth grade.

But the state was desperate for teachers, so they hired me with the understanding that I would complete coursework to become certified. I've been working on that since January 2001. Nine courses, plus student teaching, are required. I'm attending a private college; tuition is $645 per three-hour course. You can do the math to figure out how much debt I'll have accrued by the time I complete the coursework and student teaching, because you have to pay tuition for student teaching, too. And don't forget the cost of books and materials. Our school system provides something like $50 a year in tuition reimbursement.

Once I become certified, I'll have to take continuing education workshops to maintain my teaching license. Our system does a fairly good job of providing enough free workshops to maintain licensure; however, if a teacher wants to pursue some other continuing education not provided by our district, there are no funds to pay for that.

The whole time I was working in corporate America, I went to seminars periodically, but the company would pay for me to go, and I would do it on company time, not on my own time. I would sit down each year and create my own goals for professional development. Let's say one of my goals was improving employee morale. If I saw a seminar on that subject, I could nearly always get the company to pay for me to attend, travel, and be lodged for the seminar. If I reached the goals, there was a bonus attached. In education, the school system sets the goal—x number of credits to maintain licensure—and the school system provides some avenue for achieving the goal, but only if done within the system. You get no bonus for completion.

I think about leaving. The money is a huge, huge factor. If I had to say there's a single biggest factor, it's a combination of the salary and the hours required and the stress required to do the job well. I think there's a misconception out there that teachers have a short day, because school ends at three o'clock, and everybody in the corporate world thinks we have two hours of playtime in the afternoon that they don't get, and that's not the reality. There's also the perception that we get all this time off, but you pay dearly for it.

Money is a big factor. Money combined with disillusionment with the whole test-driven model that is so prevalent in our state. There's a lot of "drill-and-kill" in preparation for testing. If I'm sitting up there teaching a lesson that is boring to me, I can't imagine what it's doing to my students. I didn't come into this profession to take all the joy out of learning for children, but some days I feel like I'm doing just that. And then you combine that with the fact that in the meantime, you can barely pay your bills, and quitting definitely crosses your mind.

Duane A. Richards, 29, Fifth Grade—Avocado Elementary School, Homestead, Florida

This is my sixth year teaching. At my school in South Florida, close to 90 percent of the students are on free and reduced-price lunch. Most of the kids are of Hispanic background, about 85 percent, but we have a lot of Haitian Creole, some African American.

When I started out, I knew I was never going to make any

money. I wasn't going into teaching for the money, and I know that I'm not ever going to be rich. I'm going to have to invest and spend wisely and save my money. My wife and I have been putting away money since we've been married—now going on three years—so when we do finally have a child, she can stay home for six months. That's our big goal. We've just about reached it.

But what's happened is the school board put a halt to all teacher raises for two solid years. We went two years with no raise. We finally got raises approved, but there's been no effort to go back and pay us for the years that we've gotten nothing. My annual raise was $150. In addition to that, our medical benefits have declined; our coverage is not as good as it used to be. Now we're faced with paying higher deductibles for every office visit. Our dental coverage used to be included within our medical benefits package, but now we have to pay a portion of that. By the time I pay that, my $150 is gone.

We've been saving all this time to have a child, but the stars had to align for us financially to be able to do it. We had to pay off one of our vehicles. We've had to consolidate our bills. I'm trying to get our bills to a point where we can have a child. We live in a little two-bedroom, one-bathroom house. We would love to get a bigger house, but right now a three-two house in this area is $250,000. On our salaries, it's not really feasible.

I consider myself an excellent teacher, but I've been looking around at other fields. I've been trying the federal Department of Justice to teach inmates in federal prisons, because I've found that their pay is so much better. I would start at $39,000; I'd be guaranteed a 3-percent-a-year cost-of-living raise that's just automatic. That's in addition to any real raise I might get. We're just not keeping up with the cost of living down here.

Right now, being in my classroom with the door closed and being with my students is the only thing I even remotely enjoy about teaching anymore. In this district, even that is being taken from me; our autonomy is being taken away. There's so much emphasis on testing that they're even taking away my ability to choose what kinds of strategies to implement in my classroom. I'm no longer treated as a professional. It's hard, because I love being with those kids. I knew I wanted to do this. I started with the school district when I was sixteen years old doing after-school care, and I knew at that time that I wanted to teach. That's what I've always wanted to do. It kills me that I'm wanting to leave.

I feel like I was born to teach. Every year, the joy of life has been sucked out more and more. The morale of teachers in our district has gotten so bad. We have to fight for everything. I loathe the system for which I have to work, but it's the only way for me to do what I love to do. We have to fight for everything right now. If the pay were there, then it would be worth fighting for. If I was going to work and knowing at least I was going to get a cost-of-living raise, knowing that every year I'm going to make enough money to keep up with the economy, I could handle this. Now you walk away feeling defeated. Quite frankly, the only reason I'm considering leaving the profession is because of the pay, because the pay and benefits aren't sufficient to start and raise a family. Otherwise, all the other headaches and hassle would be worth it, because I would still get to teach.

Jeffrey McCabe, 34, Math—Wootton High School, Rockville, Maryland

I'm considering leaving teaching this summer. I haven't had an interview yet, but I've talked to a couple of companies, and one company basically told me, "Come and work for us, we want you." I'm not ready to make a commitment because I'm doing a lot of soul-searching. I don't know whether I'm ready or not to leave this wonderful profession. I really can't say I'm going to

leave teaching to become this or that. I don't know what I want
to do.

Actually, I know what I want to do: it's teach, because when I
wake up I think, "I can't wait," and as nerdy as this sounds, I can't
wait to teach finding the focus of an ellipse—I can't wait to teach
the kids that. I can't wait to see the look in their eyes when I show
them this completely technical, ridiculously complicated concept
and we break it down in forty-five minutes so they can go home
and do perfectly on their homework. Providing that they do their
homework! But that's a whole other story.

I daydream about teaching. That's why I left the business
world to become a teacher. I hate to sound greedy, but if I could
make it more than paycheck to paycheck and be able to start saving some money, I think I'd stay in this profession.

When I graduated college with an economics degree, I went
into business. I was working in technical sales for Bell Atlantic. I
was selling digital data services and working with businesses to
connect data lines. This was before DSL, before the Internet ex-
ploded. In '94, I cleared about $45,000. I was on pace to making
about $52,000 my second year. I left to go to graduate school to
become a teacher. Currently I am making $55,000. After almost
nine years in the classroom I'm now making what I would have
made the year I left private industry.

Tish Smedly, 53, Pre-kindergarten—Metro Nashville Public Schools, Nashville, Tennessee

You work 7:30 in the morning until 7, 7:30 at night. Then you
bring your work home. It's a twenty-four-hour-a-day job if you
do it the way you should. You get used to it and you go on and
you do it, because you know that's what the kids need. We get
very little spending money. There are little incidentals we spend

a lot of money for. If you plant seeds, you've got to buy seeds. If you are going to plant seeds, you've got to buy dirt. Rarely do I go a day without a bag of something from the grocery store, department store, the K-Mart, the Wal-Mart. So then you think, where is this going, money-wise? Do you ever make enough money? No. My first principal said, "If it weren't for us, the doctors, the lawyers—nobody would be anywhere." They don't realize that. They had to learn to read somewhere.

Everyone says, "You're not paid enough." But do they really know that, or do they think that's what you are supposed to say? I have mixed feelings about that. I have a friend who teaches in Atlanta. Another teacher boards her dogs for her, and he is actually going to quit teaching this year because he can probably more than triple his salary boarding dogs! Here we are, and he's just going to give up teaching. A teacher who works with me said, "You know, I make more money painting houses than I can teaching."

Brad Coulter, 43, Fourth Grade—Lakeview Elementary, Kirkland, Washington

I've taught for seventeen years in the Seattle area, in a suburban district. I've taught elementary school, anything from first to sixth grade. I have a geology degree, and out of college I worked in northern California, in the geothermal industry up by Santa Rosa. I went back to school and got my teaching credential, and I've been a teacher ever since.

My original plan, even as a twelve-year-old, was to be a teacher. I worked with kids in junior high and high school, I tutored, and I worked in special education classrooms. I worked in preschool. I did a lot of work with kids since I was on that path already, but I wanted to give something else a try before I decided to go into teaching. I think my gift has been working with kids.

I was in college in the early '80s, and I remember teacher pay being something like $14,000 a year. That was pretty laughable compared to some other disciplines in the sciences and engineering, but at the time, money didn't seem like that big a deal. It was an issue, but I was too young to understand what it really meant. I wanted to work with kids.

The issue of burnout is a huge one to me. I've gone through phases where I've been fresh and excited, working night and day. My first few years, I was so motivated. I can remember riding my bike around Seattle—all I could think about was what I was going to do Monday morning. I got married, had a couple of kids, and didn't have the kind of time that I did early on. I got tired of the daily grind of teaching and burned out after awhile. Boy, it's tough to teach when you don't have the spark. With all those kids and all the demands, the planning and correcting and so on—that can eat away at you. I've been burnt out a couple of different times, and that's been tough. A couple of times, I've thought about leaving the field, but I haven't quite gone that far.

It's tied to raising my own kids, the demands on my time, especially when my kids were babies. It's very hard to find extra time for working on things for school. Not sleeping, not having enough energy to do the job right. If you don't do the job right, you've got piles and piles, and you never catch up. Now, even though the demands on my time are pretty high with my kids, I'm back at the point where I have a lot more energy for my job and what I teach.

I do have cable TV, but I have the lowest level of cable TV. I pay $12, and I feel pretty good to have this cable TV, but I only get about five extra channels. When my kids come to school and they tell me they get this channel and that channel, it's strange to have to be this penny-pinching teacher who can just squeak out low-budget cable. Things like that come up all the time. I don't mean to be complaining. I'm a happy person. I just see these differences.

There are two things that really bother me. One is that with my salary, to be able to get back into the housing market is really tough. I'll find out this summer if I can even get back in at all. The other thing is that in most districts, once you reach a certain number of years of experience, your salary stops going up. My salary has gone up about a thousand bucks a year. Every year you survive, you get a thousand-dollar raise, more or less, in my district. But once you get to seventeen years, it stops. And that's where I am right now. Seventeen years. Then you just flatline. I've still got twenty-two more years before I can retire. I've got twenty-two years with no raises, unless the state grants us a raise, which is pretty rare. That's the toughest part for me right now: this idea that at age forty-three, I'm looking at twenty-two years with little chance of any kind of pay raise at all. What does that say to veteran teachers? It says we don't value you, we're going to stop paying you. So, you either leave, or put up with it.

I like what I do, but when I see some of the bright young kids I've taught coming out of college and saying they want to go into teaching, I just say, Ugh, maybe you should pursue something else; be a doctor, be a scientist. When they say they want to be teachers, I think, Hmm, that's too bad. You can get so burned out.

TEN

THEY LEFT—
HERE'S WHY

GREAT TEACHERS LEAVE THE PROFESSION
EVERY YEAR—THOUGH IN MANY CASES
THEY WISH THEY DIDN'T HAVE TO

The statistics about those who leave teaching get repeated so often that we risk inuring ourselves to what they represent. In 1999, Texas had to replace 57,000 teachers. Research by the Texas Center for Educational Research suggests that as many as 43 percent of new teachers in Texas leave within the first three years of teaching. Similar figures in Tennessee bear out this national trend; the Southern Regional Education Board reports that 41 percent of new teachers leave in the first five years. Nationwide, the aggregate figures seem somewhat less daunting. The National Center for Education Statistics puts the figure at around 20 percent.[1]

University of Pennsylvania sociologist Richard Ingersoll has found that the yearly rates for teacher turnover overall are close to 16 percent, a figure significantly greater than the 11 percent average across all occupations nationwide.[2]

While the effects of turnover are felt in most workplaces, the costs of turnover are highest in workplaces built on cohesion and continuity—the kind of workplaces we expect our public schools to be. In urban schools with high concentrations of poor students, the public school may be the only place in their lives where students can depend on a modicum of continuity. But in those very schools, according to estimates based on NCES figures, about 50 percent of teachers leave within the first five years.

There are many reasons people leave teaching in their first years. Some of this seemingly high rate of turnover can be attributed to teachers relocating to other schools in other states, but a large portion of these people leave the profession entirely. The NCES reports that starting a new career is the third most common reason teachers leave, behind retirement and pregnancy.[3] If we're talking about new teachers, then it's the second most common reason. There are many reasons to seek a new job, and most of the teachers interviewed for this book say that pay was often the single most important factor.

Bethany Morton, 32, Personal Trainer at the Spartanburg Athletic Club, Spartanburg, North Carolina (Former German Teacher—West Charlotte High School, Charlotte-Mecklenburg, North Carolina)
My last year teaching was 2002–2003, and leaving was a decision that took me over a whole year. I put a lot of thought into my decision to leave teaching. Money was a huge factor. I was teaching for six years. I have a bachelor's degree and was working on my master's and was halfway there. With six years of experience, after taxes, my monthly paycheck was $1,700. When you start thinking about buying a house and what it costs to buy a car and what it costs to live, $1,700 is peanuts. I don't understand how people do it. I'm single, and I live very modestly, and that was a struggle. You have to watch everything very carefully. If I ever

want to have children, that kind of money's just not going to cut it, not for the amount of work that you're putting into it. It's not eight hours a day with an hour lunch break. It's nine, ten, eleven, twelve hours a day, weekends sometimes, with nothing extra there. When I took a look at my personal goals in terms of family, home, material goods, there was no future there.

Even looking long-term at the pay scale, I thought, Well, if I get my master's degree, what will I have? It was a difference of $700 or $800 a year. It wasn't even what it cost to get a master's degree. How long would it take to break even? And then you're talking about a bigger time investment.

When I looked at investing my time in other ways and what I could earn, it helped in the decision process.

Now, I'm a full-time employee of the Spartanburg Athletic Club, and also a personal trainer and a fitness instructor. My hours are crazy, but I do have a lot of flexibility in terms of setting my own schedule. I'm paid for every single minute I work. That was a huge, huge factor.

I would go back to teaching if the pay were better. But the pay would have to equal or probably surpass what I'm making now. I know it's the money.

When I first started teaching, I was with my ex-boyfriend, Brad. We weren't married, but he elected himself responsible for paying the vast majority of the bills. My money was for me and for play. We didn't need my salary. He's a computer engineer, and in the late '90s, those guys were raking it in. I remember saying that teaching was the greatest job in the world if money didn't matter.

After September 11, 2001, all of a sudden the money mattered. Brad and his partner had their own software company, and the World Trade Center was their biggest client, the anchor, the big fish. After September 11, my salary mattered. Their company could never quite catch another big fish. Brad had saved for a rainy day, but nothing could have prepared him for that storm.

As time progressed, the savings ran out. We came to rely on and, in the end, live off of my teacher's salary. There is no way in hell that two people can live off of a teacher's salary. We lived modestly, too. Both of our cars were paid off, and neither one of us had debt. It became clear to me that if I was going to support myself and live alone, a teacher's salary was an insult. Forget it.

If teachers were paid a professional wage, or if I were to find a rich husband, I would go back to teaching in a public school rather than a fitness club.

Patrick Daly, 31, Cardiovascular Medical Representative, Abbott Laboratories (Former Science Teacher—Meeker Junior High School, Kent, Washington)

I'm in pharmaceutical sales, so I basically rep three products right now. Two are in the cardiovascular field, and one is an anti-infective. I call physicians and describe our products and teach them how to use them. I've been doing this just over two years now. I went into this pretty quickly after I finished teaching.

The salary is triple what I made as a teacher, and I work less. I work forty or fifty hours a week, just like most people in business. Occasionally, I'll work more because I have a really busy week or I have a business trip. But I'm earning triple the salary, and that was almost right out of the gate.

It seems ironic to me and sad that I don't do as much for the community at large. I'm not able to help kids the way I used to and be there on the front lines, but as far as society goes, I'm appreciated much more, as far as the monetary attachment to what I do. After awhile, I realized I was living for the kids; I was there for them, but it was just sapping my energy. This is a much healthier choice for me.

Compared to teaching, the stress load is easier, and the hours are much better. The appreciation is much better, and that's one thing for me that was very important. I'd work really hard as a teacher and there was basically no recognition. In teaching, the only feedback you get is negative—from your administrators, from teachers. Oftentimes, that's it, especially in junior high and high school.

Gosh, in this job, they're constantly looking for ways to recognize you. If you work hard, you're rewarded. If you're doing well, you're rewarded, you're recognized, you're given awards, certificates, recognition, monetary rewards, anything like that. That was disheartening in teaching. You'd put in a lot more hours. There's no advancement; there's no recognition.

It was an easy choice in a lot of ways. I taught for four years. The whole time, it was a struggle. Money was obviously an issue. I always had to struggle with the paycheck, and to circumvent some of those problems, I coached. As a young teacher, you're typically called on to lead a lot of activities, including coaching, advising, or running clubs. So my first year in the junior high, I coached all three sports seasons—fall, winter, and spring—which really adds to your day, but it does give a little bump to the paycheck, which is pretty necessary.

At the end, I realized not only did I have very little money, but I didn't have any time to socialize with people my own age. I was spending my whole time in school with the kids or late at night at school by myself, getting lesson plans together. I was at school as late as eight or nine o'clock at night, and I was there every morning at seven. There's no such thing as a forty-hour week in teaching. I've never had that. I got frustrated with working sixty-hour weeks or more and then over the weekend not having any money to go out or do anything or even go skiing with friends or anything like that. There was no way that I could have done anything like that when I was teaching. That was hugely frustrating.

Part of me doesn't want to support a system that doesn't support its teachers. That is also a reason I left: the low pay scale is, I feel, disrespectful to the hard work that teachers do. The whole thing's a mess, and I decided nothing's going to change until people start flat-out leaving the profession. As long as you stay in, even if you go on strike or do walkouts, people have been doing that forever and nothing has changed, nothing appreciably anyway. We had a walkout in my district and they came back with a small pay raise. What it basically amounted to is they had us work as many extra days as we were getting paid for. They didn't really raise our rate, they just made us work more days in terms of teacher workshops. That was their answer.

It got difficult for me because in our state and in many states, legislators like to talk about holding teachers accountable for ongoing learning and about keeping the best-trained people in the classroom. So they have ongoing education requirements for us, and for me to go back to school, not only would that cost me more money that I didn't have, but the time spent doing that would prevent me from keeping my second job. And I couldn't afford that. That was also why I quit after four years, because in our state, after five years you had to have some additional coursework completed, and more every few years after that. I wasn't going to give up a summer job or an evening job to pay more money to just do something that I had to do to keep my job. Most employers—like mine now—if they require me to have additional training, they'll not only pay for it, but they'll have me on the clock when I go, and I can even go back and get a master's degree on them. It really is strange that teaching doesn't do that, but that's a whole other issue, I guess.

Now that I've made the switch, my life is completely different. I can leave work at work. I have time to socialize and spend with friends. I have money to go out and do things with just enough to have a good quality of life, instead of living for my job. That's basically what it is as a teacher. If you want to do a good job, you have to live for your job. That has to be pretty much the number-one priority. That's the way it was for me, anyway.

I miss it all the time. If I magically had my standard of living and I didn't have to go out and find an additional paycheck to make the house payment and the bills, I would teach. That's my first love and that's definitely where my heart is.

Todd Werner, 26, Math Assessment Development Specialist at Data Recognition Corporation, Minneapolis, Minnesota (Former Math Teacher—North Kansas City High School, Kansas City, Missouri)
I never did any student teaching. I did some substitute teaching while I was going to college, and I was getting my certificate during my first year teaching. So, the first day I started teaching in Kansas City, I was the full-time teacher of record, and when I walked into my first hour of class, I had never been entirely responsible for a group of high school students until that very moment. I never got that student-teacher experience where you observe your mentor teacher and then slowly take over duties. It was "Here you go, it's all you." It was really hard.

I taught there for a year. I knew I wanted to move back to Minnesota, where I grew up, but it was hard for me to even get interviews in Minnesota. I was teaching under a provisional teaching certificate and finishing up my master's in education. I didn't have a Minnesota teaching license and couldn't apply for one until I finished my master's.

I moved to Minneapolis, but I didn't get a teaching job. The school year started, and at that point I decided I didn't want to be a long-term substitute. I never really liked substitute teaching. So I stopped looking for teaching jobs once the school year started, and I started doing temp work for American Express. It was just data-entry work. I worked there forty hours a week, and with my first paycheck, I realized that while I wasn't getting benefits with the temp job, I was going to make the same amount of money that I would have made teaching if I worked full-time for a year.

A lot of teachers don't go into it for the money; they go into it for the reward they get back from the students and seeing students grow—that satisfaction, rather than the monetary compensation. I never got that feeling when I was teaching. So I said, if the money's not doing that for me, and that wasn't happening either, there's really no point in going back. I knew I didn't want to stay at this temp job, but I said, There has to be something else out there.

Now, I write and edit math questions to go on assessments. With No Child Left Behind, every state has to test their students every year from grades three to eight. I am making 50 percent more than I was making in Kansas City, and I've been with the company a year and a half. Careerwise, this job is a great thing. It's a good résumé builder for me.

Frank Barnes, 34, Senior Associate at Annenberg Institute for School Reform (Former Social Studies Teacher)

It wasn't the hours that drove me out of teaching. The issue wasn't money, either. It was quality of life. After teaching at a large comprehensive school and a small alternative one, I thought I had pretty much experienced the spectrum of instructional settings. One setting was traditional and ineffective/dysfunctional, and the other setting was alternative and somewhat effective. Yet the latter came with such a personal cost I decided to leave.

I was told it was all about the kids, but in the endeavor, I was losing my humanity, becoming an object instead of a subject. Parents distrusted you, students resisted you, administration overworked you, and no one appreciated you. Not to mention the predetermined schedule that was far more regimented and unforgiving than even the schedule I had as a K–12 student. I needed a place where I could be a good friend, son, and hopefully one day a good husband and father, as well as a good professional. Teaching in a Boston public high school didn't offer me this. So I left. I like teaching and I like young people. It was school I disliked.

Lizabeth Barnett, 29, Private Music Instructor, Denver, Colorado (Former Music and Choir Teacher, Vickery Middle School, Cumming, Georgia)
Nobody ever goes into teaching to get rich. I knew it was going to be hard, and I knew I wasn't going to make a lot of money. I hate to say it was harder than I thought it was going to be, because I was prepared; I knew I'd have administrative stuff to do and all these other duties. But I became overwhelmed by all the extra stuff, and there's not a lot of support for teachers in schools, unfortunately. Administrators are really busy, if they're available, and unfortunately I was not under a great administration. I was tired all the time. I worked constantly, and I didn't make a lot of money, which shouldn't bother me, but I saw other people who weren't working very hard at all making the same amount of money. Before my divorce, when my husband and I transferred out to Denver, I decided to give up teaching and became a secretary. I was offered more money to do that—to be an office administrator, something I could have done with a high school diploma.

I threw in the towel and decided, it's a noble profession, but I don't have time to be noble right now, and I gave up.

It was awful. It made me sick. Literally. I got sick. It was a horrible decision. I felt like I was giving up. I still feel like I was giving up, in a lot of ways, because there are plenty of teachers out there who make it, who do just fine. I was devastated, but at the same time, I'm still a realist. I'm pretty pragmatic, and I knew that I had to make a living, and this was the best way to go about doing it, and I needed to put my ideals aside for a little bit. I also thought I would pick it back up, when things got better, maybe if I got married again—I know that sounds awful, but if I ever wound up with some other source of income, I would go back to teaching. That's really what I love doing. Teaching in a public school. Because I want to teach every kid. I want to be a part of the community and be somebody that matters to these kids. It's not just about pride, although that does have something to do with it. I was too tired.

I was at my wit's end. I threw in the towel. It was a really, really low moment in my life, probably the lowest moment in my life. It was worse than my divorce. I know that sounds awful. My marriage was not a viable relationship, and being an educator was viable for me. I had a great rapport with my students, and I worked hard for them. To realize that I didn't have the resources I needed to keep doing this was hard.

It wasn't just one thing. I realized I couldn't keep doing this. It wasn't an attractive enough offer for me to stay, even though I knew it was something I'm really good at. If there's one thing on the planet I'm really good at, it's that, being a choir teacher, being a general music teacher. But I couldn't say, Sure I'll stay at $30,000 a year, which is an okay salary, but they're paying me $40,000 to be a secretary and not have all the stress and not have the same problems. Eventually, I want to buy a house and all these things that everyone else wants, and you can see your salary—they print it in the paper every year. You can see what you're going to be making in ten years, and it's not a whole lot of money.

My company knew that I wanted to start teaching again, and that's when they analyzed what I would be making as a teacher. They wanted me to stay on, so they gave me a lot more salary, just at the idea that I might leave. They decided, We can pay you this much more, and that was really seductive. So I stayed. That would never happen if I were still teaching. If this could happen to me, just because I smiled, why would I go back? I'm not guaranteed to be in a school with a good administration, or to be in a school with a budget for music. There are so many variables that are negative, so why would I? Being noble is one thing. It makes me feel ill to say that. But I had to. I'm not going to blame anybody, because there are plenty of teachers out there who can make it, but they're made of tougher stuff than I am.

ELEVEN

"I DIDN'T WANT TO BE POOR"

WHY MANY WHO WANT TO TEACH
CHOOSE OTHER PROFESSIONS

In 2000, the nonprofit research organization Public Agenda surveyed 802 college graduates under age thirty who chose professions other than teaching. Some said they had considered teaching at one point. Others had never seriously considered the profession at all. Their reasons varied. Among the statements respondents agreed with most often were these three:

• Teachers are seriously underpaid (78 percent).

• Teachers do not have good opportunities for advancement (69 percent).

• Teachers do not get a sense that they are respected or appreciated (66 percent).

Many respondents also said they believed teachers have to worry about personal safety when they work and that they are often made the scapegoat for society's problems. Researchers also found that 47 percent of respondents "would be a lot more likely

SOME WOULD CONSIDER TEACHING[1]
If the opportunity were to present itself, would you consider becoming a public school teacher?
(respondents: young graduates in other careers)

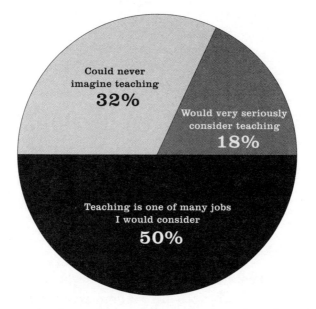

Could never
imagine teaching
32%

Would very seriously
consider teaching
18%

Teaching is one of many jobs
I would consider
50%

to consider becoming a public school teacher if teaching paid more than it does now."

The writers of the report eventually drew the conclusion that though money is important, it's not the determining factor in how the teaching profession is viewed by those considering it. To assume that it is, they wrote, is to assume the current generation of prospective teachers is purely materialistic and ignores the many reasons people are attracted to, and stay in, teaching.[2]

Money may not be the most important issue for many, but it plays an important role in the choices people make about their careers and their futures. In this chapter we hear from a variety of people who wanted to become public school teachers, most of whom were very serious about pursuing this path. Several of them even went so far as to take teacher licensing exams. But each of them decided against teaching when they realized the profession couldn't provide them with the future they had envisioned for themselves.

Amy Nichols, 27, Landscape Architect at Cummin Associates, Stonington, Connecticut

We do high-end residential design all over the country. I travel a lot. It's interesting, but I still want to be a teacher. Originally, going into college, I knew where I was going, but I didn't know what I was going to study. I only knew that I wanted to teach. I was leaning toward teaching art or English in high school. But my mother seriously warned against doing that. She was a special education teacher in both high school and elementary school. She felt as if she didn't get paid enough; she felt as if she didn't get enough recognition for the work she was doing. She said there were so many other things out there to do that I'd be much happier doing. I have a really, really close relationship with my mom, so anything she told me, I was definitely going to take to heart. I took her advice seriously and I chose to do something else.

She retired last June, and it concerned me that she had more relief than sadness. I know that a lot of times, I see people who work for forty years and don't want to leave their jobs and don't ever want to retire. For her to be waiting for that date to come was sad.

I might teach eventually, but to go into teaching would probably cut my salary in half. Realistically, I couldn't do it. I'd have to work two jobs. I'm single right now, raising my daughter on one income. If someday I were to meet Prince Charming, and there were two incomes, it would probably be fine. But right now, I couldn't imagine living on what they pay teachers starting out.

I might have gone into teaching after college if there was a higher starting salary for new teachers, and maybe if there was a system based on your performance. Everyone gets paid the same, whether you're a brilliant, amazing educator, whether or not you have your credentials. That concerns me.

Lisa Smith, 33, Public Interest Lawyer, Baltimore, Maryland

I'm proud of what I do, but I always had teaching in the back of my mind when I was growing up. Even when I was young, I idolized my teachers. I loved learning.

The big inspiration for me came in high school. I had just moved to Maryland from Texas. I didn't want to be in school. I was one of those angry, sullen teenagers. I was in the advanced classes, but I never wanted to be there. I was always leaving. Some days I didn't go. There were a couple of teachers there who took an interest in me, and I really liked them. I made sure I always went to their classes, even if it was the only class I went to all day, because they made the subject come alive for me and everyone else. They saved me. As smart as I was, I could have ended up not graduating high school if it wasn't for these people.

By the time I got to college, I was thinking, Wow, that's something I'd really like to do. They had changed my life, and I always hoped that by being a teacher, I could do that for a kid like me. But I didn't want to major in education. I was in school to learn, and education didn't feel like a real subject to me. My college professors in English were amazing. They made the subject come alive. I was devouring everything I read in those classes, and that was it. I loved reading, I loved words, and I wanted to be a teacher more than anything else. I was sure about it.

I got a chance to teach in grad school. They trained us for a week, and then gave us a class of twenty-five students to ourselves. It was a great experience. I loved it. I loved my kids. I had a really good time. I had no doubt that was what I was meant to do, but I

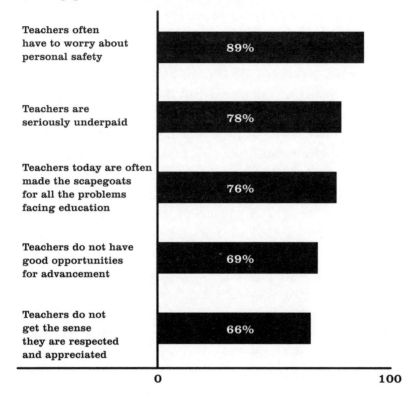

DRAWBACKS OF TEACHING[3]
% of young college graduates who say:
(Young graduates in other careers)

Teachers often have to worry about personal safety — **89%**

Teachers are seriously underpaid — **78%**

Teachers today are often made the scapegoats for all the problems facing education — **76%**

Teachers do not have good opportunities for advancement — **69%**

Teachers do not get the sense they are respected and appreciated — **66%**

0   100

wasn't making any money. Thank goodness I was living in Alabama, and it was cheap to live there. But even then, I was buying ramen noodle soups six-for-a-dollar and eating one a day. I never bought anything luxurious. I never ate meat. I never bought sodas or any snacks. I was basically just trying to stay alive.

I started doing a lot of thinking right after my master's exams. I considered going on to a PhD, and I thought about getting a teaching job. I thought long and hard about how poor I was going to be if I did that. It wears on you, eating noodle soup day after day, or eating saltines and peanut butter. I wanted to be independent. I didn't want to have to rely on somebody else to be able to live from day to day. I couldn't do it on my own, being a teacher, so I decided not to do it at that point, and I applied to some PhD programs and to law school, and I chose law school. That was in 1996.

Now I make between $55,000 and $60,000, but I could make a lot more money if I chose to. I'm at the low end of pay for attorneys because of what I've chosen to do. If I wanted to go work for a corporate law firm or a firm that represents insurance companies—that's usually who we go against—most people at those firms start at double what I make.

I still want to teach. Once a month, I start to think about ways I could teach, how I could still do it. I love what I do now, but I still want to be a teacher. I just don't see how I could do it. A lot of the people I know who are teachers worry about everything. When you visit their homes, you can see the scars of being poor. It's like they all have post-traumatic stress disorder, freaking over every paper napkin used, every soda consumed, always talking about money. "How many sodas did you drink today? That's too many. We can't afford that." That's what you hear when you go to their houses. It seems like a lot of pressure, especially for the children living in that house, to constantly hear from their parents who are teachers, "You can't do that because we can't afford it."

I don't want to be rich, and I don't want a fancy wedding, but I don't want to be so poor that worrying about money takes over like it has done to people I know. Living on my own on a teacher's salary would be hard, but how would you have a family?

I think it's one of the sickest things that teachers get paid so little given how important a teacher's job is. I'm not the only one I know who's had a teacher completely change the direction of their life. Look at how much athletes and movie stars get paid. One of the things we talk about in closing arguments is what is someone's life worth? What value do we put on other people's lives? Why do these sports players get paid $12 million per contract, and what is this kid's life worth? There seems to be misplaced value.

David Shoemaker, 26, Assistant Editor at Basic Books/ Counterpoint Press, New York, New York

When I was finishing with college, I was looking for a way to give back and have my life all at the same time, and teaching seemed like a good opportunity for that. Al Gore's promise to teachers had a huge thing to do with it. He had that plan for teacher sign- ing bonuses and a vague plan for increased salaries—I don't even remember how much, but it seemed significant at the time. I re- member saying that if he got elected, I would move to whatever city I most wanted to live in and be a teacher. He didn't, and so I didn't.

My mother was a teacher, and I always had a connection and good associations with teaching in my mind. When anybody in a position of power does something to take that career seriously, it always changes the outlook of a lot of people, and it definitely changed mine. I think the signing bonus was a big indication that he was taking it seriously. It boded well for what might have fol- lowed. I feel very strongly that more than the money is the lack of opportunity for advancement, and the fact that everybody in the country knows how little teachers make. There's incredible stigma attached to the fact that we've all decided that teachers don't de- serve more than $30,000 a year.

To me, it's weird. It's almost un-PC to be negative about teach- ers and their actual position, and everyone seems to be in some kind of agreement that teachers deserve more than they're making, but it doesn't translate. I worked for a while in a bookstore and often made this same statement there, but more in a joking manner. I'd say, "I'd love to do this job for the rest of my life, but I'd be working at a bookstore for the rest of my life." There's a whole lot of similarity between the two jobs. I could be the smartest bookstore employee in the country, and people would walk in off the street and still look at me as a bookstore employee. I think there's a lot of that in teaching, too. People are willing to say, "Oh, what a great job you're doing," but you're still just a teacher. There's something very invasive about other people knowing how much money you're making in our incredibly capitalist culture. There's a lot of interpersonal comparison that goes along with that sort of thing. So it takes a real saint or servant of a teacher to transcend that monetary classification.

Looking at the job I have now, it isn't the specific amount of money—I'm making only very slightly more in this job than I would be making as a teacher—but if I were to talk to anyone I knew then and probably anyone I know now, and say, "I want to go into book publishing," I would get a completely different reaction than if I said, "I want to be an elementary school teacher." It's just a completely different scale in society, which is really, really sad.

If I ever decided to become a teacher—and I do still think about it—it would definitely involve me flipping the bird to the world and saying, "I don't care what you think, I just want to live my life for me for a change." I guess it sounds coy and cliché all at once, but I think that falls into everyone's decision-making process. It would almost be the equivalent of moving to a cabin in the mountains and working in a coffee shop and playing my guitar for four hours a day. It's a decision you make without much regard for what people would think. That's the only way I could see myself falling into teaching at this point. It would be a philosophical decision and a break from what my life's been so far.

Nicole Reyes, 34, Executive Assistant at Hellman and Friedman, San Francisco, California

I always wanted to be a teacher. I remember loving reading and writing when I was a kid. So the teachers I looked up to were the ones who praised me constantly about what a great writer I was. I looked up to them. As I got older, I started realizing that I was good at explaining things to other people. I was tutoring other kids. I got moved ahead in class, and part of my responsibility was to teach the other kids, and I was pretty good at that.

When kids talked about what they wanted to be when they grew up, I always wanted to be a teacher. It seemed like a real and reachable goal, and it was something that was encouraged by teachers and parents. But I got an idea very early on, whether it was through the griping of teachers and so on, that they just never made enough. I was probably in high school when I started to think that that wasn't going to be for me. It wasn't that I wanted to be rich. It just didn't seem like it fit into what I wanted to do with the rest of my life.

I was pretty independent. I had to work from when I was pretty young, and I was paying for all the things I wanted. I got used to making money early, and to seeing how I needed it, so I was aware of the importance of money and how I would have to take care of myself—which included going to college and paying my own tuition. I was hyper-aware of how much things cost, and I was worried about getting into debt through student loans.

I never seriously let myself make up my mind to become a teacher; I never believed I could do it. Thirteen years ago, when I was twenty-one, I was making between $55,000 and $65,000; it's a great amount of money at that age. Looking back, I probably didn't need all those shoes and all the other things I spent money on then.

I probably could have become a teacher. I would have gone to school longer, and I would have left school with some pretty large debts that I would have been worried about paying. But now I'm a mother. I have a daughter; she's two-and-a-half years old. It'd be a risk for me to teach now. But it's similar to thinking "I want to join the circus, but I can't because I have a two-year-old." Financially, we could swing it, but it would be different than the lifestyle we have now. I bring home between 50 and 80 percent of our household income. My husband owns his own business, so it fluctuates. It would be different if he were in a corporate job and we could rely on something. It's something I've always wanted to do, but it's something I should have done when I was single because it would just change the way we do everything. If we're going to save $300 a month for college, I don't see how we would do that. It's hard to weigh those factors.

As much as I would love to make a difference in the lives of many children, I feel like I would be sacrificing my own child's education for my goals. Had I really gone after it earlier, maybe I could have worked it in, but now I don't know if I can. There shouldn't be this kind of risk involved.

I think about it a lot now, especially with my friends who are teachers. I do hear a couple of them say, "Oh my god, the money, there's no way you could do this." And I hear a couple of them saying, "You'd be too exhausted. You'd be mentally and emotionally drained, and you'd have nothing for your daughter," which is surprising to hear. I never thought about that. One friend of mine says, "You could do this, it's great." She lives in a house that her husband's father owns. They don't have to pay rent. Her husband works for his father and the father takes care of every expense related to the house. Realistically, they have no bills. She's a teacher at a Catholic school. She seems to have it made in the shade, but she also doesn't have to make any money.

Aaron Tassano, 31, English Teacher at MLS Language Institute, Busan, South Korea

After five years writing at a daily newspaper in Oakland, California, I decided I wanted to go into elementary school teaching. I attended an informational meeting at San Francisco State University and arranged to volunteer at two schools in the Bay Area. Ultimately, I stopped short of applying to SF State full-time because of the experiences I had. One school, in a poor area of East Oakland, was underfunded, understaffed, and laying people off. The teacher I worked with was a beaten-down woman, so cynical about her school and teaching in general that I quit after logging sixteen hours, for fear that the experience would turn me off teaching for good.

The second experience was different but ultimately didn't convince me to stay. It was a rich neighborhood in the San Ramon hills. A sort of utopia, I thought. I remember driving there for my first day of work and scowling as I passed the golf courses with towering fountains, the luxury strip malls, the Tuscan-style faux mansions. But regardless of my opinion of that sort of living environment, the school itself was undeniably exemplary. The buildings were new and clean, the teachers and students were happy and well-behaved, and the education itself was varied and solid.

The principal lived in Pleasant Hill, in a house she owned with her husband. Everyone else I met lived on the other side of the Caldecott Tunnel—that is, in Oakland or Berkeley. One teacher I knew did live in San Ramon but in an apartment with her two children. She'd moved into it less than a year before, because she and her husband had divorced. For a young teacher to buy a house in San Ramon would be virtually impossible, ditto for nearby Dublin and Pleasanton. I specifically asked if any of the teachers lived in the community where the school was, and the answer was "no."

The principal had overseen the school from the beginning. Before the school had opened she had hired her staff of teachers and worked with them to design a curriculum that all of the teachers followed, but with room for creativity. The two teachers I worked with had widely different styles, but both seemed perfectly at home. Only children from the surrounding community attend the school. The principal described it as a "small-town atmosphere." At first I rolled my eyes at the notion, but I was quickly won over by the high-level education these children were getting.

In Korea, teachers are well paid and highly respected. Koreans put a rabid emphasis on education, and teachers hold a similar place in society in terms of pay and reputation as firemen and policemen do in the U.S. I'm earning about $3,000 per month here, and my rent is free. I save between $1,500 and $2,000 per month. I can't imagine doing that in California. It's difficult to compare the two. English has a cultlike status in Korea. People are willing to spend $40 to $50 an hour to have someone come to their apartment and speak English to their kid for an hour.

The public perception of teachers makes a huge difference to me. My students work very hard, and in turn I admire them greatly. They sometimes thank me at the end of class. I wonder how many parents in America thank their kid's teacher. For some reason, in the United States, the perception of teachers is really low. My guess is that it's because they don't earn much money. It's like doing social work—something for bighearted types who couldn't get into something more profitable, like being a doctor. The Confucian rule that a teacher should be given a high level of respect is a good one. Teachers shape societies.

In the United States, when a person makes a decision to be a teacher, he accepts the fact that he will never make much money, that his life, unless there is some other contribution, will be a financial struggle. In Korea, teaching can be lucrative. Aside from tutoring, teachers open new schools all the time. I've been here nine months, and I plan to stay here at least two years. Once I finish my master's, I'm eligible to teach as a university professor of English here. It's conceivable that I would stay here and continue to teach here. Not likely, but I could if I wanted. I've thought about getting my credentials and teaching elementary school back home, but the idea of it is discouraging for all those financial reasons. I have thought of doing something like real estate, though.

BETTER SCHOOLS BEGIN WITH BETTER PAY

TWELVE

SUCCESS IN REFORM

WHAT HAPPENS WHEN DISTRICTS AND
SCHOOLS START PAYING TEACHERS MORE:
THREE EXPERIMENTS THAT WORKED

There are district administrators throughout the country who, in wary acknowledgment of their chronically dissatisfied labor force, have become desperate to make a change in the ways they define and pay for teachers' work. The difficulties that teachers outlined in the preceding chapters translate to very real consequences in terms of the human resources available to individual school districts.

Superintendents and human resources directors find themselves put upon to use every recruiting tool imaginable, from television ads designed to enhance the perceived status of the schoolteacher to offers of discounts at local stores to stretch the meager salary. School districts from New York City to Houston have worked with international recruiters to find teachers from Southeast Asia and Eastern Europe to teach math, science, and special education, jobs many qualified Americans won't do for such low pay.

There are districts where administrators and teachers are addressing the problem of low pay directly and focusing on improving salary structures by changing how much teachers can earn and how they earn it. These are communities where everybody—teachers, union leaders, administrators, and school board members—agrees on the central premise that in order to attract and retain the teaching force the district wants and needs, salaries must be higher. Further, pay should be tied directly to work that fulfills the community's educational needs and goals.

The people who have been central to some of these changes talk a lot about breaking out of traditional labor-management relations. Brad Jupp of the Denver Classroom Teachers Association speaks about "giving up old intellectual turf" to find places where teachers and administrators can agree. Similarly, Bruce Messinger, superintendent of the Helena, Montana, school district, has become completely enamored of the consensus-based model that moved contract negotiations "far away from the traditional bargaining approach" and resulted, eventually, in Helena becoming one of the most attractive districts in the Northwest. And at the Vaughn Next Century Learning Center in Los Angeles, Principal Yvonne Chan offers her teachers performance incentives of up to $17,000 in yearly bonuses, rather than simply expecting teachers to meet her exactingly high demands with little or no increased pay.

While the reforms profiled in this chapter cannot simply be used as off-the-shelf solutions for troubled school districts, they are all effective responses to local concerns, designed, for the most part, by collaborative teams and agreed on by all the interested parties. They were neither dictated by administrators nor the result of direct teacher lobbying. What they have in common is that they substantially raise teachers' earning potential, and they provide incentives for teachers to do the work administrators need teachers to do, work that has traditionally been outside teachers' official contracts.

One of the largest-scale reform projects is under way in Denver, Colorado, where the local teachers' union broke ranks with the NEA to advocate a new kind of performance-based pay.

CASE STUDY NO. 1

PROCOMP: DENVER'S REVOLUTION-IN-PROGRESS

WHEN UNIONS AND DISTRICTS WORK TOGETHER FOR CHANGE

Becky Wissink's life is focused on overcoming inertia. On the wall of her office at the Denver Classroom Teachers Association is a shadow box displaying some twenty medals and a small trophy sword testifying to her inertia-overcoming skill. She won the awards for throwing telephone poles—about fourteen feet long, weighing forty pounds each—in Scottish Highland Games competitions. She routinely wins amateur contests throwing various stones and weights for whatever's called for, either height or distance.

In her day job, as president of Denver's teachers' union, she struggles against less quantifiable resistance. For the last five years, Wissink has worked to build support for a teacher pay system that defies traditional union thinking and, at first glance, might seem to enact her members' worst fears about who holds them accountable and for what.

"Basically, we had to change the beliefs of the individual union members," she says.

In 2003, union members voted 59 percent in favor of having

an alternative to Denver's current "lockstep" salary schedule. Though the new pay program has been approved, it will not go into effect until 2006, and only then if voters approve the $25 million yearly tax increase to pay for it. If they approve the new tax, Denver's 4,700 teachers will see an additional $250 million in their collective pockets by 2016.

As do most school districts around the country, Denver Public Schools currently pay teachers on a schedule that provides raises only for years of service and postgraduate academic credits. Like many similar schedules, it tops out after thirteen years of service. At that point, a teacher with a master's degree and a total of sixty units beyond a bachelor's degree would see her salary stall at about $68,000—and likely see only cost-of-living adjustments for the last half of her career. Under the new system, she can keep earning raises until she retires, effectively putting her career-end salary as high as $90,000.

If the tax increase is approved by Denver voters, the new system—called ProComp, short for "Professional Compensation for Teachers"—will be considerably more ambitious than most current salary schedules. For all new hires and current teachers who opt in, pay raises and bonuses will be tied to performance in four areas:

• the knowledge and skills teachers demonstrate,
• satisfactory yearly evaluations from administrators and peers,
• teaching in "hard-to-staff" positions or "hard-to-serve" schools, and
• measured student growth in the classroom and on standardized tests.

Brad Jupp is the former Denver middle school teacher who left the classroom in 1999 to lead a team of administrators and teachers through the research and design of the compensation alternative. He describes the new plan this way: "It will pay people for learning new stuff on the job, for performing well in their classrooms, for getting results with their kids, and for working in schools and positions most teachers don't want to go to."

These are four areas in which Denver schools have been struggling to encourage teachers to perform. Before this system was proposed, teachers had little incentive beyond their own altruism to work in difficult schools. Performing well and getting results with students was what everybody hoped was happening, but the only systems in place for ensuring this were administrator evaluations that everybody acknowledged were mere formalities. As far as "learning new stuff on the job," only teachers' individual notions of professionalism or urgency encouraged them to make meaningful choices about the graduate courses they took in order to move up the salary schedule.

Both union leaders and district administrators hope Pro-Comp will help them reach certain other goals. The union, of course, wants to see members as well compensated as possible, but they also hope this new system will help professionalize teaching and create improved classroom experiences for all students. The district shares this last goal, banking on the new pay system to attract and retain high-quality teachers in order to improve the experiences of all of Denver's students.

HOW THEY DID IT:
A COMMITMENT TO COMPROMISE

In the late 1990s, the nation embraced standardized testing as the best solution to public education's problems. There were regular calls from politicians for the results of these tests to carry with them rewards and stern punishments. The climate was polarized. On one side were those upset about the perceived low performance of schools. They were looking for anything to spark change. Some wanted to tie school funding or teacher pay to student performance on standardized tests. On the other side were teachers and their allies, claiming they were doing the best they knew how and asserting that test results were not accurate indicators of how much students were learning, much less how well teachers did their jobs.

It was clear that neither politicians nor the public at large wanted to continue the status quo of paying teachers for their seniority or the number of graduate classes they had taken. It was also clear that change was on the way. In 1999, Denver's teachers' union decided to *make* that change happen rather than *let* it happen.

"If we didn't do it, someone else was going to do it for us," said Wissink. "I don't know if it would have come from the district, but it could have come from the legislature in the state of Colorado. In 1999, the talk at the time was about pay for performance and merit pay and all those things. Instead of just debating it and saying, 'No,' it's more powerful if you say, 'Maybe.'"

Saying "maybe" required a re-imagining of how unions work and what their goals actually are. Though teachers' unions have traditionally focused on pay and specific working conditions (like number of classes per day and the number of students per class), the strength of what Denver did came from recognizing that despite the fundamental management-labor adversity, the union and administrators actually share some important goals, the most important of which is that students learn.

"I think it's a mind-shift—the realization that the teachers' working conditions are the students' learning conditions. Those are one and the same," Wissink says. "It's not about time and the minutes you should get paid for. It's about the work you get done."

In some respects, that's a heretical thing for unions to talk about, much less agree to.

"When I wake up in the morning, I don't open up my NEA book to see what I can and can't do," Wissink says. "I wouldn't turn down $250 million to go into members' pockets over the next ten years, and that's what this means. What this also means is that we need to [negotiate with the district] differently in order to get more for teachers, to bring back the profession, and to have a livable wage."

Not surprisingly, agreeing to negotiate differently turns out to be a long process, and it involves sitting down with the people one might normally oppose. As Brad Jupp tells the story, when the teachers, union leaders, and site- and district-level administrators first came to the same table, their early efforts were characterized by failure. They couldn't solve the problem. They thought about add-ons to the current salary schedule or creating a salary schedule with only one column. Nothing satisfied them, and nothing looked viable, but instead of giving up and declaring the task impossible, all the parties involved—teachers, union leaders, and district representatives—decided to learn as much as they could about all the issues involved.

They met with experts outside of education—actuaries, human-resource analysts—and people inside the education world. They read all the relevant literature they could find about salary reform. Jupp says these eight months of research "changed not only our ability to think, but our ability to work together. We really gave up old roles. We gave up old intellectual turf and had a kind of intellectual bonding that became necessary if we were going to go any farther. That was really helpful."

There were surprises and challenges along the way, most notably around the issue of the role of evaluations. Traditional union thinking holds that administrators are not to be trusted, that they are potentially inept or inclined to play favorites, and therefore, pay should not be tied to administrator evaluations. Consequently, a system of ineffectual and largely irrelevant evaluations had been allowed to take root in Denver, and teachers rarely, if ever, were found to be unsatisfactory. But the teachers on the Pro-Comp design team were actually interested in beefing up the administrators' role in evaluations.

The rest of the design team's work involved negotiations and trade-offs on both sides. Teachers agreed to accountability associated with student gains on standardized tests, and they also created an accountability system in which teachers determine the criteria by which they are measured. The district got to keep administrators as evaluators, and the teachers brought their peers into the evaluation process. The district asked for teachers to take relevant professional development courses, and the teachers got a tuition reimbursement and a raise for doing that.

Although they were able to agree on the design, they felt they needed to put their ideas to the test. They did this in two ways.

TESTING THE
"PAY FOR PERFORMANCE" MODEL

The whole notion of changing the way teachers are paid rests on the assumption that pay can provide an incentive to change behavior. Denver tried to test this assumption with a pilot program called "Pay for Performance." From 1999 to 2003, teachers at sixteen schools across the district had an opportunity to earn an additional $1,500 for learning how to write objectives, putting their objectives to work in their classroom, and documenting student achievement of those objectives.

For example, a high school French teacher discusses possible goals with her principal. They agree that she should set a goal for her first-year students of acquiring 1,000 new words over the course of the year, in addition to mastering the simple past, present, and future tenses of regular verbs. She gives her students pretests and post-tests and aims for 80 percent of her students getting a C or better on the post-test. If that happens, she has met her goal, and she receives $750. For the first year of the pilot program, each teacher worked on two objectives.

To many people in the private sector, goal-setting and reward based on performance appear elementary. But public education has had difficulty applying this simple behavioral model to schools. Ann Bailey, principal at Thomas Jefferson High School, a middle-class school in a middle-class neighborhood twenty miles south of central Denver, has spent thirty-six years in public education. It was only through this pilot that she understood how useful objectives could be. "As a teacher and an administrator, I found objective writing always ineffective," she says. "Either you wrote them too easy or you wrote them too hard. I never really had proper training in how to write objectives, and therefore, I never really saw the worth in them."

Her staff, she says, agreed to participate in the pilot only because it seemed like "easy money." What they found, though, was that the training was actually valuable. Coupled with the increase in available and useful data about student progress, teachers began to improve what was happening in the classrooms.

"There were many teachers for whom it gave more of a push to see how they could begin to get things done differently, not to use the same old notes or the same old worksheets—to be more creative in their instruction," Bailey says. She added that this model also led to an increase in collegiality among her already friendly staff.

At many of the schools that piloted Pay for Performance, the program's success seemed to go hand in hand with improvements made across the district in collecting data on student progress and making that data available to teachers. Mary Romero, principal of Colfax Elementary School in Denver, says the focus on objectives and the availability of data allowed teachers and administrators to track individual student progress.

"It helped us to fine-tune how we wrote objectives and the actual impact on each kid," she said. "That was the good part for us, that every child was considered at the beginning, at the end and during the process. That's a great plus, not only for the child but for the child's family and, ultimately, for society."

Like Romero, Jupp and other ProComp boosters say the pilot shows that if you offer teachers money to change their behavior, you'll get what you pay for. Some teachers, however, feel ambivalent about the program's efficacy.

TESTING ASSUMPTIONS ABOUT THE ECONOMY

Denver Public Schools assistant superintendent Rich Allen has spent his entire career in educational finance. In spring 2004, as ProComp was receiving national attention from the *New York Times*—shortly after the union approved the program but before Denver voters cast a ballot about the new tax it involves—Allen was hammering out the General Fund budget for the 2004–2005 school year, of which teacher salaries accounted for 40 percent, or about $200 million. He was on the design team, and he has some knowledge of how difficult paying for change can be.

"When we did the literature review on innovative pay systems around the country, what we found was the landscape littered with dead bodies of these pay plans. School districts had implemented them and then figured out they didn't have the money to continue it in the long term because the costs in these systems build up," he said.

The design team worked with an actuary to create a model to cost out their program over the long term, something they say they hadn't seen done by anyone else in education. "We did the model, and it's only as good as its assumptions, but we did create a fifty-year equilibrium," Allen says. "If the assumptions are correct, it will stabilize at a $25 million increase in teacher compensation."

That's a nice, round number, Allen says, and it happens to also be the most they can ask for from a property tax levy under current law. But they factored that into their system, building a system of raises that can be sustained on that specific amount of yearly revenue.

In November 2006, a year and a half after the union approved ProComp, Denver Public Schools will ask voters to fund it with a tax increase that translates roughly to about $60 more per year on the median Denver home price, currently worth about $245,000. This is a tough sell, particularly given an uncertain economic future and the need to tie the tax to the rate of inflation. Most education-related expenditures that come to voters are often for one-time projects, like improving school facilities or enhancing technology. Because this is for salaries which will be adjusted for cost of living, the revenue source must grow proportionally. Simply put, as inflation rises, so will the need to pay higher salaries.

Allen says Denver voters can be assured the tax revenue will not be squandered on something other than ProComp. The revenue generated by this tax hike will be held in a trust overseen by a board of teachers and administrators, designated solely for paying teachers. The trust will be responsible for making any necessary adjustments to the program. They may redefine the value of professional development or a hard-to-staff position, and they might identify new district needs and create incentives for teachers in different areas.

DENVER'S PROCOMP SYSTEM AT A GLANCE

If Denver voters approve the property tax increase to pay for it, all new teachers and any current teachers who opt in will be paid under this completely new system.

Teachers who…	will receive:
…demonstrate relevance of successful recent coursework	2% raise ($659)
…complete a relevant master's degree	9% raise ($2,967)
…complete National Board Certification	9% raise ($2,967)
…spend their own money on their education (up to $1,000)	3% bonus ($989)
…teach in a hard-to-serve school or a hard-to-staff position	3% raise ($989)
…receive a satisfactory evaluation	3% raise ($989)
…teach a class in which students meet CSAP benchmarks	2% bonus ($659)
…teach in a school with "distinguished" CSAP results	1% raise ($330)
…set and meet performance objectives with their students	1% bonus ($330)

Note: Percentages and dollar figures are based on Denver's 2004 starting salary of $32,971.

THE FUTURE IN DENVER PUBLIC SCHOOLS, PART I: TEACHERS TAKING COURSES THAT MATTER

Here is how most districts currently work: If a teacher wants to improve her earning potential, she has to move herself over to a new column on the salary schedule. She does this by accruing a certain number of graduate credits, usually around fifteen, which means she has to take four or five graduate classes. Teachers can take classes in anything, from any university, as long as someone will sign off on it as graduate credit. Though many teachers make professional decisions to take relevant courses, a cottage industry of distance-learning universities, including Chapman and Fresno Pacific, has cropped up to fill the market niche of providing quick and easy graduate credit for teachers. Recent federal legislation such as No Child Left Behind has put more restrictions on what can be offered in these so-called teacher professional development series; nevertheless, teachers can still relatively easily get credit for history-related "travel courses" to Oahu or Great Smoky Mountains National Park, regardless of whether or not they teach history. Of course, in most districts, teachers pay for these classes out-of-pocket and attend them over the summer or in the evenings or on weekends.

"That's a pretty cynical system, to make somebody pay for his own pay raise," Jupp says. "What we see is that as teachers pay for their own pay raise, they let the market do the talking, and they go for the cheapest credit and the easiest credit," said Jupp.

Districts make large investments in providing on-site professional development for their teachers, but there is often little incentive for teachers to apply what they learn and make changes in their own classrooms.

If the tax increase is approved by voters in 2006 and ProComp goes forward, teachers will be able to earn raises for successfully completing relevant university courses and district-offered professional development. Where traditional pay schedules paid for any and all courses, ProComp puts the emphasis on relevance. Teachers will be required to demonstrate in their work how they've applied what they learned from the courses. In exchange for this demonstration of relevant new knowledge and skills, teachers will earn an additional $659, or 2 percent of the district starting salary ($32,971). Teachers who earn a relevant master's degree (in education or a teacher's discipline) will receive a 9 percent raise, almost $3,000. Another 9 percent raise is offered for becoming certified by the National Board for Professional Teaching Standards, a rigorous, yearlong process in which teachers assemble an extensive portfolio containing documented daily instruction, student learning, and their own written analysis.

Education policy wonks like Jupp refer to this as "job-embedded staff development." The central idea is to render the professional development choices made by schools and teachers relevant to the work of the school and then to reward successful participation. They see this as an antidote to both the problem of buying raises with irrelevant graduate credit and the squandering of resources in on-site professional development efforts that come with neither carrot nor stick. This program is essentially all carrot. It even involves $1,000 a year in tuition reimbursement.

It's a simple calculus, really—ask teachers to do what you want them to and then pay them for it—and it's what drives other elements of the pay system, like the market incentives for working in hard-to-staff positions or hard-to-serve schools.

DENVER'S FUTURE, PART II: PAYING MORE FOR TEACHERS IN HARD-TO-STAFF SCHOOLS

Colfax Elementary School is about three miles west of downtown Denver. It is a classic "hard-to-serve" school. It is housed in a somewhat nondescript building—brown-bricked, boxy, two stories tall—and it provides a strong center for a troubled and challenged community. The staff run book, food, and clothing drives every year for the families that make up their clientele. In 1995, teachers, staff, and administrators felt their current calendar

HIGHER SALARIES FOR SOME?[2]
Do you think it is a good or bad idea to:
(respondents: new teachers)

...Pay higher salaries to teachers who work
in difficult schools with hard-to-educate children?

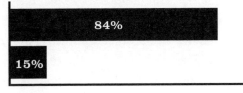

Good Idea — 84%

Bad Idea — 15%

...Pay higher salaries to teachers who prove to be
highly effective in improving academic performance?

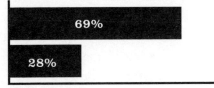

Good Idea — 69%

Bad Idea — 28%

...Pay more money to teachers in subjects like math
and science, where there are severe shortages?

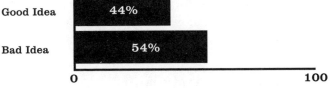

Good Idea — 44%

Bad Idea — 54%

0   100

meant the children spent too much time on the streets and out of
school during the summer. Colfax then became the first school in
Denver to move to a year-round calendar, and it did so with 85
percent approval from the community.

Like many urban schools, Colfax has a large number of
English-language learners. Some classes at every grade level are

taught in both Spanish and English. But the statistic that tends to impress people about Colfax is this: 80.9 percent of the students receive a free or reduced-price lunch. In other words, four out of five children at this school live in households surviving below or just barely above the poverty line. Last year, the figure was more like 90 percent. These are the children of residents in a nearby battered women's shelter. They are the children who share a single room with their parents and brothers and sisters in the cheap motels that line Colfax Avenue a few miles west of downtown Denver.

The other thing people at Colfax talk about is the high "mobility rate" of the students. It's a statistical category that seems hampered by connotations of the "upwardly mobile," which these children are anything but. The word *transient* seems more apt.

Union president Wissink cut her teeth teaching at Colfax and spent a significant portion of her career trying to understand the impact this mobility was having on the school, where she taught bilingual fourth grade and ran the Title I program. She analyzed the student turnover and mobility data "just for fun," and found the reality of the data startling. Although 70 percent of the student body was relatively stable, the other 30 percent was so rootless that the actual number of students entering and leaving mid-year was far greater than the number of students who were stable. "That 30 percent would turn over again and again," Wissink says.

Of the fifty-six children in the 1998 fifth-grade class, only nine had attended kindergarten at Colfax.

Mobility like this is extremely common in poor communities. Families are often renters, and parents may be marginally employed. Teachers at Colfax say that when a child stops coming to school, it's often because his family has been evicted and they spent the day moving to a shelter.

Maggie Willett has seen these patterns in her classrooms at Colfax for the last twelve years. On a Thursday in the middle of

May 2004, she had twenty-eight students currently in her first-grade attendance book. One student had just begun that day, one month before school was to end. She had entered five other new students in the past month. During the same time, three other students had left.

"The mobility is the most challenging thing," Willett says. "My son's girlfriend is an elementary school teacher as well, but she's had the same twenty-two children the whole year. That's very different. This is just the way of teaching here, and, actually, it's what I'm comfortable with."

Under the ProComp system, in recognition of the adversities teachers face at schools like Colfax, Willett and teachers in her school can earn an additional $989 bonus every year they teach in a hard-to-serve school like Colfax or in a hard-to-staff position like special education or bilingual education.

DENVER'S FUTURE, PART III: ACCOUNTABILITY AND EVALUATIONS THAT MATTER

In some public schools, the administrator evaluation is a traditionally perfunctory ordeal often involving a distracted principal, a checklist, and a rubber stamp. To correct this in Denver, a team of administrators and teachers is designing a new evaluation system that will focus "only on what teachers do in their classrooms," said Jupp. Teachers will be rated by both their peers and their administrators, and a "satisfactory" review will result in another 3 percent pay raise, or another $989.

This piece of the new system has yet to be finalized, and, at the time of the union vote, it wasn't much more than an idea and a promise. To be successful, the design team will have to create a set of criteria both teachers and administrators can work with and buy into.

But all sides have agreed to two safeguards for the evaluations:

• They will be evaluated by their peers as well as by administrators

• There will be an appeals process for teachers who feel they have been evaluated unfairly

Bonuses are attached to the goals and objectives teachers write for themselves—the legacy of the "Pay for Performance" pilot. Teachers who participate get a 1 percent ($330) raise in their salary as well as a 1 percent bonus (another $330). Though this seems small, it has had substantial effects. Not only does it acknowledge that there is a great deal of progress that students make that cannot be measured by standardized tests, but it also gives teachers a voice and some degree of control over how they will be held accountable.

The piece of the new system that was the most troubling for many teachers was the tying of another 3 percent raise ($989) to students' achievement on the Colorado Student Assessment Program (CSAP) test. Teachers at any school designated as "distinguished" because of schoolwide performance on the CSAP can receive a 2 percent ($659) bonus. Though some teachers had a difficult time with this, any system trying to get the support of the district office and the Denver voters has to take into account the results of standardized testing.

"That was an important political piece," says school board president Les Woodward. "It represents a very small part of the total overall compensation, and it's not easy to acquire a pay increase for achieving [those gains]. But, when we go to the public for more money, it's too easy a question to ask to say, 'Well, why didn't you think the achievement of students as demonstrated by the state test was important enough to count it in the compensation system?'"

In early versions of attaching economic stakes to student performance on tests, some states threatened underperforming schools with funding cuts. What is different, and in some ways more benign, about Denver's approach is that there is no way for a teacher to be punished for poor student achievement. A teacher whose students don't meet benchmarks doesn't get that additional 3 percent raise, but neither does a teacher who is assigned to a grade level or subject other than those tested by the CSAP. The CSAP scores account for only a part of one of the four areas in which teachers can earn raises. This made the bitter pill easier to swallow.

DENVER GOT IT DONE BECAUSE EVERYONE AGREED SOMETHING NEEDED TO BE DONE

There are many lessons to be drawn from Denver's experience, the most important of which falls under the idea of process. In creating a reform of this scale, there is little reason to believe any off-the-shelf solution will succeed in a given district, and less reason to believe that what works in Denver will work in Duluth. What people in Denver did well, however, was talk to each other and listen to each other. In wanting to test their ideas, they were not afraid to ask for help from people outside education.

They also allowed themselves to move forward with a work-in-progress—a risky move for stakeholders on both sides—which requires trust among all players over the long haul. When the union voted, the evaluation system wasn't in place, nor were all the criteria for professional development credit or student scores on standardized tests. But they moved forward anyway, saying and believing these were all achievable tasks. At the same time, they put into place structures like the board of trustees to oversee the tax revenue and to evaluate and improve the system.

People in Denver seem to understand there are no quick fixes and that the alternative they're offering may not even be the ultimate answer.

"I don't think we're the new paradigm," says design team facilitator Brad Jupp. "I think we're the people that opened the door widest to the new paradigm. What we did was to move away from a two-dimensional matrix or a salary schedule, so individuals become their own reference point for their own salary."

Everyone involved acknowledges there are still problems with the system, and the fact that not every teacher will be eligible for a raise in each of the four areas is one of them. The likelihood that teachers in hard-to-staff special education or bilingual positions will also see their students' standardized test scores rise to the benchmark for a raise is fairly slim, but then again, they get the extra pay for that hard-to-staff teaching assignment. There is balance in that all teachers are eligible for professional development raises, as well as raises for their evaluations and meeting their own goals. While this doesn't solve every problem, it does offer a new way of thinking about how teachers can be paid.

Maggie Willett, first-grade teacher at Colfax Elementary, is like many teachers in this book. She is smart, dedicated, and motivated more by a desire to help children than to make money. She has taught for thirteen years and has reached the top of the salary scale at $61,012.

Without ProComp, she says, "I would basically be staying at the same level, going up once every five years for the rest of my career. It's maybe a few thousand dollars. I can't imagine staying at this salary with the cost of living increasing. In fifteen years, I'll be out there getting second jobs again. I did that for many years, and it's only been in the last few years that I've been able to live only on my teaching salary."

Because she is already at the top of the schedule, she stands to gain a lot from opting into ProComp. For satisfactory yearly evaluations, she can get a 3 percent raise ($989) on top of the starting teachers' salary. She is also eligible for the market incentive for teaching in a hard-to-serve school, another 3 percent bonus every year. She'll earn both of those without changing her work at all. Any professional development units she successfully completes will get her another 2 percent ($659) raise, and, if she decides to get a second masters degree or become certified by the National Board for Professional Teaching Standards, she can earn herself an additional 9 percent ($2,967) raise. If she chooses to continue working on her own objectives in the classroom and documents student progress, she can earn a 1 percent raise ($330) every year she does so. Because she doesn't teach in a grade level where the CSAP test is used, she won't be eligible for those raises, however. Nevertheless, when she adds it up, Willett will get a $989 raise and a $989 bonus every year for doing the same good job she's doing now, and she will have the option of working toward an additional $989 raise every year.

"It'll have a substantial effect on my retirement," she says. "Those last three years you're working, everyone knows you want to make your salary as high as you can possibly make it." If she plays her cards right, by the end of her career, her salary could top $90,000.

Of course, the same isn't true for all teachers in Denver. Because of the quirks of the pay system, a large group of mid-career teachers may see only a $10,000 difference between what they'll make when they retire under ProComp and what they would have made under the old system. However, new teachers coming in under ProComp can expect their careers and savings accounts to grow quite differently than they might have. The more important point, though, is how this will change the future of students in Denver public schools—how a community places value on the work teachers do, and, ultimately, improves the lives of students and their teachers.

Renee Barela is a parent of a Colfax Elementary student and

happens to work in Denver Public Schools' payroll department. It goes without saying that she knows how much teachers bring home now, and she believes this new program will help the district keep good teachers. "When the kids come up to the fifth grade, it's nice if they have a teacher they've been seeing there since they were in kindergarten," she explained. "It makes your child feel safe. Knowing that things are going to be steady makes me feel safe as a mother. Just like living in the same home for a number of years, you feel comfortable there."

If Denver Public Schools can keep good teachers around longer, that may turn out to be the most important legacy of the work they've done on pay reform.

"We need to get competent, well-trained, good teachers here," says Willett, "and the long-term effect is that we will retain quality teachers, and we'll be able to bring in quality teachers from outside. My students only have me for one year. If they can continue to have quality teachers along the way, that will have a positive impact on them."

*   *   *

What seems most remarkable about Denver's ProComp system, beyond the scale, is the manner in which it seems to satisfy the desires of all advocates of teacher pay reform—those who simply want higher pay and those who want to see increased pay tied to very specific outcomes. The traditional idea—that the only way to raise salaries is to raise everyone's salary—is often countered in the political arena with the argument that a universal increase provides no incentive for teachers to focus on improving student achievement nor to become better teachers.

Chester E. Finn, president of the conservative Thomas B. Fordham Foundation and former assistant secretary of research in the U.S. Department of Education, is an unofficial education spokesperson for the politically conservative. He has long been an advocate for differentiated pay for teachers (i.e., providing substantial increases for only certain teachers, and cutting pay for others). "Raising teacher salaries needs to be joined with some profound changes in how teacher salaries are determined and administered and meted out," he says, "or else it's not actually going to do any good and it's not going to be either politically or fiscally viable. I think that we should be reformulating the whole teacher compensation and personnel system in fairly radical ways, and part of that should include more pay for highly effective teachers, teachers of scarce subjects, and teachers who take on challenging circumstances."

Denver's reform seems to meet Finn's criteria for who should qualify for increased pay. Because it is optional, only teachers willing to meet the demands of the new contract will opt in or choose to work in Denver. At the same time, as Becky Wissink has said, the new program will put millions of dollars a year into teachers' pockets.

CASE STUDY NO. 2

CHANGING PAY AND INCREASING STUDENT SUCCESS IN LOS ANGELES

VAUGHN NEXT CENTURY LEARNING CENTER

In Los Angeles, there is a principal at a charter school dedicated to getting more and more money into her teachers' pockets, in exchange for asking them to help her create a more effective school than any of them had ever seen before. This is a different kind of reform. It's not district-wide, and it isn't dependent on $25 million in new taxes. It is based on a common vision at the school and made possible by the tenacity of the staff and their leader.

The Vaughn Next Century Learning Center is a public elementary school in the San Fernando Valley serving predominantly Latino, low-income students. Fourteen years ago, Vaughn was a struggling school. Test scores were in the bottom 10 percent of the state; students were truant and most had very poor English skills. The classrooms were overcrowded, in dilapidated buildings with a crack house next to the school grounds. Demoralized teachers were often absent from work. Today, it's an entirely different place, in large part because teachers at Vaughn earn a great deal of money for being effective.

One could easily mistake Vaughn for a private school. At ten in the morning some 300 students play in a huge open courtyard the size of a city block. There are three basketball courts, picnic tables, and a grassy field for soccer. The courtyard is clean and the surrounding buildings—beige, tall, handsome—are remarkably free of graffiti. The bell rings. The fourth- and fifth-grade stu-

218

dents, dressed in gray, white, and maroon uniforms, with gold medallions of St. Michael, St. Christopher, and the Virgin Mary peeking out from under their white collars, file off in lines behind their teachers.

Fourth-graders return to Susie Oblad's class, chatting happily. They look at the day's agenda and meander to their chairs. The front of the class is decorated with crayon-colored maps of California. Next to those is the "Hooked on Books" board, where the students recommend their favorite titles to their classmates. Another wall is filled with their reports on dolphins. The students, unprovoked, sit at their desks and pull their workbooks from their desks.

"Yo, yo, yo!" Ms. Oblad calls out.

"Yo, what's up?" is the response, in unison, from her eighteen students.

This is their routine. It gets the class's attention and signals the beginning of class. Ms. Oblad announces the beginning of "appreciation/concern time." Two students pop up to the white board and grab dry-erase markers. Many students in the room have their hands raised. The two students in the front of the class write some of their classmates' names in a list on the white board: 1. María; 2. Franky; 3. Hector; 4. José. María reports she is happy because her presentation for the following day—about the San Fernando Mission—is ready. Franky bemoans the fact that he has had to return his defective Play Station 2 to the store. The boys in the class groan. After each student speaks, the entire class says "Thank you" to the student who has shared. One boy explains he's happy because over the weekend his family surprised his father with a birthday cake, and at the party, he gave his father a gift of fifty cents. "It was all I had," he shrugs.

Ms. Oblad is also invited to share. Standing at the back of the class, relaxed, she registers her pride in the fact that the class posted 100 percent attendance the previous month. She pushes her blond hair behind her ear and adds that she knows the next day's presentations on California history are going to be strong, and she is looking forward to seeing them. This is all she has said during this ten-minute activity. Her nine-year-old students have run the entire affair themselves.

Thania Torres, a seventh grader, comes in the door. All upper-level students at Vaughn have to do service hours in the school, and Thania, a former student of Ms. Oblad's, serves as teacher's assistant.

"Yo, yo, yo!" Thania says.

"Yo, what's up?" is the response.

Thania has taken over the class. It's time to go over their math homework, so the students already know that they should turn to page 79.

Hands are immediately raised to answer questions. Hector wants to answer so badly that he waves his arm desperately; his entire body is out of the chair. The class moves quickly, with Thania running through the answers. Hector gets called on for number seven, and is finally able to sit down again and relax.

Several students have gotten question number twelve wrong. Ms. Oblad steps in and asks for a student to read the word problem. Irene, the young student who was at the board earlier, volunteers. The problem deals with temperature and involves subtracting from negative numbers. Once the problem is read, Ms. Oblad goes to a bright poster with numbers lining the wall. She starts working through the problem by walking next to the relevant numbers in the poster. As she stands at "−12," she asks the students, "Which direction should I move in if you need to subtract?" The students call out that she has to walk backward. Seeing her walk in that direction appears to help students understand where they've gone wrong. Together, they have understood the problem and its solution. Ms. Oblad checks in with several students, to make sure that they've understood. Thania then takes the floor again.

Another few questions are answered correctly. At number sixteen, several students are stumped again. Ms. Oblad guides them to the right answer and then asks something unusual: "Who would like to explain their thinking on their wrong answer?" Several students raise their hands to elaborate on their mistakes. Oblad calls on Carlos, who explains that he added 5 and 12, took away 4, and got 13. She asks him to look at the problem again and see if he notices anything about the numbers that may have led him astray. There is a patient pause while other students wait. He calmly says that the first number in the word problem is a –5, not a 5, as he had thought. She smiles, and Carlos scribbles in his notebook.

In Oblad's class, the students know that it is safe to make mistakes. They even seem to understand that knowing why they make mistakes is an important part of the class.

Later, when the school day is over, Oblad's blue eyes smile as she watches the class trail out of the room. "I'm very proud of them," she says. "There's a lot of growth they see in themselves."

Best of all, because her peers are paid well, she doesn't fear for her students' future. "I can be sure that they're going to have a good fifth-grade teacher," she says.

Oblad has been teaching for eleven years and will make about $70,000 this year. Her base salary—calculated according to the years she has taught—is $52,900, and bonuses will add up to just over $17,000. This makes her one of the best-paid public school teachers in the state for her level of experience. The base pay at Vaughn is less than it is for a teacher of equal experience in Los Angeles County, yet with bonuses, the teachers take home significantly more.

There are five areas in which Vaughn teachers can earn bonuses on top of their base pay:

• Evaluations: Every teacher's performance is measured by evaluations from other teachers, from administrators, and from the teacher him- or herself. Scores from these evaluations are averaged to determine the teacher's overall score. Depending on the score, this bonus, the largest possible, can reach up to $13,050 per year. However, a teacher may take home nothing in this category if a bonus is not merited.

• Student attendance: If the school's overall attendance is 95 percent or better, each teacher receives an additional $250. Student attendance of 98 percent or higher earns them $1,000 each.

• Teacher attendance: Teachers who have perfect attendance themselves receive another $250. (They are allowed ten sick days a year.)

• Performance goals: If the school's overall goals are met on the Average Performance Index (the measurement used to rate all California public schools), all teachers earn another $2,000 each. Goals are set based on the previous year's scores, plus agreed-upon goals for improvement.

• Extracurricular activities: All teachers are compensated for taking leadership roles on campus. Serving as committee chair or faculty chair is worth $500 per year. Serving as team leader for teachers at a given grade level is worth $750. Serving as peer reviewer brings in an additional $1,000.

The evaluations, which are assessed using guidelines established by the teachers and administration, make up the largest portion of the bonus. This is how it works: Each semester, another Vaughn teacher visits the class. This "peer evaluator" sits with the class for a large portion of the day, taking notes. On another day, an administrator—the grade-level coordinators, the assistant principal, or the principal—sits in the class for a large part of the day, also taking notes. In order to evaluate the teacher and assign a score to her performance, they look for evidence of the teacher's effectiveness in class and ways in which the teacher can improve her practice. Each evaluator places the teacher into one of the following categories: distinguished (4), proficient (3), basic (2), or unsatisfactory (1). The teachers are also given the opportunity to assess their own strengths and weaknesses in a self-evaluation. The three evaluations—administrator's, peer evaluator's, and self—are then averaged to become the teacher's score for that semester's performance. This numerical score correlates to the bonus the teacher will receive for that semester. This process is repeated in the following semester.

Oblad rates at the highest level, that of a "distinguished" teacher, with a top score of 4. This means when her peers and administrator are in her classroom, they see the following behaviors, listed on Vaughn's evaluation paperwork, with which all teachers are familiar:

• Teacher seeks reasons for student misunderstanding.

• Students produce high-quality work that they exhibit with pride.

• Teacher's directions and procedures are clear to students.

• Students assume considerable responsibility for the success of discussion, initiating topics.

• Students assume responsibility for productivity.

• Pacing of the lesson is appropriate for all students.

• Teacher-student interactions are friendly and demonstrate general warmth, caring, and respect.

• Teacher addresses students respectfully.

• Students demonstrate genuine caring for one another as individuals.

• Teacher displays extensive content knowledge.

• Teacher consistently uses, where appropriate, knowledge of students' varied approaches to learning in instructional planning, including those with special needs.

• Assessment criteria and standards are clear and have been clearly communicated to students.

• Planning of learning activities, interactions, and the classroom environment convey high expectations for the learning of all.

When Vaughn teachers demonstrate their excellence, they are paid well. The most significant result of tying increased teacher pay to specific performance objectives has been a dramatic increase in student achievement. Before Vaughn revamped its pay structure, Vaughn students were testing in the bottom 10 percent of all California students. Teachers began to be evaluated using the pay-for-performance model in 1998, and in 2004, they're testing above the 50th percentile. Students who in 1990 had an 88 percent attendance record now come to school at least 95 percent of the time. Just as crucially, teachers themselves boast an almost perfect attendance rate.

VAUGHN'S CHALLENGES

Vaughn is located in the town of Pacoima in the San Fernando Valley, twenty miles northwest of downtown Los Angeles. The students are 96 percent Latino and 4 percent African American. They are mostly immigrants; 97.4 percent qualify for the free or reduced-price breakfast and lunch program. (In California, a family of four earning less than $24,505 a year qualifies for the free lunch program. The two meals received at school each day are sometimes the only food the students eat.) Sixty-nine percent of the parents do not hold a high school diploma; 78 percent of the students are learning English only outside the home. Most of the students' parents work in factories, in construction, as gardeners, or in the service industries, and many of the children come from single-parent families. Many of Vaughn's students have not gone to school in their home country and do not have strong language skills in Spanish, let alone English. In many cases, students come to Vaughn with deficiencies in both languages. In this community, it is not unusual for up to ten students to be living in the same home.

In 1990, the Vaughn Street School, as it was called at the time, was riddled with problems. The school served students from kindergarten through fifth grade, and was overcrowded. There were no services for students with special needs, so several hundred were bused to other public schools, often separating siblings. State funds tied to student attendance were reduced because of student truancy. Teaching vacancies were difficult to fill, and students were often taught by teachers with emergency credentials or with less than three years of experience. Violence and drug abuse among the adults in the neighborhood were commonplace. Not surprisingly, students were performing poorly on standardized tests. The school's rating issued by the state was in the single digits—among the very worst in California.

Not only were the students performing poorly, but there was tension between the bilingual teachers and the English-only teachers. The bilingual teachers believed that the students would be more successful if they were taught in both English and Spanish, while the English-only teachers favored full immersion. Teachers blamed one another for the students' lack of success.

Suzanne Llamas taught third grade in the '90s. She is a tall Latina woman with short, dark, curly hair. She recalls that era as she escorts her class across the courtyard to lunch. "The school was very divided," she says. "There was a lot of uproar. There was a lot of money spent unwisely. The principal had seen a lot of injustice both in the classes and within the system."

Unable to make progress with the school's problems, the principal resigned. Dr. Yvonne Chan, then principal at another elementary school in the district, was asked to lead the school.

"The district felt that this Chinese woman would be the middle-ground person," Llamas says. "She wasn't black. She wasn't white. She wasn't brown. The district thought she would be able to pull people together."

THE REINVENTION OF VAUGHN

In 1990, Chan began to shift the school culture. She and her teachers quickly realized that they needed freedom to make changes, and found the Los Angeles Unified School District's bureaucracy too challenging to work within. The teachers learned about the then-new charter school movement and embarked on the application process to become one. As a public charter school, they would be free of some of the constraints imposed on traditional district-run schools. The "charter" is an actual contract with the district that allows schools to manage their own budget, hire whom they wish, and make their own pedagogical decisions.

In 1993, Vaughn became a charter school and changed its name to the Vaughn Next Century Learning Center. The Vaughn charter included the following goals:

• To increase attendance to 95 percent
• To ensure that students speak and write fluent English
• To include parents in leadership decisions and in their children's academic lives
• To provide meaningful professional development for teachers
• To help students raise their average test scores by 15 to 20 percentage points on California state exams

Vaughn's charter comes up for renewal every five years, when they must bring evidence of their success to the district school board. In an effort to facilitate success, Chan and her staff made the following immediate changes in 1993:

• The school year was extended by twenty days, to a total of 200 instructional days for all students.

• Special education programs were created so those students would no longer have to be bused to other sites.

• Parents were required to sign a contract saying they would commit thirty hours a year to participation in school life and their children's learning. They could meet this requirement through monitoring the playground, volunteering in classes, or even taking their children to the library. Parents were also required to be available to teachers to discuss their children's performance whenever necessary.

• To save money, the school cut unnecessary administrative positions, and began to contract locally for food service and building maintenance.

• New portable classrooms were brought in to alleviate overcrowding.

In 1997, with the charter up for renewal the following year, Chan knew that still more improvements were needed to achieve the academic goals they had outlined. She recognized that the traditional salary scale on which she paid her staff encouraged mediocrity and that some teachers were well paid despite lackluster performance. New teachers faced three years before they saw their first, modest raise, which discouraged many from staying even that long. Even good, dedicated teachers considered a future in administration the only reliable way to increase their earnings.

Chan suspected that financial incentives might provide the impetus some of her staff needed to improve their performance and extend their stay at Vaughn.

"We had many teachers who had been here for many years," Suzanne Llamas remembers, "and they weren't doing what they were supposed to be doing, and yet they received quite a bit of money. Just because the teacher has been here for fourteen years doesn't mean they should be making a lot of money."

There was some discussion about changing the compensation system to reward teachers for their abilities in the classroom. But there was resistance to the new ideas from some of the older teachers.

"This was really innovative thinking at the time, and they said, 'No, we don't want to do something like that!'" says Llamas. "There was fear because teachers and administrators were going to come in and monitor them. Teachers were reluctant to lose money or to try something different."

Despite ambivalence on the part of many teachers, Chan was able to garner enough support to test a pilot program to reward teacher effectiveness with increased pay. In 1998, the charter was renewed and the new teacher compensation program was initiated.

HOW THE PAY-FOR-PERFORMANCE PROGRAM UNFOLDED

In the 1998–1999 school year, ten out of a total of fifty-five teachers on the staff became the first to test out the performance-pay plan. The school started with a small number of teachers both to learn the pitfalls of the design and to be able to plan financially before initiating the program with the entire staff. The idea was to fold other teachers into the program over a period of years.

Two groups of teachers comprised the first ten pay-for-performance teachers: teachers new that fall, and a handful of teachers with less than five years of experience.

The ten teachers who went through the program the first semester earned bonuses ranging from $150 to $1,650, depending on how well they performed on their evaluations. By the second semester, more teachers opted into the system. That second semester, the school paid fifteen teachers sums ranging from $650 to $1,650. In addition to rewarding individual performance, Chan hoped to reward the school as a whole for the group effort of the entire staff. When overall student scores on the state assessment met the growth target, the entire staff, including the administrators, received $1,500 on top of their salary in the spring of 1999.

As the first year of the performance-pay plan unfolded, three issues emerged. First, veteran teachers not participating in the program saw that the people on the plan were earning more money, and they wanted to participate. Second, newer staff felt that they had to work harder to earn their money, because their pay hinged on their evaluations. But a staff survey found the process had hurt school morale.

Oblad remembers the challenging times. "We lost some staff because of it," she says. "They went back to the district. They were fearful that [the evaluation process] would be too subjective or that someone might be harmed in an evaluation. They felt the process might be too human."

While these tensions existed, there was an important upside: the teachers believed that the process had a meaningful impact on their work, and that the evaluations were authentic and connected to student learning. At the end of the year, the staff voted to continue the program, and more teachers joined the program that fall.

For the 1999–2000 school year, all teachers were given the

choice to opt into the performance-pay plan. A handful teachers joined the program. The following school year, in 2000–2001, all teachers—whether they were on the performance-pay plan or not—were evaluated using the same system as the people on the plan. Many teachers received strong evaluations and were able to see how much money they might have earned on the pay-for-performance plan. They were losing bonuses, they realized, by not being on the plan. By the fifth year of the new pay plan, 2002–2003, all of the teachers at Vaughn were on board.

FUNDING THE PAY-FOR-PERFORMANCE PROGRAM

A first-year credentialed teacher in the Los Angeles Unified School district is paid $41,177 for a year's work. At Vaughn, a first-year credentialed teacher is paid a base salary of $38,900 but with bonuses can earn $47,700. Today the school operates on a $12.6 million budget, which means it is spending about $8,400 per student—$1,000 more than the statewide average in 2004. Chan anticipates spending between 5 and 8 percent of that on teachers' bonuses.

Vaughn, like all public schools, receives state money based on the "average daily attendance" of students. This accounts for 90 percent of its operating budget. The rest of the school's budget is the result of Chan's fund-raising efforts.

"She sits around a table with people like [Bill] Gates," says Oblad. "I walked in to the office the first year I was here, and I overheard Chan on the phone saying, 'You will get me our money!' That is how she is: she won't let up."

Oblad says that sometimes Chan will find out about a funding grant in the evening and will have the application ready the next morning—even if it requires a fifty-page proposal. But grants alone do not solve all of the school's challenges. Chan is a fiscal hawk and directs a significant amount of energy at cutting costs at the level of virtually every line item. She halted unnecessary textbook purchases. The school now buys paper from local vendors rather than the more expensive district office. When it comes to maintenance and construction needs, the school uses local contractors—which provides the double benefit of saving money and supporting the parents of Vaughn students.

THE IMPACT OF PAYING FOR PERFORMANCE

Through outside research done by the Consortium for Policy Research in Education, Vaughn has confirmed that teachers' performance does affect how well students do. Specifically, the study found a positive relationship between teachers' performance evaluations and the achievement of their students on standardized tests. The better a teacher scored on her evaluation, the more academic gains her students made.

Louise Larson is the coordinator of instruction for Vaughn's middle school and is one of the administrators who evaluates teachers. She says that beyond providing teachers with an opportunity to earn money, the evaluation process has helped teachers improve their practice.

"We can target the skills that directly correlate to the learning environment the teacher is creating," she says. "You can document it and say, 'Here's an area in which you are not scoring well.' Then you provide strategies and alternatives. You can actually give teachers constructive recommendations for improvement, and it's reflected in the salary in turn."

Because Vaughn teachers are given freedom in their curriculum and paid well, overwhelming numbers of high quality teachers apply wherever Vaughn has an opening.

"We'll have seventy, eighty résumés for only five elementary openings," says Claudia Delgadillo, the coordinator for instruction for the second and third grades.

This kind of competition was unheard of ten or fifteen years ago, when the school could not find credentialed teachers to fill the classrooms. The caliber of the teaching staff has improved with this kind of competition.

"The school attracts people who are going to work a little harder," Delgadillo says. "They're people who are a bit out-of-the-box thinkers, who aren't afraid, and don't need to be tied to a specific curriculum or a scripted way of doing things. What's attractive about our program here at Vaughn is that teachers definitely get paid if they have skills. They will make a considerable amount more than if they went with the district. We do have a group of teachers, brand new, year one, who are going to make good money because they score so high on everything. They're such amazing new teachers."

THE ROAD AHEAD FOR VAUGHN

Chan is happiest when her teachers receive the credit for Vaughn's success, but it's her leadership and her willingness to work long hours and get her hands dirty that have set the tone for the school. Her teachers seem ready to follow her anywhere.

"I see her picking up garbage and wiping down white boards," Delgadillo says, pointing to Chan's office across the hall. In Chan's eyes, however, much of her success lies in the implementation of her salary scheme. Chan, Delgadillo, and all the administration staff are also paid according to their performance.

"With the pay-for-performance plan," Chan says, "the bottom line is that we are able to put student achievement as our burning focus on our school site. Vaughn is truly a community of learners where everybody and everything is connected. We always put student achievement at the forefront of all the work we do."

These changes have brought far-reaching effects to the school and the surrounding community.

"Vaughn has created a stable atmosphere within the neighborhood," says Larson, the middle-school coordinator. "This used to be a very transient place, and now people are more permanent. We have students who've been here since pre-kindergarten—there's longevity. I think part of that is a result of the performance-pay in our charter. There's a lot of commitment here."

That sense of commitment has extended beyond the traditional work of the school. To better serve its 1,500 students and the community, Vaughn has begun an early childhood development program and a school-based community health clinic. The school is also planning to expand to encompass a high school. When Chan is able to implement her vision, the Vaughn community will have cradle-to-college education from some of the best-paid teachers in the country.

As Chan sums it up, "We've been able to solve a lot of problems associated with poverty and urban poor schools. Against all odds."

Allen Odden, who oversees the teacher compensation research at the University of Wisconsin's Center for Policy Research in Education, says that Vaughn's approach to paying teachers better is the kind of reform that might be most applicable to small rural school districts. It was large reform in a small community where all teachers and parents were invited to be decision makers along with administrators. Many of the successes were made economically viable by Principal Chan's fiscal restraint and fund-raising acumen.

Some districts try to do this without raising extra money, however. Administrators in Helena, Montana, as we'll see in the next section, had no money to fund the salary increases they wanted to offer their educators. For teachers and prospective teachers, the Helena school district was one of the employers of last resort. That is no longer the case.

CASE STUDY NO. 3

BETTER SCHOOLS IN HELENA, MONTANA—NOW, EDUCATORS CLAMOR TO TEACH THERE

HELENA'S PUBLIC SCHOOL DISTRICT

"**Y**ears past, we would get twelve applicants for each position, and that would be about it," says Principal Randy Carlson of Capital High School in the Helena Public School District. "So out of the twelve, we'd be looking at interviewing five or six at the most. Oftentimes, people will apply, and they don't really have the qualifications. They say, 'I'll be getting my degree; can I get a provisional certificate?'"

In 2004, Carlson had to fill three social studies positions, and he had over one hundred applicants to choose from.

"It was miserable making the decision. It was hard," Carlson continues. "But out of a hundred, we got down to forty, and then out of the forty, we wanted to cut it down to twelve to interview. That was extremely difficult. Then we did the twelve interviews, and out of the twelve, we were looking for three. There were nine we were ready to hire."

Carlson's experience was paralleled all over the district, where a total of almost 900 applications were received for a mere fifty positions. Though most of the applicants were coming from within Montana, the positions had attracted a large amount of interest from out of state. "Let's see, there was Waco, Texas; Augusta, Georgia; Nampa, Idaho; Surprise, Arizona; and Gresham, Oregon, and there's Washington, Wisconsin, Oklahoma, Kansas . . ."

says Jean Horne, assistant to the personnel director, reading a spreadsheet on her computer's monitor.

By the beginning of June, the file cabinets and boxes storing the applications and video tapes of interviews had outgrown the district's modest personnel offices. They were filling storage closets and peeking out from under administrators' desks. The administrators doing the interviewing—many of them long-time veteran teachers of Helena Public Schools—were regularly joking with each other that they didn't think they ever would have been hired if they had faced similar competition for their own jobs twenty or thirty years ago.

"We put everything else on hold, and this has been our priority. We knew we had to reformat how we used to do things," says director of educational services Keith Meyer, a former elementary school teacher whose walrus mustache and ready smile give him the impression of having just stepped out of a children's story.

"We wanted the majority of our hiring done by the end of school. That's a first for us. Usually we don't get done until the end of July. Now, it's the beginning of June, and we're going to be done," Meyer explains.

This is what happens when district administrators and union officials decide to become leaders in the area of salary reform. Teachers everywhere hear about it, and what was once a school district like any other in Montana finds itself the first choice of educators across the region.

They have had to respond accordingly. They called in retired principals to help screen applications. They created a new database to keep track of everyone who applied. And they began what personnel director Bill Rasor described as the "welcome chore" of identifying "the best of the best" to fill their vacancies.

What attracted these 900 applicants was, in the simplest

terms, better pay and a better pay system. Many applicants had interest in being in Helena already, having grown up there or having some other connection to the town, but prior to the introduction of Helena Public Schools' salary reform (called the Professional Compensation Alternative, as seen previously), most teachers were unlikely to have chosen to teach in Helena public schools. After all, the starting salary in 2003 was barely over $23,000.

"I couldn't afford to teach there," says new hire Brandon Price, twenty-nine, who left Helena after college to pursue his teaching career elsewhere.

When he started to teach, he says, he "could go out of state and start at $30,000 or $32,000, so there was a $10,000 difference to move out of state. That's pretty significant coming out of college with loans."

Back in the late 1990s, Price moved to Texas, then Oregon. But he says Helena's alternative compensation plan was his "opportunity to get back."

In the summer of 2004, Price and his wife moved 500 miles back to Helena so he could start teaching eighth-grade science at C. R. Anderson Middle School. They sold their home in Gresham, Oregon, a middle-class suburb of Portland, knowing that even though his new salary in the $30,000s would only be $10,000 less than what he earned in Gresham, it would suffice in Montana, where the average is around $25,000. They were confident that with this salary, plus whatever his wife brought home from her work as a real estate agent, they would be able to buy a house and start a family.

The story of why teachers like Price are taking a second look at Helena schools begins in 2002. It is a story of a school district finding a new way of doing business, finding a way to do what everyone wanted but no one knew how to pay for. Interestingly, it's a story about how they did it without costing the district or taxpayers a penny more than they were already spending.

* * *

In 2002, district officials were sure of a number of things. They were sure they weren't attracting high-quality candidates in the numbers they wanted, and they were sure they needed to start doing that. They knew they were among the lowest paying districts in the nation, and they were sure that needed to change. If not, they knew they'd be consigning themselves to an ever-shrinking and increasingly shallow pool of qualified candidates applying for their teaching vacancies. They were also sure they couldn't afford the massive pay raise both administrators and teachers wanted to see.

Helena Public Schools had been trying to cut spending for years. Board of trustees president Julie Mitchell said they had cut from between several hundred thousand dollars to $1 million a year for several years in a row. They were facing a decline in enrollment, and over the preceding decade, the state had gone from providing a 70 percent share to a 61 percent share of their budget. They had reached the limit on what they could raise in local taxes for operating costs, and the city residents had gone even further, taxing themselves to the tune of another $1 million annually for a building fund to cover district infrastructure and physical plant needs.

To cut management costs, the district had tried asking some principals to run two schools at a time. (Apparently, that's not a successful management strategy. After two years of suffering with a half-time school leader, teachers at one school demanded the superintendent reassign her to her former full-time assignment at that school.) They had cut administrative support staff down to a virtual skeleton crew, and they were preparing to cut new text-books out of the budget, hoping there might be money to spare in their contingency fund at year's end. They outsourced the after-school sports at the middle schools to the Helena YMCA. Throughout the cuts, they remained sure that good classroom teaching was still the most important resource on which they could spend money.

"Schools are about teachers and teaching students," says per-sonnel director Rasor, summing up the sentiments of the admin-istration and board members. "That's what it came down to. There are two things you have to have—students and teachers—so that's where we put the priority."

Teachers were already the first priority in the district. Educa-tor payroll accounted for about two-thirds of the annual budget, and though there had been some teaching positions cut in recent years, tenured union members had remained somewhat insulated from the pains of fiscal belt tightening. Class sizes still averaged about twenty-five, and teachers still had their jobs. But in Novem-ber 2002, administrators were going to meet with the teachers' union to negotiate a new contract. Members of the board and the administration knew they would have to offer a raise, but they had no idea how they could come through with the money.

"We've watched a lot of things go away in our district because of a lack of funding," says board president Mitchell. "So, when we were going into negotiations, we had cut about $1 million, and from the board's perspective, we were thinking, Where ever are we going to get money?"

When the teachers' union leaders and administrative repre-sentatives sat down to negotiate in 2002, it was unlike any previ-ous negotiation. The fiscal problems were nothing new, but the way they talked and what they talked about were completely dif-ferent. For starters, they couldn't talk about the "bargaining table." There literally wasn't one. They also didn't have notes, and they sat in a circle. These were all characteristics of the consensus-based process the board of trustees had suggested and to which the union somewhat skeptically agreed.

During his first five years in Helena, Superintendent Bruce Messinger had been slowly trying to change the climate of the district. He had arrived after a slew of superintendents hired to fix the district's problems, who had stuck around for two years and then left the district generally a little worse off and more antagonistic. To counteract this, Messinger sent members of his administrative team to seminars on conflict resolution and building consensus. These administrators had been making tiny waves in committee work around the district ever since. The board of trustees had also been using this consensus model with considerable success, so when it came time to talk about the new labor contract, they decided to ask the Helena Education Association if they would agree to use it to negotiate. Union negotiators agreed only under the condition that all nine members of the board of trustees participate in every day of the negotiations.

"That was a huge paradigm shift from how we had done negotiations previously," says Mitchell.

For years, the teachers and administrators at HPS had hammered out contracts the way unions and management traditionally do—starting on extremes and continuing with deep mutual distrust. Now, with the facilitation of the consensus guru who trained Messinger's administrative team, negotiators began by talking about their concerns and goals.

Randy Carlson is the principal at Capital High School, and he's been involved in negotiating contracts for a long time, on both the management and teacher sides. In the old way, he says, "you were still sitting around the table; you have papers in front of you, with notes, which all do nothing but contribute to keeping you in a position and keeping you from moving. When you take away the table and you take away the notes and there's just you and there's just the group and you're just there with one another, you don't have something to hold on to, physically, so that allows you emotionally and psychologically to let go and explore new ideas."

One of the first things they did in negotiating the contract was talk about their worst fears—that is, the outcomes they least wanted to see. For most people in the room, their worst fear was being played out 176 miles away, in Billings, where teachers had just broken off bargaining and gone on strike.

"They were the poster child of what can really go wrong in contract negotiations. So, there was a lot of fear that we couldn't figure this out," says Messinger. "Bozeman was nearly into a strike, so our peer districts were in trouble. We all said, 'We can't go there. There has got to be a better way.'"

After identifying what they didn't want to see happen, both parties started to talk about what they did want to see happen, and a raise for teachers was on everybody's minds. The facilitator had them write down what they each thought the starting salary should be. The figures seemed clustered around a target: $30,000. There was agreement, but when they ran the numbers, moving the current salary matrix to start at $30,000 and end in the low $60s meant a 22 percent total increase. Because Helena currently had so many veteran teachers at the top of the salary scale, the cost of such a raise was exorbitantly high, around $7 million. It was essentially impossible. So they kept talking.

"When we began the discussion, it was a different kind of talk than we had ever had before," Mitchell explains. "It wasn't just about different components of the current contract. We got to spend more time talking about what things we'd like to see happen. Everyone got to talk about that. Out of that was born this concept that we could have a whole different pay plan with a different set of criteria in it defining how people would move through it."

It took six full days of negotiating, but in the end they agreed the district needed a new way of paying teachers starting at $30,000 and topping out at $65,000. District number crunchers suspected they might be able to afford a new system if they somehow didn't have to pay for some of the more expensive veteran teachers. In 2002, almost 40 percent of the teaching force was eligible for retirement. If any new compensation system had a chance, they had to find a way to encourage some of these people into retirement.

Negotiators also agreed the details should be worked out by a committee of teachers and other certificated staff (nurses, librarians, speech pathologists, and so on), along with administrators, board members, and members of the community. They wisely decided participation in any new system would be optional for current teachers. They set a goal of moving this plan from idea to implementation in less than two years.

Negotiators had also managed to agree on new figures for the current salary schedule, which, similar to other traditional systems, was a matrix that paid for years of service and graduate credits beyond a bachelor's degree. In the end, they agreed on what they felt was necessary to keep good teachers and immediately attract some new ones: a hefty 9.5 percent raise over two years. Like any politicians worth their salt, they piggybacked the new pay system onto a raise that would be too sweet to turn down. A Yes vote meant yes to the 9.5 percent raise and yes to a new alternative compensation system that would start at $30,000 and end at $65,000, that would be optional when it went into effect, would be designed by committee, possibly altered by the negotiators, and had absolutely no details worked out. A No vote meant no big raise and no pay alternative and would send the negotiators back to work out a new agreement.

Few unions turn down a 9.5 percent raise, and the contract won handily. By April 2003, two important steps had been taken. First, the district offered a retirement incentive of $5,000 cash and another $5,000 toward health insurance to any eligible teachers who would commit to retiring at the end of the following year. Thirty-six teachers took the bait, and the district calculated that would free up about $1 million to help fund the new system. The second step was the formation of an Alternative Compensation Committee, made up of ten educators, ten administrators, and three community members. The committee was co-facilitated by a district office administrator and an elementary school physical education teacher. No committee member had been involved in the contract negotiations.

"To sell this to the union and to the community, we had to keep broadening the circle of involvement, and the way to do that is to simply increase the number of people involved," said union president Larry Nielsen. "We also didn't want bargaining conversations to influence what the design team came up with."

The design committee was given three parameters: work by consensus, make it start at $30,000 and end at $65,000, and finish the design in eight months. They started as the negotiators had, sitting in a circle, talking about their "worst fears" and their "best hopes."

"When we first got together, we had a lot of diverse viewpoints, people that were not sure about the consensus process for one thing, and they weren't so sure about the alternative compensation plan. We had them do their research," said Mary Seitz, the physical education teacher who co-facilitated the committee.

They worked tirelessly, meeting weekly to review literature on compensation reform and listen to presentations from people who had done similar work, like the design team that built Denver's ProComp system. By the summer, they agreed the pay system ought to reflect and encourage development of teachers' careers, and it ought to reflect and encourage the work that good teachers do "above and beyond" their current official contract. They broke the task down and handed the pieces off to three subcommittees who worked through the summer—one to design a framework for the new system, one to determine how to use the system to encourage meaningful career development for teachers, and one to define how the work teachers do beyond the existing contract could be reflected in the new compensation plan.

In the subcommittees and when the larger group met together, ideas were proposed and revised, some were disposed of and some were revisited. One idea that never saw much play was tying teacher pay to student achievement on tests, as happens in many other alternative compensation schemes, like that in Denver or at the Vaughn Next Century Learning Center.

"I don't think there was ever much support at all for tying this to student performance," says Superintendent Messinger. "Not that we shouldn't talk about it, worry about it, and work on it, but that's different than to connect your salary to it. We never went there. We talked about it, and we looked at plans that incorporated it. We think it's the Achilles' heel of these plans. I don't think anyone wanted to go there; particularly now with No Child Left Behind, there's a fear of this obsession with standardized tests."

As the work progressed, committee members were routinely in contact with the constituencies they represented. They worked quickly, and after ten months, they proposed a new compensation system to the negotiating team that placed teachers on a career continuum from novice to master, required teachers to commit to certain kinds of professional services "above and beyond" the previous contract, and also asked educators to write and follow their own career development plans that would help further the district's goals of meeting the needs of all students.

In many ways, what they presented to the negotiating team was still very similar to the old system. Most notably, it looked a lot like a traditional salary schedule. The number of units beyond a bachelor's essentially determined whether a teacher was a novice, an apprentice, or somewhere else on the continuum to master teacher. Also, like the old salary scale, any teachers without a master's degree would never be able to move more than halfway up the scale.

Personnel Director Rasor took from that proposal everything that was new and innovative and left behind most of the vestiges of the old lockstep salary schedule. He designed a single-column salary scale of twenty-four steps and accompanying criteria for raises. The negotiating team approved, and a full 60 percent, or 300, educators in the district are now being paid under the plan.

In order to earn the yearly raise of $1,350, teachers must:

• Fulfill a certain number of "professional service commitments."

• Write and follow their own Career Development Plan, a comprehensive outline of professional and student-centered goals, which is reviewed and approved by a council of teachers.

• Receive a satisfactory evaluation from their principal.

Master's degrees are not required, but they are encouraged by the possibility of receiving a yearly $2,000 bonus. Another yearly $2,000 bonus is available to teachers who receive and maintain certification for the National Board for Professional Teaching Standards.

The notion of paying teachers for their work "above and beyond" the old contract became, in the new plan, teachers' "professional service commitments," which are now simply an expectation of the job. Teachers and other staff on the plan are expected to extend their job outside of their classrooms. They may choose to participate in district-wide work (curriculum-development committees, for instance), work in outreach-to-parents programs, or staff an after-school tutoring program. Teachers themselves decide where and how to do this, and they submit their choices for administrator approval.

"In the years that I've been on the board," says Mitchell, "it's really become a very small segment of teachers who have worked beyond the classroom on committees and things like that. With three hundred people signed up, that's a whole lot more people than we've had. We're not talking about just committee work. We're talking about them investing time in things that they might see that need to be done with students outside of the student day. We need their expertise outside the classroom in our district discussion on things. Now we are compensating teachers to do that."

Teachers generally see this as a good thing. "It's a paradigm shift. Most teachers, when they come into the profession, take on lots and lots of responsibilities, and they get to the end of their profession and they say, 'I did that when I was younger. I'm tired of that.' It doesn't happen in all cases, but it does happen," says union president Nielsen.

"The unfortunate thing about that," Nielsen adds, "is that when they get to the end of their career, that's when their expertise is the greatest. That's when they've got twenty-five, thirty years behind them. It's important to keep those people involved and motivate them to be involved in mentor programs, for instance, or advancing curriculum development. We need to keep folks and their expertise involved."

Greater involvement in activities beyond the school day turns out to be something that attracted new Helena educators like Oregon transplant Brandon Price. "You want to be involved, but you're already involved up to your eyeballs teaching 130 kids all day long," he says. "Being a part of a committee is something you need to do if you're going to have any say in what goes on in your school district. If they're going to give us credit or possibilities of increasing our pay because we're being involved, it's going to encourage more people to become more involved, and I would assume the school district will be better for it, and a better place to work."

So, in Helena, responsibility will grow with a teacher's career. In the first nine years, only one professional service commitment is expected. From years ten to twenty, teachers will participate in two; beyond twenty, three. Nielsen calls this an "all-American" plan in which "more responsibility equals more money." Educators may fulfill their service commitments through their work as union representatives or as active leaders in professional organizations, such as the National Council for Teachers of Mathematics. Of course, with 300 educators now offering to work outside the classroom, the district and the union had to find some new places to direct these newly willing participants and their energy. In the 2004–2005 school year, the district started two new task forces—one for reading, another for math—and a mentorship program to support new teachers. Interested educators need to apply for spots in these programs. This is a big shift from the days when ideas like these might have foundered for lack of participation.

This makes a huge difference in the culture of the district—just imagine every single teacher in one school actively engaged and willingly participating in some important project outside of the regular day, then multiply that by sixteen schools. But for Superintendent Messinger, the keystone to the new system is the Career Development Plan—a document each teacher will conceive him- or herself, outlining that teacher's professional goals over one to three years. The goals will relate to the teacher's specific classroom assignment and to district needs. Teachers will also be asked to explain the impact their own professional development will have and is having on their classroom practice and how they will use available data to measure their success and to inform modifications to their efforts. There are educational requirements to the plan as well, aligned with Montana's teacher license renewal requirements. This is a combination of graduate credits and attendance at professional development seminars. These graduate credits and seminars must be aligned with a teacher's Career Development Plan, which, in turn, must be aligned with the district's goals and higher student achievement.

"This will mean having hundreds of teachers working at a high level, focusing their training, their professional development, their efforts to further refine what they do with children in the classroom in a way that's aligned with where we're going as a district," says Messinger. "That's what will take us to a different level."

Plans may be based on individual or collaborative work, and the compensation committee designed a crucial element that will ensure these don't become just another piece of perfunctory paperwork. Every year, each educator's plan will be reviewed by their peers on Career Development Councils at the elementary, middle, and high school levels. These councils will provide teachers with feedback and guidance and ensure that these plans are relevant and that teachers are following them. Teachers who write the plans and those who sit on the councils will be guided by a comprehensive but usable rubric created by the design team. The rubric prompts teachers to describe the demographics of their classes and to align their goals with the U.S. Department of Education's guidelines on effective professional development.

The last piece of the plan—the third requirement teachers must meet to earn their raise—is a satisfactory evaluation from their administrator. In the past, these evaluations have carried little weight. A teacher found to be unsatisfactory one year not only still had a job the next year, but also received a raise. Under the new system, a $1,350 raise is riding on the evaluation. That means both teachers and their administrators will have to take them more seriously.

"Now your evaluation means something. It's no longer just a fluff piece, a love letter at the end of the year that you sign and I sign and we send on its way," says Tim McMahon, principal of Warren Elementary School and member of the alternative compensation committee. "But it also means something to us as administrators. I'm not going to write a poor evaluation for a teacher and hand it to them on May 15 and say you're not going to get a pay increase, not unless I've really done my homework all year long. I'd better have been working with that teacher. I'd better have been identifying things I have concerns about, given ideas for how to improve that and offered specific training and ways to help them become better at what they do."

Throughout the district, administrators say they are excited about the way this will change the part of their job that has to do with managing teachers. Not only has it changed the way they hire—choosing three social studies teachers from among one hundred applicants is quite different from choosing from twelve—but they also know it will mean there will be a greater number of teachers working on projects outside of the classroom.

"I'm very excited," says Capital High principal Randy Carlson. "There are going to be all these teachers working on interesting projects, and I get to talk to them about all of them."

McMahon knows the new system comes with challenges and benefits. "It does make my job both easier and harder. Ultimately, we recruit the very best, we keep the very best, we help the very best to get better," he says.

*　*　*

People in Helena are proud of the Professional Compensation Alternative. They know their design is not perfect, but it's not the design they're proud of. They're proud of the process they went through and of their ability to come together to create something so successful that a majority of existing teachers have chosen to participate. Over 300 teachers are now paid under the Professional Compensation Alternative. In 2004, some 200 teachers remained on the old system, many for financial reasons—they stood to make more money in the short term. Some of these may eventually move over to the alternative plan. Others may soon retire.

There are a few who fear that the new system has not been completely thought through. High school English teacher Colleen Hansen says she won't ever move to the compensation alternative. "My concern as a union rep was that the alternative system is not clearly defined. Having helped with grievances—and I've had my own personal grievances—if you don't have language in the contract, it will be almost impossible to grieve any situations," she said. "If there are any issues, related especially to unfair treatment or unfair opportunities, it's going to be really hard to resolve."

Hansen says, though, that she will likely retire within five years, and part of the motivation for her stance is political—she believes the old system protects teachers better, and that was the central issue in her campaign when she ran against Nielsen in the last union election.

Members of the compensation committee hope fears held by Hansen and those like her will be assuaged by the existence of the Transition Team, an eight-member board of teachers and administrators who are charged with working out the kinks the new system will undoubtedly develop. They will work by consensus.

Just as there are those who fear this change, there are others, some quite close to retirement, who have switched to the alternative pay plan. Mary Kay Senden teaches fifth-grade math and science at Hawthorne Elementary School and is within five years of retirement. She knows her job well, and some might think she would eschew the hassle of a career development plan and professional service commitments. But she is participating, eager to talk about the work she hopes to do on the new district task force for math. She says she went to a number of meetings at which she heard about the new alternative pay system, and she asked a lot of questions. By switching to the new system, she can extend her salary beyond the $55,000 cap on the old schedule.

"I thought about the money, of course, right away. But then, the more I thought about it, I thought this would be a good opportunity for me to turn to some specific areas of concentration and hone in on my teaching of math and science skills. So I take it as an opportunity to zero in on some math and science that I could do on my own, but now it looks like we'll have some support and possibilities for connections with other people to do that. I've always been involved in committee work. To have those things recognized as being important in our job and not so much taken for granted is enticing, too."

*   *   *

Helena's successes are numerous. The city managed to build a pay system that attracts teachers from all over the country and turned getting a job in Helena public schools into a highly competitive venture. They created a new way to recognize and encourage the exceptional work teachers do, effectively transforming the district into a place where being exceptional became the norm.

Those who were involved in the negotiations and the design of the Professional Compensation Alternative speak of it as a transformative experience. They don't talk about their "bargaining positions." Instead, they refer to their "worst fears" and "best hopes." They talk about overcoming fear and mistrust. They talk about building trust where there had been only deeply entrenched antagonism. They talk about the consensus-based process not so much with the zeal of the newly converted, but with the enthusiasm of former rivals who have just found that by being on the same team, they'll sweep the league. They've simply found a more effective way to do business than they ever knew existed, and their success has spread beyond Helena's schools. In Helena's city government, the parking commission is now using the consensus-based model. And, in the Bozeman school district, negotiators used the same model to reach agreement on the 2004–2005 contract.

People in Helena are proud of the work they've done, but they don't see it as completed by any means. Superintendent Messinger says he imagines the future will involve some significant revisions to what they've designed.

"The jury is still out on this. The question is, will it work?" he said. "Anybody can do this, whether it's Denver or here. It's our best thinking. And what we think will take us down the path."

*   *   *

What Denver, Helena, and Vaughn have in common is that administrators and teachers were all keenly aware of the problems their schools faced: they were not attracting and retaining enough teachers of the caliber they wanted, the level of pay they offered was not perceived as sufficient incentive to motivate teachers to do the work they needed from them, and they saw their students suffering as a result. Turnover rates were high, and many teachers were frustrated. Many administrators and teachers across the country are desperate to make a change, and many will grasp at any reform they think might make a difference. There are smaller class sizes, small schools, scripted curricula, block scheduling, year-round school calendars, computers in every classroom. Sometimes these help, but these reforms have their limits.

In her research on why teachers leave the profession, economist Caroline Hoxby says many studies have documented a steady decline in teacher aptitude over the last forty years. Her findings suggest this is due to the combined effects of the limited earnings in teaching pushing teachers out while teachers are simultaneously lured away by better paying opportunities outside of education.

"I think there's a pretty simple solution," Hoxby said in a phone interview. "If you want to attract people into teaching, you have to pay teachers more like other professionals. We need people going into teaching who are good at doing school, and that means we have to devote more of the total budget to them. We have to reallocate money from other things and towards teacher salaries. But we've also got to be willing to pay teachers more if they look like they're better teachers."

The people who worked for these reforms seem to understand this clearly. They have offered teachers more competitive earning potential, and they've tied increased pay to what they've defined as better teaching. In Helena, part of better teaching is having a career development plan tied to your teaching assignment and participating in programs outside the classroom. At Vaughn, it's motivating children to be at school and teaching like Susie Oblad or other "distinguished" teachers. If the tax increase is approved in Denver, better teaching will involve setting and meeting goals for student achievement, and better teachers may find themselves competing for positions in the toughest schools.

The primary lesson of these reforms turns out to be surprisingly simple. Raising teacher salaries doesn't have to be a labor-management conflict. It can be an opportunity for teachers, parents, administrators, and community members to identify goals for their schools, and it can be a tool to reach those goals.

Summaries of the programs described in this chapter appear on the following pages.

DENVER PUBLIC SCHOOLS

PAY FOR PERFORMANCE
AT A PUBLIC CHARTER SCHOOL

Problems:

• Typical of many urban districts, Denver has its share of "hard-to-serve" schools with transient student populations and high turnover among teachers.

• Recruiting for special education and bilingual education positions had found limited success.

• Administrators were frustrated that some long-time veteran teachers were stagnating in their teaching practice and were unmotivated to innovate or change.

• All stakeholders were aware of mounting pressure from state government regarding testing and teacher accountability.

• There was general agreement among union leaders and administrators that, while teachers are underpaid, an across-the-board pay raise would not likely solve the problems.

Solution:

The Professional Compensation System for Teachers, designed by a joint task force of union leaders, rank-and-file teachers, and district administrators, will pay teachers a base salary with raises and yearly bonuses tied to market conditions, student growth, acquired knowledge and skills, and professional evaluations.

Old salary structure:

Starting salary: $31,320

Top salary: $64,919 (thirteen years' experience and a PhD)

New salary structure:

Base (starting) salary: $31,320

Top salary: $85,000–$95,000

This is dependent on the career trajectory chosen by the teacher. A teacher who never earns an advanced degree, never takes on difficult assignments, and meets only the minimal requirements to retain her job would earn only about $50,000 after thirty years.

Results:

A pilot of the "pay for performance" part of ProComp, which paid bonuses to teachers in exchange for successful participation in a sort of self-accountability program, resulted in teachers changing their practice and students achieving at higher levels. In 2003, the Denver Classroom Teachers Association voted to approve ProComp, allowing the task force to begin transition work and generate support for the proposed property tax levy to pay for the program.

How they pay for it:

In November 2005, Denver voters will be asked to vote on a $25 million property tax levy—roughly $60 per year on a $245,000 home. Revenue from the levy will go into a trust fund to be managed by another joint committee of teachers and district administrators who will be tasked with setting levels for raises and bonuses and redefining criteria for raises and bonuses when necessary.

VAUGHN NEXT CENTURY LEARNING CENTER

PERFORMANCE PAY
AT A PUBLIC CHARTER SCHOOL

Problems:

• Student performance was among the lowest in California on standardized tests.

• Student truancy was rampant, causing reductions in state funding.

• Classes were overcrowded.

• Teachers were growing accustomed to infighting over responsibility for the students' poor performance.

• Families felt extremely disconnected to the school and teachers.

Solution:

In 1993, the school became a charter school, allowing the staff more flexibility in changing policy. Vaughn administrator Yvonne Chan started by piloting a system of bonuses for performance on bi-yearly evaluations. The pilot gradually expanded to include all teachers. Now, though teachers have a slightly lower base pay than the rest of the school district, bonuses from successful evaluations and other criteria mean they are among the best-paid teachers in California.

Los Angeles Unified School District's salary, 2003–2004 school year:

Starting salary with a teaching credential: $35,904
Maximum salary with ten years' teaching experience: $62,587

New salary structure, "performance-based pay," 2003–2004 school year:
Starting salary with a teaching credential: $38,900

Vaughn teachers can make a significant amount more than this amount through their evaluations, student attendance, the state's growth target for student testing, and for good attendance.

Salary with a teaching credential with fifteen years of experience:
The base salary is $51,400, yet teachers are eligible for another $19,050 in bonuses and for taking leadership roles on campus, raising their total earning potential to $70,450.

Results:
Teaching positions at Vaughn have become among the most sought-after teaching jobs in the Los Angeles area. Before these reforms, Vaughn struggled to find teachers with credentials to teach their students, and today each position is highly competitive. On statewide tests, students are outperforming their peers in similar schools in California. Vaughn has made such progress on student achievement and teacher quality that they can now focus on other projects to serve the community, such as expanding to include a health center, an early childhood development center, and a high school.

How they paid for it:
In addition to using their allotment of regular state and local funds, Vaughn applies for many grants under Yvonne Chan's leadership. To free up funds for salaries, they also cut every bit of fat out of their operating expenses and made teachers' salaries a priority.

HELENA SCHOOL DISTRICT

ALTERNATIVE PROFESSIONAL
COMPENSATION PLAN

Problems:

Helena schools faced millions of dollars in budget cuts in recent years. More than 50 percent of the teaching force was within five years of retirement, and Helena found their applicant pool dwindling. A vacancy would typically generate interest from ten applicants, only one or two of whom might be truly qualified. Starting salaries were among the lowest in one of the lowest-paying states.

Solution:

The Professional Compensation Alternative starts and ends significantly higher than the old system. It offers yearly increases of about $1,350 in exchange for successful evaluations, relevant professional development and education, and taking on responsibilities outside the classroom (on district committees, in after-school programs, and so on). It is an optional program for current teachers and required of all new hires.

Old pay:

Starting: $23,000
Top salary: $55,241

New pay:

Starting: $30,000
Top salary: $65,000

Results:

In 2003, the Helena affiliate of the Montana Education Association approved the alternative plan (along with a 9.5 percent raise on the old pay plan). By fall 2004, more than 300 of Helena's 500-plus teachers were signed on to the new system and writing their own career development plans, as well as joining committees and creating new programs, including a district-wide mentoring program for new teachers.

How they paid for it:

In exchange for $10,000 each, thirty-six teachers took early retirement, which freed about $1 million to start up the new system. District-hired accountants predict the new system will reach equilibrium as soon as the retirement wave passes.

THIRTEEN

SOLUTIONS THAT AREN'T

MANY PROGRAMS HAVE BEEN CREATED TO
ADDRESS TEACHER SHORTAGES, BUT NONE
WOULD BE NECESSARY IF EDUCATORS
WERE PAID PROPERLY

I f you're a teacher in a DeSoto County, Mississippi, chances are
you're not well paid, but you are entitled to a fantastic tan. In
DeSoto County, where a teacher's salary tops out at $53,000, the
tanning salon has a special discount for educators: 33 percent off a
full-body browning.

Offers like this exist in communities all over the country. Businesses and districts will often do everything they can think of to
make their teachers' lives a bit easier—everything, that is, but raise
their salaries. The efforts to provide corollary perks often result in
a further diminution of a teacher's prestige: Taxpayers would
never approve of salary increases, but how about free muffins
every other Tuesday?

When school districts hire a veteran teacher, if they use a traditional salary scale that pays in part for years of seniority, they will usually honor only seven years of that teacher's experience for pay purposes. That means that whether a teacher has taught for ten years or twenty, he or she will be paid only as a seven-year veteran. This strange market pressure is a direct way of coercing career educators to stay put in the district where their career experience will be honored, discouraging moves to other schools or districts where their expertise might be greatly needed.

District leaders go to similar lengths to recruit new teachers. They form partnerships with teacher training programs to gain access to prospective new teachers; they create teacher academies in their high schools to get teenagers interested in becoming teachers in the future; they create fast-track alternative certification programs for mid-career professionals who want to switch to education. Generally, these efforts make sense, and they're the kind of plans any forward-thinking human resources recruitment group would put together.

But there's also another kind of effort made to overcome the human resources problems that plague public schools. Across the country, districts have put into place and come to rely on a number of stopgap solutions that often have the appearance of last-ditch efforts. Think of the emergency teaching credentials issued in California in the late '90s, an effort to overcome staffing shortages created in part by the class size reduction implemented there. It was a quick fix that addressed only the immediate fact of the shortage but did little to address the long-term issues of teacher quality and retention. Policy makers and human resources directors say these are the solutions of last resort, but they aren't really solutions at all. They postpone the need for real solutions, and they deceive us into believing that the problems of attracting teachers, and paying them well, are virtually solved.

IMPORTING TEACHERS FROM INDIA

In 2001, Cleveland public schools needed to hire 850 new teachers. During the preceding year, they had interviewed over 1,200 applicants, but only 45 were qualified to fill the math and science positions presenting the greatest need, says Carol Hauser, executive director of human resources. So, like the HR directors of high-tech corporations scrambling for warm bodies to write programming code, Cleveland public schools looked to India and tried to recruit teachers with the offer of a work visa and a U.S. salary.

"It was the choice of last resort," says Hauser. "At that time, the economy was booming, and over half the people graduating in math and science were hired by people in business and industry. So, people would start in education schools, intending to teach math and science, but when they got out, they met such sophisticated recruitment efforts and had such sophisticated employment packages offered to them—compared to what they would get in a school district—that they ended up going into industry."

So teacher-recruiters looked abroad. Similar efforts were under way around the country, and recruitment consultancies were springing up in New York and Houston, placing classified ads in newspapers in New Delhi and Mumbai, promising districts to fill math and science positions with well-educated instructors more than happy to work for a salary in the low $30,000s. It was, after all, three or four times the going rate for teachers in most developing nations.

USA Employment is a Houston-based placement agency for teachers from India and Mexico. They have placed over one hundred teachers in various districts in the last two years. "Just like the nurse shortage, any time there's a shortage in an occupation because domestic people don't want to take the jobs, companies think globally," says agency director Jay Kumar.

Budget cuts in 2004 eliminated close to 700 teaching positions in Cleveland, and changes in immigration law have shifted the market for foreign teachers. Despite this, three years after their international recruitment effort, forty-seven of the original fifty recruits are still teaching in the Cleveland Municipal School District.

The same is true in Chicago, Philadelphia, and other districts that tried to solve their labor shortfall by recruiting globally.

NEW YORK CITY APPEALS TO MADISON AVENUE

In 2001, the New York City Department of Education (NYC-DOE) was looking at almost 8,000 vacant positions. They recruited in every way imaginable. Almost 800 of the teachers who began working in the fall had been lured from places like Austria, Spain, Canada, and the Phillipines. New York City employs over 78,000 teachers, and recruitment has always been a problem.

"It definitely takes a lot of planning," said Lucille Ameduri, spokesperson for the NYCDOE human resources branch. "We go to different colleges throughout the United States and abroad, and we go abroad to recruit teachers for critical shortage areas, where we can't find Americans who want to teach—for special education, math, and science."

Though their Teaching Fellows program has, in recent years, attracted 7,500 new teachers from other professions and other nations, only 55 percent actually return for a fourth or fifth year. International teachers are often limited by their visas, and others find that, while teaching was an interesting diversion, the job itself is not financially viable in the long run.

In April 2004, the Office of the Mayor and the New York City Department of Education teamed up with Hollywood director

Joel Schumacher (*The Lost Boys, St. Elmo's Fire, 8mm*) and a New York advertising agency to produce an ad campaign for the teaching profession. Schumacher and Agent 16, the ad agency, both worked pro bono and produced a handful of fifteen-second television spots featuring dedicated, good-looking educators in their classrooms talking about how much they love teaching.

In a minute-long ad for the "Join New York's Brightest—Teach NYC" campaign, schoolchildren run through the streets slapping flyers with their teachers' faces over the fashion advertisements and bus shelters and posters. As the music builds, a voice-over tells us, "Some of New York's most admired figures don't sell out concerts. They'll never be a running back for the Giants. And they probably won't go platinum. But to millions of kids, their teachers are still the biggest heroes in the world."

"I think we've reached a higher number than we've ever reached in terms of recruitment this year," said Ameduri. "Can we give credit just to the ad campaign? Probably not. It helped, but there are a lot of other things we do."

No doubt, public service announcements like this do something for the status of the profession. The teachers appear professional and dedicated, and the kids seem authentically happy to be celebrating their teachers. But when beginning teachers bring home about $2,200 a month in one of the United States' most expensive cities, no amount of positive PR can get people to choose teaching math over trading bonds, unless, of course, they've already made their killing and don't need to live off their salary.

TEACH FOR AMERICA:
TWO YEARS OF TEACHING—AND SOMETIMES MORE—
FROM THE YOUNG AND ALTRUISTIC

Although recruitment was never its primary goal, some of the most effective efforts in this area have come from the Teach for America (TFA) program. Since its founding in 1990, it reports to have placed more than 10,000 graduates from some of the best colleges in the country into urban and rural schools with the highest needs. The value of their work has been documented by national studies and the experiences of students and principals in the schools where they work, and these successes have led some to see TFA as a model for solving the teacher shortage and quality crises.

TFA recruits make a two-year commitment to teach, and they are allowed to do so through waivers of standard credentialing requirements. They receive intensive summer training, but when they meet their students, most have never done any student teaching. Inasmuch as they are supported at all, corps members are sustained and nurtured during their two years through ongoing professional development, mentoring by veteran teachers, and the camaraderie they find with fellow TFA teachers at their school sites.

Notably, about 40 percent remain in teaching, and another 20 percent continue to work in other areas of education, striving to change the lives of children.

In directing the idealism and passion of recent college graduates to correct inequities faced in the poorest schools in the country, TFA founder Wendy Kopp creates an effective way to fill a few thousand teaching positions every year that not only gets highly skilled people to teach in challenged schools but also has the ripple effect of exposing promising young people—some of whom may eventually be leaders on a local or national level—to the plight of poor urban and rural schools.

For whatever reasons—the program's success, the almost archetypal desire shared by many young college grads to make a positive impact in the lives of children, the dot-com bust, or higher unemployment in the early part of this decade—more and more college graduates are hoping to join TFA's ranks. In 2003, TFA received 16,000 applications for 1,800 spots, over three times the number of applications they received in 2001. These applicants are graduating from Ivy League colleges and the top public universities, with median 3.5 GPAs. One of the most impressive achievements of the program is its ability to attract high-quality minority candidates to teaching. In a nation of an overwhelmingly white teaching force, where recruiting candidates of color has become increasingly difficult, a third of those who applied to TFA in recent years belong to an ethnic or racial minority.

Despite these recruitment successes, Kopp says, they still have to address substantial challenges in training and supporting corps members. "What we believe is that we cannot end up with exceptional teachers unless we start with certain kinds of people," she says, "people who have an achievement orientation, who persist in the face of challenges, who are strong critical thinkers, who can influence and motivate others. We need people who have a good degree of organizational ability, and who want to work relentlessly to close the achievement gap for their kids, who have high expectations for kids and families in low-income communities. At the same time, we would never want to throw them into the classroom and just say they'll learn what they need to learn on the job, because there is so much they can learn. Why do that, if they can start out at a higher level through what has been learned about the approaches that successful teachers in low-income communities utilize? There is a huge base of skills and knowledge that can and must be learned. Some of it can be learned in a pre-service training program, and some of it has to come with ongoing management and ongoing support."

Not surprisingly, the program inspires strong feelings from all sides. The program's critics argue that however laudable the goal of getting high-aptitude people into the classroom, allowing corps members to teach without appropriate certification suggests that anyone with a college degree and a little optimism can be a good teacher. There are others, though, who would like to see TFA turned into a model for relaxing teacher certification require- ments. Principals at schools that have benefited from TFA pres- ence say corps members were often better than other first-year teachers, and, in some cases, more effective than veteran teachers. Of course, some respond, if one only plans on teaching for two years, it's quite a lot easier to devote oneself fully to the cause entirely—given that the light at the end of the tunnel is visible from day one.

"We're very clear about what Teach for America can be and what it can't be," says Kopp. "The problem we're trying to address is not the teacher shortage. The problem we're trying to address is that kids who happen to be in low-income communities are aca- demically so far behind kids who happen to be born in high- income communities, and we think, this is America? This is the land of opportunity? We feel this is our generation's civil rights movement, and we have to do something about that. If we were trying to address the teacher shortage, we would proceed in a dif- ferent way."

A study released in June 2004 found that TFA corps members were generally making an equal or greater impact in the academic performance of their students, as compared to regularly certified teachers in the same schools. If this is true, that means TFA has begun to make progress toward its goals of correcting the inequities faced by the United States' poorer school districts.

TFA's success does not mean that either the teacher shortage or teacher quality crisis could be solved by creating an ongoing supply of young, bright, and extremely motivated college graduates who might put in two years before moving on to other careers. All parties involved agree that schools need longevity from their teachers. Nevertheless, the success of TFA's recruitment strategies and the training and support for corps members they've begun to implement offer a few important lessons:

• Aggressive recruitment combined with high standards for selection can create a pool of exceptional candidates.

• Intensive preservice training and intensive ongoing support are crucial to teachers' success, regardless of how academically exceptional they may be when hired.

PAYING TEACHERS WITH COUPONS, DISCOUNTS, AND AFFORDABLE LAWN-MOWER REPAIR

In DeSoto County, Mississippi, teacher salaries start at $29,000 and top out at $53,000. The school district has to compete for teachers with nearby Memphis, Tennessee, where teachers can earn $7,000 more for doing the same job. In order to attract new teachers and hold on to the ones they have, DeSoto County is offering something Memphis doesn't—33 percent off at the local tanning salon, just for starters. It's part of the district's PERKS (Praising Educators for Reaching Our Kids in School) program—a thank-you to the underpaid but highly valued educators who stick with the community's schools. More than thirty local businesses are participating in PERKS and offering teacher-only discounts on dry cleaning (10 percent off at Watson's), lawn-mower repair (15 percent off at Harris and Sons), discount legal representation (20 percent off at Myers, Graves and Associates), and invoice-priced Fords and Chevrolets (at Homer Skelton Ford, Country Ford, and Jimmy Gray Chevrolet).

It's a symbiotic arrangement. Teachers get a break on things they might need to purchase, and local businesses reap two benefits. Not only do they build goodwill in the community by supporting teachers, but they also have direct marketing to district employees provided by the school district, which happens to be the county's second largest employer.

Of course, this is nothing new. In the nineteenth century, as public education was just beginning to become an institution, teachers were rarely paid in cash. They made what were known as "boarding rounds": each family who sent a child to school would provide room and board for the local teacher for a few weeks at a time. DeSoto County is just another example of a community trying to make their teachers feel valued.

"Your paycheck may not show that you are deemed worthy, but getting these perks helps," said seventh-grade social studies teacher Tina Stallcup. "I do feel that teachers deserve to be treated as professionals, and we don't, in many ways. This is what I do for a living. I work very hard at it, and this PERKS program helps to do what a few other things won't."

On the national level, the federal government has made its own attempts to offer teachers non-cash compensation. Back in 2000, the U.S. Department of Housing and Urban Development unveiled the Teacher Next Door program, offering public educators first crack and a 50 percent discount on HUD properties in neighborhoods in need of economic revitalization.

This dovetailed with efforts in the private sector, as Bank of America offered special first-time homebuyer mortgages for teachers. Efforts like these were replicated in the rental market, as rent and mortgage subsidies were offered to teachers in cities including Chicago, St. Louis, and San Jose. In most cases, the teachers who participated in these programs were required to remain at their schools for three to five years.

While they offer teachers significant savings, they don't always have the intended effect of making teachers feel valued. When Catherine Travelute, an English teacher at Cross Keys High School in Atlanta, was buying a home, she was surprised by the loans available to her.

"When I started investigating getting a loan, there was a lot of, 'Because you're a teacher, you're eligible for these special programs,'" she said. "They were the same kind of programs that are offered to people coming off welfare. It's not offensive; just shocking. It was a huge surprise that, as an educated person with a career and a master's degree behind me, I would be eligible for the same program as people who dropped out of high school and didn't have any real work experience. The perception that someone who was a teacher would need these programs was troubling."

There is no shortage of examples of large and small communities attempting to make up for the subtle offense of not paying teachers enough. Teachers can take a $250 deduction on their 1040 forms, an acknowledgment from those who write tax code that teachers often pay out of their own pockets to purchase supplies their schools do not provide. In Fairfax, Virginia, teachers can get bargains on service from Internet providers and moving companies, along with interest-free loans to cover moving expenses and 5 percent off their rent in certain housing complexes. Any teacher can find discounts on prescription drugs online— clearly a helpful perk for teachers whose medical coverage doesn't include drug benefits. These seemingly random examples have one thing in common: They are ways to compensate educators without paying them.

The well-meaning administrators, business leaders, and union officials who broker these deals are simply responding to market needs. Staples, the office supply chain, celebrates Teacher Appreciation Day by handing out bags of pens and crayons to teachers who walk through their doors, and they get more customers that way. Six Flags offers discounts to teachers, and more people come through the gates to buy $4 sodas and $5 funnel cakes.

DeSoto County's PERKS program is also a cost-efficient recruitment tool. "It's something we need to be able to recruit the best teachers in the state and in the mid-South region—not just the number of teachers we need, but the best teachers, the top ten percent, the most qualified, the ones who are going to give the competitive advantage to our students," says DeSoto County school district spokesperson Riki Jackson.

In a certain light, all of these offers—a lower rate on one's home loan, 10 percent off one's dry cleaning, 5 percent off one's rent—appear to be ways our communities can avoid paying teachers more. But how many other professions get similar discounts like this? Garbage collectors aren't getting half off at the movies, and the American Medical Association doesn't lobby for a better deal at Kinko's. A teacher may or may not want to live in a HUD-designated revitalization area, but in certain cities, that may be the only option available to him and his family. In paying teachers with discounts like these, we exploit their dedication and assuage our consciences.

* * *

This catalog of recruitment and retention efforts is not at all meant to be exhaustive. Another entire book could be written about the lengths our communities go to in their attempts to address the very serious problems they see in being unable to hang on to the teachers they need. The point here isn't to lambaste these programs as ill-advised or ineffectual. It's clear that there are important successes associated with all of them. Many of the Indian teachers who came to Cleveland are happily continuing their careers there. They have helped the district meet students' needs in important ways. Teach for America has inspired thousands to work to improve schools and effectively changed the lives of children around the country by bringing bright people to hard-to-staff schools. And teachers in places like DeSoto County feel valued by communities that help them in tangible ways. There is absolutely nothing wrong with any of these efforts.

What is wrong is that the more we rely on discounted autos, clever HR directors, and youthful altruism to do the hard work of attracting and retaining high-quality teachers, the more we will convince ourselves the problem has been solved.

CONCLUSION

PAY NOW OR LATER

THE PROBLEM
WON'T GO AWAY ON ITS OWN

Raising teacher salaries is a popular idea, and at the same time, it isn't. Bring up the subject of compensation for public schoolteachers virtually anywhere, and a lot of people will enthusiastically agree that teachers are doing important work and ought to be paid more. When, in May 2004, Senator John Kerry promised $30 billion over ten years to raise teacher salaries if he were elected president, few blanched. It was just another piece of campaign news across the nation. Editorial pages of the major newspapers hardly took notice. If he had talked about substantially changing the way teachers are paid—something that might require $30 billion a year, rather than $3 billion a year—people would likely have had a different response. In the abstract and on a small scale, salary boosts for educators always sound like a good idea. Politically, however, real salary reforms for teachers seldom fly. This is because politicians are loath to push for expenditures whose benefits might not be seen for a decade after they've left office.

Senator Kerry's was a moderate plan, proposing signing bonuses for new math and science teachers, along with modest raises and more testing for all teachers. He promised to fund this by repealing some of President Bush's tax cuts. Historically, salary reforms of this size tend to have only a small effect. They may temporarily attract a few more people to teaching, but they don't substantively change the way the profession works or how it is viewed by society.

As a nation, we already spend a lot on education, and we expect a lot in return. The United States spends roughly $390 billion on public K–12 education every year.[1] For that investment, we have reasonable and high expectations. Public schools are mandated to teach the entire population how to use their brains and keep students engaged in learning five days a week, for at least six hours a day. At the end of thirteen years of this process, we expect, at minimum, an employable, skilled individual who can read, write, communicate with co-workers, and count change accurately. We also hope our public schools will be able to do more than that. Schools are called on to help raise children and assist them in understanding themselves in relation to their world. Schools and teachers are asked to provide basic moral instruction, to teach children right from wrong and how to function as part of a community. Of course, we also hope schools will teach children how to be thoughtful communicators and critical thinkers, how to solve problems, and how to think about the world around them in creative and scientific ways. In short, we want our schools to help children learn to be valuable to society.

But when our public education system doesn't work as well as we want it to, society suffers, and the effects are far-reaching.

According to the National Adult Literacy Survey, in the United States, there are currently 40 million adults—21 percent of the adult population—who have difficulty using certain reading, writing, and computational skills considered necessary for functioning in everyday life.[2] Many of these are people who live paycheck to paycheck. They may run the risk of losing a $6-an-hour job because they can't reliably operate the cash register or read the instructions on a bottle of cleaning solution. Not only are there costs associated with low-skilled unemployed workers—welfare, job training, Medicaid—but there are significant economic losses when people aren't employable in terms of either the decreased tax revenue or increased burden on those who do pay taxes, depending on which side of the problem one looks at.

The connection is fairly simplistic, but few would argue with it. If more people could read well enough to be employable, fewer of them would fill welfare rolls and more of them would pay taxes, thus decreasing the burden on society. If we want more people to be able to read well, we must attract more highly qualified people into teaching so that more students can learn and achieve at higher rates.

There are other, larger costs associated with an inadequate education. When people leave school without the basic skills necessary to hold a job, some present an economic burden to the taxpayer in the costs associated with crime, both those incurred by victims and those incurred by the states in paying for incarceration and the operation of courts. Right now, over 2 million Americans are in state, local, or federal prisons. Another 5 million are on probation or parole. That means one out of every thirty-four adults is in some way caught in the criminal justice system.[3]

There are many factors that come into play to make this number so large, but the relevant question isn't, Why is this number so high? It's, What are the conditions that cause people to turn to criminal activity? And, Why do people need to break the law rather than get a legitimate job? These questions lead to others—namely, How can we change the conditions that push people toward crime? What roles can teachers play in guiding young people away from these paths?

When we ask these questions about crime and criminals, we're not talking about violent offenders or people with criminal pathologies. We're talking about two types of people. First, there are people in prison as a result of economic decisions. This includes people who are convicted of drug dealing, property crimes, and prostitution. Then there are people incarcerated for possession of drugs, a habit often associated with poor decision-making skills. These and other nonviolent offenders make up more than 50 percent of the number of those behind bars,[4] and it's not unreasonable to assume that most of this population have problems stemming in part from their K–12 education experience.

There are some relevant characteristics of the incarcerated population. The Bureau of Justice reports that two thirds of those incarcerated never completed high school. Over a third of them say they dropped out of high school because of academic problems, behavioral problems, or because they lost interest. About a fifth dropped out because they needed to work or they needed money. Only a sixth dropped out because they were convicted of a crime. Interestingly, 66 percent of those who never finished high school nor received a GED report having a learning disability.[5] The picture these statistics paint is of a substantial proportion of inmates whose educational experiences in some way failed to meet their needs.

Criminologist Mike Jacobson of the John Jay College of Law in New York says many end up in prison as a result of strictly economic decisions. Drug dealing and property theft, he says, are "akin to a jobs program."

"They're employment opportunities," Jacobson says. "For those folks, it's a business decision. It pays more than low-level McDonald's jobs. When you put all the hours together, it probably doesn't pay that much more, but it is seen as something potentially more lucrative."

The connections to education are largely intuitive. Students who leave school for the streets do so because school does not satisfy them in some fundamental way. Perhaps they have a learning disability and the special education program is staffed by full-time substitutes, none of whom has a special education credential. This happens often. Consider the Cleveland Municipal School District, which had 173 full-time substitute teachers filling special education positions in 2000. Perhaps in the elementary years, these people now in prison had a series of ineffective teachers and arrived at high school reading at a fourth- or fifth-grade level. High school presented too great a challenge, and eventually, they left.

Economists often speak in terms of distributions, and in this case, uneven distributions. Caroline Hoxby, professor of economics at Harvard, says she sees these sorts of problems as linked to education. "A lot of the problems in the United States are indirectly related to what I would describe as an uneven distribution of skills among the U.S. population," she explains. "If everyone was highskilled, I don't know that very many people would end up in prison. That's really the result of inequality of skills and inequality of opportunities, which result from inequality of skills."

It seems obvious yet important to remember that those with low skills and those who end up in prison are often former students from poor, urban, minority schools, schools with high turnover in what are often called "hard-to-serve" communities.

What, if anything, can be done? How much of the answer lies in education? Although there are an enormous number of studies on the educational level of prison inmates, on adult literacy, and on the current state of education, very little has been done to analyze the long-term effects of high-quality K–12 education. Some relevant work has been done in the field of early childhood development and its long-term impact on the lives of students.

From 1962 to 1965, in Ypsilanti, Michigan, fifty-eight children identified as "born in poverty and at risk of failing in schools" were given an opportunity to attend a high-quality preschool program before they entered Perry Elementary, the local primary school. In addition to two-and-a-half-hour classes daily, the program also included weekly home visits by teachers. Teachers were of the highest quality, trained in providing children with the best environments for fostering learning through their own play. In their home visits, teachers were able to show parents how they could help their children and reinforce learning.

The families participating in the study had been identified as low socioeconomic status by virtue of their educational levels, household income, and the number of rooms in the home. There were other children in the study, too. Another sixty-five children in the control group—also of low socioeconomic status— attended no preschool program. Researchers tracked the educational progress of these children through primary and secondary schools and college, and continued to track the subjects' careers and successes and challenges in life, interviewing participants at ages nineteen, twenty-seven, and thirty-nine to forty-one.

Forty years after they had attended preschool, participants were exceeding their control-group counterparts in every aspect considered economically valuable to society. Compared to the control group, a greater percentage had graduated high school. They demonstrated higher aptitude on standardized tests. They were employed at higher rates and made more money in their jobs. More of them owned their own homes and second cars. This means more of them were leading healthy lives with options and opportunities.

The successes of the preschool experience also presented—if we're talking about purely economic measures (and it should be part of the equation)—significant savings to society. The children who went to preschool, who had been at high risk of failing in schools, were entering the criminal justice system and the welfare system in fewer numbers and with less frequency than those who didn't attend preschool.[6]

The RAND Corporation analyzed the results of the Perry Preschool Study in 1998 and found the cost-benefit savings to be the same as those reported by the primary researchers. Every dollar spent on the preschool education of these children resulted in seven dollars saved to society at large. There were savings in education because these children required fewer special education services. There were savings on welfare, because, as adults, they had less need of assistance programs. Most significantly, there were savings from reduced criminal justice costs.[7]

Logic suggests that if these kinds of benefits to society can be realized by investments in early childhood education, similar benefits can be reaped by targeted investments in public K–12 education. Critics of this logic might argue that the Perry Preschool Study is too small a sample. Because it provided an educational opportunity to children who otherwise would have had no such opportunity, it was guaranteed to create improvements and benefits. Critics might also suggest that because teachers at the Perry Preschool taught children in addition to their parents, the effects are more far-reaching than anything we could expect from K–12 teachers who don't have time for regular home visits. All are legitimate concerns and rightly call into question whether this study is applicable to fixing K–12 education.

Little argument can be made about the size of the sample. One can only agree and say, yes, it's small; we should keep that in mind and try not to exaggerate our conclusions or extrapolate too much from them. But if we say the conclusions ought to apply to only pre-kindergarten interventions, we severely limit our own thinking on this matter. Last, providing an opportunity for children and parents where one was absent may make an extrapolation suspect, but it's certainly not a reason to cease examining the possibilities. The questions raised suggest the need for more research, perhaps a study into the effects of teaching by high-aptitude teachers over two or three decades.

If investments like those at the Perry Preschool can have such substantial effects over the long term, there is at least a significant likelihood that similar targeted investments in the K–12 system may well produce similar outcomes. But regardless of what might happen and whether any educational researcher is going to take up this project, society pays for these problems at one time or another. When we cut funding to education and reduce the number of opportunities available to students in public schools, we consign ourselves to having to face certain problems eventually.

*　　*　　*

Teachers are not the only cost in education, nor are they the only important cost in education. But good teaching is one of the factors that has the most important influence on student achievement and is the one factor that can counteract the forces of low socioeconomic status, despite how powerful and predictive those forces can be.

We've mentioned this elsewhere in the book, but it is worth deepening our discussion of this point with a quick review of some important recent research. Economist Eric Hanushek

EDUCATIONAL ATTAINMENT FOR CORRECTIONAL POPULATIONS AND THE GENERAL POPULATION[8]

Educational Attainment	Total incarcerated	Prison Inmates		Local jail inmates	Probationers	General population
		State	Federal			
Some high school or less	41.3%	39.7%	26.5%	46.5%	30.6%	18.4%
GED	23.4	28.5	22.7	14.1	11.0	(not available)
High school diploma	22.6	20.5	27.0	25.9	34.8	33.2
Postsecondary	12.7	11.4	23.9	13.5	23.6	48.4

writes, "The difference between a good teacher and a bad teacher can be a full level of student achievement in a single school year."[9]

A study in Boston shows student learning gains in both reading and math to be, on average, far superior when they work with an effective teacher than when they work with an ineffective teacher.[10] These types of gains are mirrored in a Tennessee study that shows that effective teachers can help the lowest performing students make gains of as much as 53 percentile points on standardized tests in a single year. Over three years, students with effective teachers show as much as an 83 percent gain.[11] These studies also found that effective teaching counteracted the often predictive effects of low socioeconomic status.

All of these deductions—that good teachers improve the learning capabilities of students—seem intuitive and common-sensical, but what's lost in the shrill demands for more testing of students and teachers is that it takes great teachers to get struggling students to pass tests. Simply adding more tests won't improve scores. Teachers have to be uniformly excellent. And regardless of one's feelings about standardized tests, this research definitively demonstrates that good teachers make a difference in students' learning. As researcher Steven Seidel of Harvard's Graduate School of Education says in Chapter 6, "teaching and learning are profoundly human enterprises . . . [and] there are a lot of human relationships in teaching and learning." The academic and personal success of students rests on those relationships.

When we talk about the experiences of children dropping out of school, we're talking about students who are marginalized and don't feel connected to their schools. Teachers are some of the people who connect children to schools and to each other. There may be activities or sports or certain clubs, but these are run by teachers and coaches. Teaching is a human business, and it requires intelligent, sensitive, caring, and demanding individuals, who understand the challenges their students are facing.

Barbara Broderick, chief probation officer of Maricopa County, Arizona, says she believes powerful teachers can dramatically change the lives of students and steer them away from poor decision making. But even greater effects, she says, can be made with investments in children's early lives.

"Most of the research now is pointing to the fact that cognitively, the way offenders were thinking is very poor. They do a lot of faulty thinking in terms of not being able to take responsibility for their own life," Broderick explained. A substantial difference could be made, she went on, "if we can get in early and improve some of the pre-K and elementary training so that we're really teaching values and right from wrong—things that we take for granted."

* * *

Fiscal savings in the realm of criminal justice and costs associated with poverty aren't the only reasons we need to invest in effective teaching. Another crucial reason is the changing labor market. Economist Richard Murnane, co-author of *The New Division of Labor: How Computers are Creating the Next Job Market*, says that while low-skilled service-sector jobs at the bottom of U.S. income distribution—Wal-Mart custodian or Starbucks barista, for instance—have expanded somewhat in recent years, the economy has lost large numbers of better-paying low-skilled manufacturing and clerical jobs. There are two causes, he says. The market for those low-skilled jobs has either disappeared as computers have been made to perform those tasks, or the market has moved overseas. What remains for U.S. workers are two types of jobs: service-sector jobs that don't pay a living wage because, as Murnane says, "all humans can do them," and jobs toward the higher end of income distribution, which require higher skills than most high school graduates currently learn.

"The big question for high school graduates," Murnane says, "is are they going to leave high school with the skills to be able to succeed in the post-secondary education and training they need to get access to those jobs? Because if they don't, they'll have to compete for these service jobs that just don't pay enough."

Murnane explains that as computers have taken over routine problem-solving and communication tasks, what remains for many workers who want to earn a living wage are jobs requiring what he calls "expert thinking" and "complex communication." To illustrate this, he gave the example of an auto mechanic trying to repair a defective car alarm. The mechanic runs the computer diagnostics on the car; the computer reports the car is fine, but the car's owner insists it's not working correctly. The diagnostic computer has already done the routine checks the mechanic might have done in a similar situation twenty years ago, and in order to repair the car alarm, he must be able to solve the problem in a new way.

As this labor market shifts, so does the need to change our education system. This isn't the kind of change that can be achieved by raising standards or implementing a new battery of tests, however.

That's been done, and there's only so far that can go. The U.S. education system is not irreparable, and it's not terrible. Given the magnitude of the tasks it attempts to complete, it's actually phenomenal, and, despite the complaints that one often hears—that schools aren't as good as they used to be, for instance—studies show that despite changes in school culture, students' math, science, and reading ability remain about the same as they were thirty years ago.[12]

But our schools need to get better. Recently, economists at the University of Maryland found a steady forty-year decline in teacher aptitude.[13] It's not that teachers are somehow becoming less intelligent. In fact, these economists found that the average teacher today has only slightly less verbal and mathematical aptitude than her counterpart forty years ago. The most significant finding, though, is that those who graduate at the top of their classes are now much less likely to become teachers than they were in the 1960s.

Caroline Hoxby has found that the blame for this can be attributed to two places—low earning potential and wider job opportunities for would-be teachers—with the lion's share of the blame attributed to low earning potential.[14]

If we want to attract exceptional people to the teaching profession, we must pay them substantially more. Examples elsewhere in this book, most notably in Chapter 12, about Helena Public Schools and the Vaughn Next Century Learning Center, illustrate this. Higher pay works to attract a higher number of better candidates. How that higher pay is determined, how it is meted out, how high it ought to be—those are all questions that may only be answered at a local level.

It doesn't take policy superheroes to make this happen. It simply demands that people take risks. It demands that our elected representatives be forward-thinking, creative, and willing to truly support educators and those who run school districts. Real salary reform demands that people be willing to give up old ways of thinking about how teachers should be paid. To make this happen, though, communities must be vocal about how important good teaching is to them. People must be clear that spending money to find, keep, and support the best teachers is simply the most effective investment they can make in the future of their children, their communities, and their country.

IF ONLY THE BEST TEACHERS COULD KEEP TEACHING

I WISH K.C. FULLER, MY GRADE-SCHOOL FRIEND AND AN EXTRAORDINARY TEACHER, COULD AFFORD TO TEACH

I grew up with a girl named K.C. Fuller. We met in fifth grade and became friends when I dated her friend Stephanie. (Dating at that point involving calling each other on the phone nightly and talking about who or who wasn't *queer*. The word had a different meaning then.) K.C. had round red cheeks and a crazy-happy smile and seemed always to be in a particularly good mood. Actually, she was, and remains, one of these people whom I can't remember ever being upset, or angry, or even the least bit off-balance. I'll go one further: I've known her for twenty years now, and I honestly don't know if I've ever seen her even mildly annoyed. Calling her "sunny" or "peppy" or "the light in any room" would be accurate—she was one of those very smart and well-liked people about whom everyone wondered, "I wonder what she'll do with her life."

During and shortly after college, K.C. and I weren't in touch much, but in our mid-twenties, we found ourselves living about five blocks away from each other in San Francisco. We got together on her back porch one day in early August, and I asked her what she was doing, in terms of a job, because almost no one I knew had any sort of career in the works, it being San Francisco in the early '90s and we being confused about everything.

"I'm teaching!" she said, slapping my knee, which is something she does. "You didn't know I was teaching? I got a teaching credential! I taught last year—junior high. I start again this fall. I didn't tell you that?"

I shook my head. I didn't know she'd been teaching. She slapped me again on the knee.

"Well, it's amazing," she continued. "I'm teaching math and science and it's just such a blast. I just got back from a conference in Arizona, where I studied desert ecosystems and local medicinal plants, and so I'm going to incorporate that in my lesson plan. Oh wow, I've been working on that all summer, and I'm almost done, but school starts in a few weeks and I have to get the classroom ready, too, and I'm going kinda cuckoo but I can't wait. I'm just so anxious to get back into school and see the kids again—"

K.C. tends to talk very fast sometimes, and after I slowed her down and asked some questions, it dawned on me that I didn't know anyone else our age—we were both about twenty-five at that point—who was so clearly and profoundly inspired by their work. She hadn't been on a teaching track in high school or early college, but at some point she'd fallen in love with the profession and now she, and her passion for all this, was something to behold. Most of the people I knew were temping—I was temping myself—or were working for marketing firms, but K.C. was in charge of the science program for about 120 junior high students. It was a revelation. I was inspired and jealous. I asked her what a job like hers paid.

"About $22,000," she said.

I knew teachers weren't well paid generally, but still, I was floored. And I wasn't so jealous anymore.

"But this year I'll be the assistant soccer coach," she added, "so I'll get an extra $500."

I couldn't believe it. As a temp, working about three days a week for random San Francisco companies who needed Macintosh-oriented help, I was making much more than that. K.C., with a master's degree, was earning about $10 an hour, while I was making $18, rarely doing more than designing interoffice flyers for Pac Bell.

Over the course of the schoolyear, I would often visit K.C.'s apartment, and we'd talk about whatever she was working on in her classes. One day it was astronomy, for which she'd taken her students to the Exploratorium and had made a solar system from coathangers and fruit. The next week it was oceanography; her classes had gone to the beach to go tidepooling—wading through the rocks to find crabs, algae, and sea anemones. Again and again I found myself getting an impromptu lesson in something that she was teaching or planned to teach: alternative energy sources, or rocket design, or storm systems. She was, clearly, a fantastic educator. If I could have fit into the school uniform, I would have snuck into her classes to watch her work.

Later—about five years after that first talk on her back porch—I asked her about her plans for the upcoming schoolyear. She was, at that point, teaching high school and coaching the soccer team.

"I didn't tell you?" she said. "I'm not going to teach this year. I just can't do it anymore. I'm so sad, but I really have to try to make some money. I still have student loans, and I'll never afford my own place in this city on what I'm making. It's so frustrating. I just—"

This time she wasn't slapping my knee. Her departure from the profession wasn't without bitterness: she'd done everything she was supposed to do, and excelled in every way, but after five years in the classroom in one of the most expensive cities in the country, she was still making less than $30,000. She felt that the system was rigged against people like her: unmarried and ambitious and unwilling to live a spartan life indefinitely. She was looking for a job that valued her teaching experience but that would allow her to earn money tied to her performance, her innovation and drive.

After looking for a few weeks, K.C. found a job at an educational software company in the city, in sales and marketing. The software company permitted her to make her own hours, and, within the first year, she was making over twice what she'd last made teaching. The year after, she made three times her teacher's salary. I was happy for her, but I felt sorry for her students and her school. I knew she was the sort of teacher who could make math- and science-hating students—and I was one of them—interested in, even inspired by, those subjects. She was the life-changing sort of teacher that a school just can't afford to lose.

K.C. was one of the people I consulted when I was trying to shape the idea that would become 826 Valencia. She and I talked about ways to alleviate the burdens on teachers, and ways to get other people—especially, in my case, writers and editors and such—involved in the public schools. K.C. helped with the notion of offering after-school tutoring to English-language learners in the city, and of sending tutors into schools to work under the guidance of teachers, assisting with large classrooms where students needed more one-on-one attention than a teacher with thirty-two students can always provide.

In 2002, 826 Valencia opened its doors in the Mission District of San Francisco—a neighborhood with a high percentage of immigants from Mexico and Central and South America—and we began to help at our namesake location, and also in schools all over the city. Nínive Calegari became the executive director of the organization, guiding its curriculum, goals, and day-to-day operations.

Very early in our in-schools work, Nínive partnered our organization with Leadership High School, a public charter school, the majority of whose students planned to attend college, often against great odds. We worked with Kathleen Large to help her students write essays about what their teachers should—and often didn't—know about students' lives and dreams and obstacles. One day about thirteen of us tutors, Nínive among us, were sent to Leadership, and in a trailer-classroom in the parking lot of the school, we worked with the students on their ideas for their essays.

This was one of my first times in a public high school in the city, and though I'd heard a lot about Leadership—about how ambitious its teachers and student body were—I was saddened when the first student I spoke to was anything but upbeat about her school and her prospects. She was a junior, African American, a good student and an excellent writer. But she was down on her school that day; she said that Leadership had changed a lot since she'd been there. When she'd arrived as a freshman, it was inspiring and fun, she said, but it wasn't much anymore. I asked her for more details, but she said it was hard to explain. I wanted so badly to get at what it was in the school's culture that had been altered, because it was obvious that she'd once loved school and now didn't. In some way, her love of the school—of school itself—had been taken from her.

I didn't see that student again, and only now, two years later, I've finally put everything together. This afterword is being written after the rest of the book is complete, and it was just a few days ago that I finally realized that we came to Leadership that day shortly after the departure of Jonathan Dearman and two other

African American teachers. I didn't know Dearman's name at the time, and only learned of his existence—and of his influence and legacy and his decision to leave teaching to sell real estate—when Daniel Moulthrop and Nínive Calegari decided that we should profile him in the introduction. But now knowing his story, and knowing firsthand how profoundly the departure of a popular and inspiring teacher can affect the mood of a school—and its students' interest in learning—it underlines for me how simple the problem this book espouses really is.

At 826 Valencia, we give a monthly award to a Bay Area teacher; it's a no-strings-attached $1,500 check to reward excellence in teaching. It's fulfilling to be able to honor and meet these educators, but we constantly wring our hands about our inability to do more. We've discussed, many times, what it would take to be the sort of organization that could pay someone like Jonathan Dearman the salary difference that would be necessary to make it possible for him to teach at Leadership again. We really think about this: about how we might raise $50,000 so that the 350 students of Leadership can have this "strong, gifted, funny and brilliant African American teacher" back in the classroom.

I'd also like to get K.C. back in the classroom. (K.C., by the way, is now selling real estate, too.) Perhaps because K.C. was a science teacher, she and I have spoken about the "ecosystem" of a school, how interdependent all of the elements of a school are, and how important it is to the students to have a sense of stability and continuity. But we rarely hear policymakers talk about such things. So much effort is devoted to bringing new people into the profession—from other professions, from other countries—while so little is done to keep the K.C. Fullers and Jonathan Dearmans of the world in the schools that need them.

It might come down to private individuals, companies, and foundations to step in and sponsor these teachers. Maybe, just as

wealthy donors provide the funds to re-sod this high school football field or to fix that community pool, it will be the private sector that will step in to pay the teachers what they're worth, and
thus prevent the school-culture malaise that can occur when great
young teachers leave.

I'm cautiously optimistic that the day will come when teachers
are treated with the respect given to doctors and architects and
judges, and are paid commensurately. I do think that it will happen, though it will take decades to change perceptions of the profession, and to make people see the fairly simple and irrefutable
correlation between teacher quality and teacher salaries, between
teacher retention and teacher salaries, between student performance and teacher salaries, and the prospects of our youth and the
future of the country and teacher salaries.

If there are signs of hope in all this, they are small but significant. I
was recently in Los Angeles, at the opening of 826LA, a small tutoring center we're operating with the help of Amber Early, Pilar Perez,
Steve Irvin, and the educators in the area. At the event, I met a number of teachers from the Green Dot Schools, a group of small public-
charter high schools started all over L.A. by education visionary
Steve Barr. After meeting the principal of one of these schools, and a
few of the teachers—all were young and extremely inspired—they
introduced me to a woman named Rosa. She was a longtime teacher
at another school in Santa Monica, and she had been brought out
that night as part of a recruitment effort. The Green Dot staff knew
of Rosa's talents, and wanted her to work for them. Rosa's boss had
heard that she was being wooed by Green Dot, and offered to top
whatever salary Steve Barr was dangling. There was, in effect, what
amounted to a bidding war going on for this teacher, who at the time
was teaching fifth-grade science. It had never happened to Rosa before, but she was clearly loving the attention and the acknowledg-

ment of her talents. I'm not sure where Rosa will be next year, but even if she stays where she is, having been fought over, she will feel more valued—and she'll be better-paid to boot.

Speaking of fifth-grade science teachers, an update on my friend K.C., one of the most talented teachers you'd ever know: she just got her real estate license, and she's selling houses like crazy.

—Dave Eggers
MARCH 2005

ABOUT THE TEACHERS

MORE INFORMATION
ABOUT THE TEACHERS FEATURED

Richard Adelman

Richard Adelman is from Philadelphia and has taught at John Bartram High in southwest Philadelphia for his entire thirty-year career. He holds a degree in teaching and a master's in communication. He has taught English for about twenty years and also teaches English and computer applications.

Scott Arnold

Scott Arnold is from Portland, Oregon, but has lived in Boise most of his life. He teaches Western civilization and AP European history, and has been at the same school for over ten years. He received a bachelor's in history from Boise State University and a master's in European integration (the study of the European Union) from the school of international service at the American University in Washington, D.C. He has a wife who also teaches and two sons, ages five and eight.

Joel Arquillos

Joel Arquillos has been teaching social studies at Galileo Academy of Science and Technology in San Francisco, for the past six years. He has served as an Advancement Via Individual Determination (AVID) teacher for the past four years and as the school's Associated Student Body director for the past two years. Before becoming a high school teacher, Joel was the director of a day program for developmentally disabled adults in Santa Rosa, California. He was also the lead singer of the punk rock band PATCH. He graduated from Hunter College, City University of New York (CUNY), and received his teaching credential at San Francisco State. Arquillos will become Galileo's director of creative arts and media, in which capacity he will provide high school students the opportunity to display their artistic and creative talents on stage and video.

Frank Barnes

Frank Barnes has taught high school social studies and humanities in the Boston Public School system and has worked with young people in various co-curricular settings as a volunteer and youth instructor. He earned his bachelor's in political science and speech and communication from Macalester College, and his MEd in teaching and curriculum from Harvard University. Prior to teaching he served as both a regional director and national network director for the Campus Outreach Opportunity League and as a program officer for the Massachusetts National and Community Service Commission. Barnes has lectured at colleges and universities across the country and has presented at regional, national, and international conferences on civic engagement, volunteerism, and urban school reform. He is currently a senior asssociate at the Annenberg Institute for School Reform at Brown University, where he researches and consults on school-district redesign and central office operation.

Lizabeth Barnett

Lizabeth Barnett is originally from Powder Springs, Georgia, a suburb of metro Atlanta. She graduated from the University of Georgia in 1997 with a bachelor's in music. Between 1997 and 2000, she taught in Forsyth County at two different middle schools. She moved to Colorado in February 2000. For about three years, she undertook office work for a company—a job that paid better than teaching. However, she missed teaching and started giving group lessons on the side. Now she works part-time in an office and part-time as a private music teacher in Denver, but plans to return to full-time private instruction.

Jeffrey Taylor Bauer

Jeffrey Taylor Bauer is from Philadelphia, Pennsylvania. He received his bachelor's degree from Temple University and his master's degree from the University of Pennsylvania. For the past nine years he has taught kindergarten, first grade, and third grade in both public and charter schools in Philadelphia, Chicago, and Englewood, New Jersey. In September 2001, an article he co-authored about kinder-gartners' responses to literature was published in the *New Advocate*. In September 2004, he will be teaching kindergarten for the newly opened Harlem Children's Zone Promise Academy in New York City.

Erik Benner

Erik Benner was born near Pittsburgh but was raised mostly in Fort Worth, Texas. He has been teaching at the same school, Cross Timbers Middle School in Grapevine, Texas, since graduating from the University of North Texas. He travels all over Texas to gather information for his classes.

Daniel Beutner

Dan Beutner was born in Indianapolis and raised in Bettendorf, Iowa. He taught third, fourth, and fifth grades, as well as gifted resource at Kyrene del Sureño School in Chandler, Arizona, from 1988 to 2000. After working three years in the private sector as a senior course developer for an e-learning company in Scottsdale, he returned to Sureño, where he currently teaches fifth grade. In 1999, he earned a master's degree in educational technology from Arizona State University. He has served as KEA representative, team leader, and technology mentor for the school, in addition to conducting numerous staff-development trainings for the district. He currently lives in Gilbert, Arizona, with his wife, Jennifer—also a teacher—and their children, Brice, Sean, Aaron, and Kayleigh.

Paul Callan

Paul Callan embarked on a teaching career in 1990 and has taught at high school area vocational centers, high school, and, since 1995, at the Kentucky Community and Technical College System (KCTCS). His primary teaching responsibilities at the KCTCS are second-year courses in National Electrical Code, electrical construction, rotating machines, motor controls, and programmable logic controllers. He also serves as the co-chair of the KCTCS Electrical Technology Curriculum Committee and the elected technical faculty regent for the KCTCS board of regents until 2006. He helped found the Technical Faculty and Staff Alliance (TFSA) Local 6083 of the American Federation of Teachers in Kentucky and is the secretary of Local 6083. Before becoming a teacher, Callan enrolled in a two-year diploma course as an industrial electrician and worked as a self-employed electrician wiring custom-built passive solar homes. In 1985, he enrolled at Eastern Kentucky University and completed a variety of related degrees. During this time, he also raised a family and lived on food stamps.

Joseph S. Center

Joseph S. Center graduated from Brigham Young University with a BA degree in English education. He completed his student teaching for his credential in Payson, a town twenty miles from BYU. He has taught at Payson Middle School for several years and recently received an endorsement to teach percussion. He is the assistant band director at Payson High School, where he teaches and writes the music for the percussion ensemble and drum line. He was recently married.

Matthew Cheeseman

Matthew Cheeseman started his teaching career at Biglerville High School, Gettysburg, PA, in 1995, where he taught chemistry and coached varsity baseball. He taught the following year at Highlands High School, Natrona Heights, PA, near Pittsburgh, where he taught chemistry and served as the Key Club co-advisor. Upon moving to California in 1997, Matthew taught chemistry and physical science at San Lorenzo High School for five years. In addition to his teaching duties, during his tenure he was employed by the district as class advisor, technology mentor, MEChA advisor, and Digital High School Coordinator. In 2002, Matthew joined the East Nicolaus Joint Union High School District, where he teaches chemistry, forensic science, biology, and advanced placement sciences. His extracurricular duties include coaching (volleyball and baseball) and the position of Athletic Director. Matthew received his BS in chemistry and BS in education in 1994 and 1995, respectively, from Delaware Valley College, PA.

He earned his MA in natural science in 2002 from San Jose State University, CA.

Brad Coulter

Brad Coulter lives in Seattle. As a boy, he attended public schools in the Seattle area. He spent his college years at Western Washington University in Bellingham, where he studied geology. Upon returning from work in the geothermal industry in northern California and Hawaii, he obtained his teaching degree from the University of Washington in Seattle. He has taught elementary school for seventeen years. He has a twelve-year-old daughter and an eight-year-old son.

Rachel McBroom Cross

Rachel McBroom Cross was born in Smithville, Tennessee, and has almost always lived in some part of the state. She attended Tennessee Tech University in Cookeville, Tennessee. Over the course of her nine-year teaching career at Oneida Middle School in Oneida, Tennessee, she taught algebra I, seventh-grade math, eighth-grade social studies, and sixth-grade social studies. She also served as head of the math department and the discipline committee, serving on committees from school dances to textbook selection. She coached high school girls' and middle school girls' basketball teams as well. When needed, she has served as a substitute principal. Cross is still employed at Oneida Middle School where she teaches sixth-grade math and algebra I.

Patrick Daly

Patrick Daly graduated from Washington State University with a degree in biology and student taught in the Kent School District. His first teaching job consisted of instructing high school algebra, pre-algebra, and biology at Kentridge High School. He was also the girls' dive coach and the head boys' swim-team coach. During the summer, he managed a local country club pool and coached the swim team there. For the next three years, Daly taught life science, environmental science, and general science to seventh-, eighth-, and ninth-graders at Meeker Junior High School (also in the Kent district). He continued to coach swimming for the high school, and coached volleyball and softball for the junior high. He submitted his resignation in May 2001, and began to work for Abbott Laboratories the following school year.

Amanda Deal

Amanda Deal is a fourth-grade teacher at Mineral Springs Elementary School in Winston-Salem, North Carolina. Prior to beginning a second career in education, she worked for ten years in corporate America. She graduated with distinction from the University of North Carolina with a B.S. in business administration. Since beginning her career as a teacher, Deal has been pursuing an MA in teaching from Salem College. She has chaired the grant committee for Mineral Springs Elementary School, where she was awarded a grant to provide professional development for her school's staff. In 2003–2004 she played an integral role in developing and writing a grant in hopes that Mineral Springs will become a Federal Magnet School. She is a member of the Forsyth County Association of Educators and of Kappa Delta Pi, an international honor society for educators.

Dave Denning

Dave Denning is from Kansas and teaches in the Grapevine-Colleyville Independent School District. He has taught U.S. history for seven years and is also the volleyball, cross country, and track coach. He received a B.S. from Kansas State University and is married, with one child.

Elizabeth Grady

Elizabeth Grady is the K–12 chairperson for history/social science for the Cambridge, Massachusetts, Public Schools. She was a classroom teacher for more than twenty years, a founder of two alternative progressive secondary schools, and a long-time staff member at a third, the Pilot School, the oldest alternative high school program in the United States. She directs staff development in history for the system, and taught in the teacher certification program at the Harvard Graduate School of Education for ten years. She is a board member at the Boston Children's Museum and a director at Cultural Survival, an organization that represents the interests of indigenous peoples. Trained as an anthropologist, she holds a doctorate in human development from Harvard. She visited and studied in Japan on a Fulbright scholarship in 2001. She is from Cambridge, Massachusetts.

Nancy Gutmann

Nancy Gutmann grew up in Portsmouth, Ohio. She received a BA in English from Duke University and an MA in English from Northeastern University. Thereafter, she taught English for three years at Marblehead High School, took ten years out to raise her children and volunteer as an ESL teacher, and then taught English and ESL for twenty-six years at Brookline High School. She has three grown children and lives with her husband in Brookline, Massachusetts.

Doug Hamilton

Doug Hamilton grew up in the Bay Area and graduated from University of California, Berkeley, with a bachelor's in history. He received his teaching credentials and master's in education from Stanford University. After teaching briefly in Palo Alto, he moved to San Lorenzo High School, where he has taught for eight years. He is married, and recently welcomed a baby boy to his family.

Linda Hamilton

Linda Hamilton is from Danville, California, and has taught at San Lorenzo High School, San Lorenzo, and California State University, Hayward. She received a BA in English (and drama) from the University of California, Davis, an MA in English from California State University, Hayward, and a Single Subject Teaching Credential from California State University, Sacramento. Hamilton is the author of *Hiking the San Francisco Bay Area* (Falcon Guides Hiking) and mother of one child, Ben.

Steven Herraiz

Steven Herraiz is a kindergarten teacher at John Muir Elementary School in San Francisco's Western Addition. Having taught for eight years, he also mentors student teachers through San Francisco State University's MATE (Muir Alternative Teacher Education) program. Herraiz is the teachers' union building representative at his school site. During his tenure, he has also worked at a popular San Francisco nightclub two nights a week. Herraiz earned a bachelor's degree in English from Kent State University (Kent, Ohio) and has been a San Francisco resident for fifteen years.

Michelle Hurley

Michelle Hurley taught first grade in the El Segundo Unified School District in El Segundo, California, for six years. She completed her bachelor's degree in history at UCLA and her master's degree along with her teaching credential program at Pepperdine University. Aside from spending time in the classroom, Hurley has served on various district committees addressing issues including curriculum development, standards-based evaluation, and literacy intervention. She has also served as a master teacher to graduate-level student teachers from Pepperdine University. After taking a year's leave of absence following the birth of twins, Hurley returned to teaching in the Tahoma School District near Seattle, Washington.

Matt Huxley

Matt Huxley taught social studies for eleven years at both the middle and high school levels. Most recently he taught world history, government, and economics, and served as a professional development coordinator at Sir Francis Drake High School in San Anselmo, California. A recent graduate of the Principal Leadership Institute at University of California, Berkeley, he is currently working as a vice principal at Berkeley High School in Berkeley, California. Active in leadership positions throughout his career, he is dedicated to disrupting the historical inequities that exist in public education. He was born in San Rafael, California.

Mark Isero

Mark Isero is from Los Altos and has taught at Leadership High for the past four years. Previously, he spent three years teaching English and history to grades nine through twelve at Irvington High in Fremont. He earned his bachelor's in history from University of California, Berkeley, and a master's in education from Harvard University.

Dawn Jaeger

Dawn Jaeger has taught social studies and German at Deuel High School in Clear Lake, South Dakota, for twenty-seven years. Before that, she taught for two years and one semester in Minnesota, two years at Biwabik, Minnesota, and a semester at Howard Lake-Waverly. Among the courses she has taught are American and world history, government, sociology, psychology, world problems, and civics, as well as German I and II. She has also served as the yearbook advisor, newspaper advisor, cheerleading advisor, and middle school oral interpretation coach. Jaeger has been a career-long member of the National Education Association and was a 1999 Library of Congress American Memories fellow. She is a graduate of Minnesota State University at Moorhead, Minnesota, and holds a master's in education administration from South Dakota State University in Brookings, South Dakota. She is originally from Nelson, Minnesota.

Eric Lehman

Eric Lehman is thirty-three years old and has taught fourth grade at Hawthorne Elementary School in Helena, Montana, for the past three years. He graduated from Edinboro University of Pennsylvania in 1992 with a BS in elementary education/early childhood education, and his first job consisted of teaching first grade at Fairfax County Public Schools, Fairfax, Virginia. Thereafter, he worked at Clancy School, dividing his time equally between his role as Gifted and Talented Program Coordinator and kindergarten teacher. He also spent a year teaching a multi-age classroom (five- to eight-year-olds) in a private community school.

Lara Lighthouse

Lara Lighthouse grew up on the South Side of Chicago. She attended Colgate University in Hamilton, New York, where she majored in English literature. She has a master's degree in special education from San Francisco State University and a number of teaching credentials. She has been a teacher at Town School for Boys, The 150 Parker School, Roosevelt School in Redwood City, and Washington School in Burlingame. Her experiences include teaching K–3, teaching a special day class, and serving as a resource specialist. Lighthouse is married and is the mother of a five-year-old boy and a three-month-old girl.

Skip Lovelady

Skip Lovelady lives in Marin County, California. He graduated from Dominican University in San Rafael, California, with a degree in biology in 1994, and received his secondary teaching credential from Dominican University in 1995. He completed his student teaching at Redwood High School in Larkspur and was hired as a full-time science teacher at Redwood in 1995. In 1998 he became the science department chair. He has also taught a curriculum development course for science and math credentialists for four years at Dominican University. Lovelady specializes in lower-division general education courses, college-level courses taught in high school, and mainstreaming special education students.

Jeffrey McCabe

Jeff McCabe currently works for the On-Line Higher Education division of Laureate Education, Inc. Before that, he was a math teacher for eight years in Mongomery County, Maryland (a suburban area outside D.C.), and taught calculus at Carroll Community College at night. He has served as the department chair of the math department at Wootton High School for the past three years, and began teaching and serving as the assistant athletic director at Damascus High School in fall 2004. He has also coached soccer and swimming at the high school level. Prior to embarking on a teaching career, McCabe was an account executive for Bell Atlantic Network Services, Inc. He is married with three children under six years old. His wife, Mary Beth, stays at home full-time raising their children.

Chris McCarty

Chris McCarty was born and raised in Seymour, Tennessee, a rural suburb outside of Knoxville. He attended Maryville College in Maryville, Tennessee, where he received a bachelor's in history for teacher licensure. He taught eighth-grade U.S. history and coached for two years at Seymour Middle School in Seymour, Tennessee. McCarty is currently enrolled in law school at the University of Tennessee in Knoxville.

Christopher McTamany

Chris McTamany has been teaching government and economics classes at Thomas S. Wootton High School in Montgomery County, Maryland, for six years. He was also the junior varsity wrestling coach for five years and is currently the varsity wrestling coach. He has been the government team leader for several years, and was the sponsor of the senior class of 1999 and the Fed Challenge team of 2001. He has been working toward his MS in finance. He was born in Baltimore and raised primarily outside Annapolis, Maryland, in Cape St. Claire. He studied at Drexel University for a political science degree with an economics minor, but before completing the degree, he changed his mind and decided to teach. He transferred to Towson State University and earned a history major with a secondary education track.

Kim Meck

Kim Meck moved to Alaska with her family when she was in second grade in 1976 and has lived there ever since. She attended second through twelfth grades in the Anchorage School District

(ASD) and spent a year in Switzerland as part of an exchange program before returning to earn a bachelor's in international business and relations from Alaska Pacific University. The opening up of Russian airspace at this time—and the subsequent decline in international trade occupations—led Kim to switch careers because she did not want to leave Alaska. Thereafter, she earned her master's in the art of teaching from Alaska Pacific University and has been teaching for six years for ASD. Her classroom experience includes first, second, and fifth grade at three different schools. Meck is currently enrolled at University of Alaska, Anchorage, to earn her administration certification. She loves to teach, even though she knows that she does not earn enough money as a single woman to secure her future retirement. She hopes to influence the people around her to make education a top priority in all ways, as it is in countries like Switzerland.

Brian Mock

Brian Mock teaches social studies (U.S. history to eleventh-graders and government/economics to twelfth-graders) at Catalina Foothills High School in Tucson, Arizona. Apart from teaching, he has co-sponsored the Ping-Pong Club and will also co-sponsor the Political Activism Club. Before this, he taught U.S. history at Canyon Del Oro High School and AP economics at University High School, both also in Tucson, and was the faculty advisor for the Gay-Straight Alliance at both schools. He attended the University of Arizona in Tucson and received a BA in sociology, minoring in economics and political science, in 1997. He received a post-bachelor certification in secondary social studies from the University of Arizona as well. He is originally from St. Louis, Missouri. He also writes record reviews and the occasional feature article as a freelance music writer for the *Tucson Weekly*.

Bethany Morton

Bethany Morton was born in Columbus, Indiana. She graduated from Wofford College in Spartanburg, North Carolina, with a BA in German and art history. While in college, she spent a semester at the University of Salzburg in Austria. In 1997 she began teaching German at the West Charlotte High School in North Carolina. She attended the University of North Carolina to obtain a teaching certificate. In 2000 she moved to Spartanburg, South Carolina, to teach German at James F. Byrnes High School, where she taught until 2003. She is now a personal trainer at an athletic club.

Alyssa Nannt

Alyssa Nannt was born in Fargo, North Dakota, and grew up in small towns in Wisconsin. She graduated from University of Wisconsin–Madison in 1990 with a BA in French and international relations and began working at the Wisconsin Department of Revenue processing tax forms. Following this, she served as a special education teacher's assistant for students with cognitive disabilities in the Madison Metropolitan School System. She worked at two high schools and was encouraged by the teachers to go back to school to get a teaching license in special education. She attended college part-time from 1993 to 1996 while working full-time for the school district, and graduated in 1996 from Edgewood College (in Madison, Wisconsin) with an MA in education and a teaching license in special education. Nannt paid for her education by working, taking out student loans, and living in a low-income neighborhood. She taught K–3 special education at Crofton Meadows Elementary School, Maryland, from 1996 to 1998 before accepting a position with Talbot County Public Schools. For the next six years, she taught grades nine to twelve special education as a resource teacher at Easton High School in Easton, Maryland. She worked with students in regular education classes. Nannt now works with kids with emotional disabilities in grades nine to twelve at North Dorchester High School in Hurlock, Maryland.

Julia Normand

Julia Normand taught English at Goldenview Middle School in Anchorage, Alaska. She has lived all over the country in her sixty-five years, and has traveled extensively. She majored in classical languages in college and taught Latin for several years at the high school and college level. Before moving to Alaska, Normand taught medieval cooking at the Cloisters in New York, worked as an au pair in Italy, and worked at summer camps. She is currently writing a book, *Mother's Awakening,* and on the weekends makes and sells applesauce and apple butter.

David O'Rourke

David O'Rourke taught grade eleven and AP English at Silver Creek Central School District (a small rural/suburban district south of Buffalo, New York) for nearly seven years. He was a political-action chairperson for the teachers' association, participated in New York State United Teacher's Leadership Institute at Cornell University's School of Industrial Labor Relations, and coached soccer and swimming. He was also a Virtual High School Inc. course developer and online instructor from 1999 to 2003. O'Rourke received a BA from the University of Toronto and an MA and 7–12 teaching certification from the State University of New York, College at Fredonia. He left teaching in 2001 to undertake post-graduate work at Columbia Teachers College in Hypermedia and Education, later serving as a staff developer/ curriculum coordinator with the Board of Cooperative Educational Services. He returned to Silver Creek this past August as director of instruction and technology. He lives in Dunkirk, New York, with his wife and two children, and is currently enrolled in a MEd/EdD degree program at State University of New York at Buffalo.

Duane A. Richards

Duane A. Richards has been employed by the Miami-Dade County school system since the age of sixteen, when he started as an after-school activities leader. Later, he worked his way through college as a substitute teacher in the district. He has been a classroom teacher since 1998, when he was nominated Rookie Teacher of the Year. He has taught third, fourth, and fifth grades and was nominated Teacher of the Year at his school in 2003. He earned his National Board Certification as a Middle Childhood Generalist in 2002. Currently, he is the grade-level chairperson and teaches fifth grade at Avocado Elementary School in Homestead, Florida, where he was born. He earned his associate's degree in elementary education from Miami-Dade Community College, and a BS in elementary education from Nova Southeastern University.

April Sharpe

Born and raised in Miami, April Sharpe has been teaching since the age of twenty-three. She currently teaches art 2D, drawing and painting I–III, and AP art history at Homestead Senior High School, where she was chosen Teacher of the Year in 2002. She also sponsors the Art Club and, each year, the junior or senior class. Previously, she developed a private painting business and served as the art director for a private enrichment center, the Learning Tree of Arts, which she has run since 1997. The Learning Tree helps students to build their portfolios and audition for art magnet programs. Sharpe received her BFA in painting from the University of Miami (summa cum laude), with a minor in biology and art history. She is currently beginning her master's at Florida International University.

Tish Smedly

Letitia (Tish) Ann Smedley is beginning her thirty-second year of teaching three- and four-year-old children. After graduating from the University of Tennessee with a BS in child development, she began her work in the inner-city area of Nashville, Tennessee, with the Head Start program. As a teacher and center director, she has worked in many areas of the city over the past nineteen years. She attended Tennessee State University to obtain certification in early childhood development and a master's of education in administration and supervision. Thirteen years ago, after being approached for the third time, she accepted a position as a pre-kindergarten teacher for the public school system. While working with four-year-olds, she has helped to develop a curriculum for Head Start and the public schools. Recently, she was involved in creating the pre-kindergarten standards for the school system (in compliance with state standards) and has trained many in these developmentally appropriate standards.

Sam Stecher

Sam Stecher is a 1997 graduate of the University of Nebraska at Kearney with a BA in education. He has taught for seven years at Horizon Middle School in Kearney. Currently he is seeking his master's in educational administration. He has also worked for Love and Logic (a company that provides techniques for parents and teachers) for the past three years.

Cindi Swingen

Cindi Swingen teaches in the Beaverton School District in Beaverton, Oregon. Over the past sixteen years she has had experience with teaching in each of the elementary grades (K–5). The majority of her teaching career has been in multi-age or blended classrooms, where students remain with the same teacher for more than one year. She has also been involved with gender-equity training, math research, site-based decision making, peer coaching, and mentoring student teachers. She earned her master's degree from Lewis and Clark College.

Shelley Szipszky

Shelley Szipszky began teaching in 1983 in Fairbanks, Alaska, where she taught first grade for two years and fifth grade for four years. She participated in the Alaska Science Consortium and taught in-services on the writing process and on math programs. She moved to Juneau in 1990 and worked for the Alaska Centralized Correspondence School over the summers. During the school year, she taught fifth grade, sixth grade, and reading at the middle-school level. She also worked at the Alaska Department of Education as an education assistant and an interim counseling specialist. She has been a part-time consultant for the Alaska Mineral and Energy Resources Education Group, helping to write curricula, doing in-service training, and teaching credit classes. In 1993, her family moved to Anchorage; she took time away from teaching to get her special education certificate and to qualify to teach the gifted. She worked for the university as the data manager of an Anchorage School District federal grant. She then worked for two years as a Public Health Specialist for Medicaid Services. In 1997, she returned to teaching in Anchorage as a teacher of the gifted. She stayed with the program for five years before returning to the regular classroom as a fifth-grade teacher. She is currently employed as a sixth-grade teacher. In addition to teaching, she helps provide technical/computer support service to the school.

Catherine Travelute

After an introduction to the educational world through the University of North Carolina–Chapel Hill MAT program, Catherine Travelute took an ESOL teaching position in urban Atlanta. It was her good fortune that Cross Keys High School had been designated the most diverse high school in Georgia; it continues to be an inspiration for her after five years of full-time teaching. She came into education after stints in publishing and construction estimating management.

Todd Werner

Todd Werner grew up in Duluth, Minnesota. He received a BA in mathematics and an MA in secondary mathematics from Truman State University. He taught high school math at North Kansas City High School in Kansas City, Missouri, and currently works in education assessment as a development specialist at Data Recognition Corporation in Minneapolis, Minnesota.

Greg Worley

Greg Worley was educated at the University of Oklahoma, where he received his undergraduate degree in elementary education. After ten years of teaching, he received a fellowship to an accelerated program for his master's degree in educational administration. He has taught fifth grade for ten years and has two children, Scotty and Madison. He has stayed in Oklahoma all his life.

Kathryn Wright

Katy Wright is a second-grade teacher at Hawthorne Elementary School in Helena, Montana. She graduated from Middlebury College in 1993 with a double major in Russian and Eastern European studies and theater. Before becoming a teacher, Wright worked as an actor in various theater companies around the country. Currently she performs at the Grandstreet Theatre in Helena and sings with the band In Cahoots. Wright lives in Helena with her husband, Tyler, the executive director of the community YMCA, and their two sons, Travis and Trenton.

INNOVATIVE SCHOOLS, DISTRICTS, AND UNIONS

Cincinnati Public Schools
2651 Burnet Avenue
Cincinnati, OH 45219
(513) 363-0000
www.cpsboe.k12.oh.us

During the late 1990s, Cincinnati implemented a new performance evaluation system for teachers and attempted to tie compensation to that system. Though the new evaluations are still used, teachers continue to be paid on a traditional salary schedule.

Denver Classroom Teachers' Association
1500 Grant Street, Suite 200
Denver, CO 80203
(303) 831-0590
www.denverclassroom.org

The DCTA worked with the Denver public schools to create ProComp, an innovative pay system, which will take effect in

2006, provided voters approve the funding. The ProComp system is profiled in Chapter 12.

Denver Public Schools

900 Grant Street
Denver, CO 80203
(303) 764-3200
www.dpsk12.org

Along with the Denver Classroom Teachers' Association, the Denver Public Schools created the ProComp system, a comprehensive salary-reform package. The ProComp system is profiled in Chapter 12.

Helena Public Schools

55 South Rodney
Helena, MT 59601
(406) 324-2000
www.helena.k12.mt.us

In 2004, the Helena school district started tying comparatively higher teacher pay to evaluations and teachers' work outside the classroom. This system attracted almost 900 candidates from across the region to apply for fifty teaching vacancies. A full profile of the reform can be found in Chapter 12.

Montana Education Association/Montana Federation of Teachers

1232 East Sixth Avenue
Helena, MT 59601
(800) 398-0826
www.mea-mft.org

MEA-MFT is affiliated with both the major national teacher unions. They provided key support to their local affiliate in

Helena in helping to create Helena's Professional Compensation Alternative Plan. More information can be found in Chapter 12.

The Teacher Advancement Program
Milken Family Foundation
1250 Fourth Street
Santa Monica, CA 90401-1353
(310) 570 4800
www.mff.org/tap
TAP offers schools support in changing the structure of teaching, teaching support, and compensation, offering teachers multiple career paths and increased pay for increased responsibility and improved student performance.

Vaughn Next Century Learning Center
13330 Vaughn Street
San Fernando, CA 91340
(818) 349-1820
www.vaughn.k12.ca.us
Vaughn became a charter school in 1993. Among the reforms implemented since then was a substantial change to teacher compensation. Studies report these reforms have had led to an improvement in student outcomes. More information can be found in Chapter 12.

RECOMMENDED
READING

The following reading list is by no means exhaustive. It is representative of some of the more compelling and worthwhile reading we did in the course of researching this book. Note that not all the texts listed here support raising teacher salaries.

Teacher Pay and Teacher Quality
Dale Ballou and Michael Podgursky
Kalamazoo, MI: W.E. Upjohn Institute for Employment Research, 1997
Economists Ballou and Podgursky advocate raises for only the demonstrably best teachers and cuts for less effective teachers or teachers in low-need areas. They agree that good teachers are underpaid, and that some lessons from the private sector can be adapted to suit public education's needs.

Enhancing Professional Practice: A Framework for Teaching
Charlotte Danielson
Association for Supervision and Curriculum Development, November 15, 1996
Danielson is an educator and consultant who has worked for the Educational Testing Service and the National Board for Professional Teaching Standards. This framework has been used by many schools and districts seeking to redesign their evaluation systems. It is a comprehensive system of some nineteen different criteria and is aligned with standards tested on the Praxis III (the test many states use in teacher licensing).

Doing What Matters Most: Investing in Quality Teaching
Linda Darling-Hammond
Prepared for the National Commission on Teaching and America's Future, November 1997
Prepared for a commission of education and government leaders, this report argues for linking teacher certification standards to student learning standards, reinventing teacher education and professional development, overhauling teacher recruitment, and revising pay systems to pay for teachers' knowledge and skill.

"A Sense of Calling: Who Teaches and Why"
Steve Farkas et al.
A research report, Public Agenda 2000
This report focuses on what new teachers and college graduates who don't go into the teaching profession have to say about the teaching profession and what does or does not make it worthwhile.

"Stand By Me: What Teachers Really Think About Unions, Merit Pay, and Other Professional Matters"
Steve Farkas et al.
A research report, Public Agenda 2003
"Stand by Me" reveals that many teachers are dissatisfied with the current state of the system governing their profession, including current tenure laws. Public Agenda reports that although a majority of teachers are supportive of alternative pay systems and would like to see their unions work toward implementing them, many are worried that salary alternatives might simply be a way for districts to pay teachers less.

"Good Teaching Matters: How Well-Qualified Teachers Can Close the Gap"
Katy Haycock
In *Thinking K–16,* a publication of Education Trust (Summer 1998, 3:2)
Education Trust publishes a number of reports on teacher quality compensation. Here, Haycock argues that "if we only took the simple step of assuring that poor and minority children had highly qualified teachers, about half the achievement gap would disappear."

"Pushed Away or Pulled Out: Explaining the Decline of Teacher Aptitude in the United States"
Caroline Hoxby and Andrew Leigh
Harvard University, December 2003
Hoxby is among the few economists who study school finance. In this paper, she and Leigh try to explain why fewer high-aptitude candidates enter and stay in the teaching profession. Their answer: they are pushed away by low earning potential and pulled out by more enticing opportunities.

"Better Pay for Better Teaching: Making Teacher Compensation Pay Off in the Age of Accountability"

Bryan Hassel, Progressive Policy Institute Twenty-First Century Schools Project, May 2002

Hassel starts with the premise that raising teacher pay can and should be done by reforming pay systems to do away with anti-quated salary schedules. He writes, "We must increase the opportunity that teaching affords teachers, but we must also ask in return that teachers accept more responsibility for results in a more professional and differentiated system of compensation."

Teacher Turnover, Teacher Shortages and the Organization of Schools

Richard Ingersoll, Center for the Study of Teaching and Policy, January 2001

A former social studies and math teacher, sociologist Ingersoll examines national data and determines that the biggest reasons accounting for teacher turnover are job dissatisfaction and teachers pursuing other jobs. Ingersoll argues that organizational change is necessary to improve teacher retention rates.

Investing in Our Children: What We Know and Don't Know About the Costs and Benefits of Early Childhood Interventions

Lynn A. Karoly et al., RAND Corporation, 1998

This is RAND's analysis of the Perry Preschool Project, in which they also analyze similar investments in early childhood education. This study's oft-quoted finding: $7 is saved in future costs for every $1 spent on early childhood development.

The New Division of Labor: How Computers are Creating the Next Job Market

Frank Levy and Richard Murnane
Princeton, New Jersey: Princeton University Press, 2004

Levy and Murnane, authors of *The New Basic Skills: Principles for Educating Children to Thrive in a Changing Economy* (Free Press, 1996), argue here that because the labor market has drastically changed in recent years, education must change to provide future graduates with the skills they need to compete in the labor market.

"Barely Breaking Even: Incentives, Rewards, and the High Costs of Choosing to Teach"
Edward Liu et al., Harvard Graduate School of Education, April 2000
This paper focuses on how groups of teachers in Massachusetts view available incentives and rewards in teaching. They find that low pay provides an effective disincentive to teachers to stay in the profession.

The Two Percent Solution: Fixing America's Problems in Ways Liberals and Conservatives Can Love
Matthew Miller
New York: Public Affairs, 2003
The most relevant chapter in this book is "The Millionaire Teacher," in which Miller advocates a set of comprehensive reforms regarding how and how much teachers are paid and how they move through their careers. He manages to find agreement among those with otherwise disparate viewpoints and offers a plan for how the federal government might actually fund substantial reform.

"Survey and Analysis of Teacher Salary Trends, 2002"
Howard F. Nelson and Rachel Drown
Washington, D.C.: American Federation of Teachers, AFL-CIO, 2003

A recent version of AFT's biennial report comparing teacher salaries over time and among states. The AFT has a number of other comparative studies, including international comparisons of education expenditures and student achievement.

Paying Teachers for What They Know and Do: New and Smarter Compensation Strategies to Improve Schools
Allen Odden and Carolyn Kelley
Thousand Oaks, CA: Corwin Press, Inc., 2002
Odden and Kelley offer a variety of strategies—from paying individuals more for particular qualifications to paying school-wide bonuses for improved student achievement. They also offer suggestions and resources for implementing salary reform.

"Higher Pay in Hard to Staff Schools: The Case for Financial Incentives"
Cynthia Prince
Prepared for the American Association of School Administrators, June 2002
Prince's argument is that targeted financial incentives are the most effective way to raise teacher salaries. She offers examples of schools and districts paying more for hard-to-staff positions and circumventing traditional objections to differentiated pay by offering extra work and commensurate pay to teachers staffing difficult positions. She also describes bonus programs, housing incentives, and student loan forgiveness programs.

"Teaching at Risk: A Call to Action"
New York: The Teaching Commission, CUNY Graduate Center, 2004
The Teaching Commission was an exceptional panel of leaders in education and business led by former IBM CEO Louis Gerstner.

Released in early 2004, their report advocates a "new compact" with teachers that would pay teachers more and pay them based on their performance, including the outcomes of their students.

"Low Pay, Low Quality"

Peter Temin

Education Next, Summer 2003, 3:3, p. 8

Temin's piece is a companion to Richard Vedder's piece, "Comparable Worth" (see page 329) in *Education Next*. His is a thoughtful and statistically sound "you get what you pay for" argument, suggesting that not until we increase pay will we begin to see improved quality.

"The Cost of Teacher Turnover"

Prepared for the Texas State Board of Educator Certification by the Texas Center for Educational Research, November 2000

This study attempts to measure the hard costs associated with teacher turnover. Texas's average teacher attrition rate of 15.5 percent costs $329 million every year, at the low end, though the costs might be as great $2.1 billion a year. The models this study uses focus on human resources and administrative costs—without taking into account the soft costs for students and the community.

The Teachers We Need and How to Get More of Them: A Manifesto

The Thomas B. Fordham Foundation, April 20, 1999

Signed by luminaries from education theory and education policy, this manifesto argues for a reduction in certification regulation and an increase in accountability as the best way to attract teachers.

"Comparable Worth"

Vedder, Richard

Education Next, Summer 2003, 3:3, p. 14

Vedder argues that teachers are, actually, quite well paid, compared to the hourly wages of many professions. He rests much of his argument on the idea that teachers work only seven hours a day for 180 days of the year. He then breaks salaries down to hourly wages and compares them that way.

"A Case of Successful Teaching Policy: Connecticut's Long Term Efforts to Improve Teaching and Learning"

Suzann M. Wilson et al.

Center for the Study of Teaching and Policy, February 2001

Wilson, Barnett Berry, and Linda Darling-Hammond offer a rigorous analysis of Connecticut's decades-long efforts to improve teacher quality. Connecticut combined an increase in pay with higher certification standards and has managed to amass what may be the most effective statewide teaching force in the country.

TEACHER RECRUITMENT
ORGANIZATIONS

California Teacher Recruitment Center
9300 Imperial Highway, ECE 104
Downey, CA 90242
(800) 875-2929
www.teachnow.la
The Teacher Recruitment Center helps prospective teachers navigate the differing hiring practices of California's school districts and charter schools.

New York City Teaching Fellows Program
The Center for Recruitment
65 Court Street, 3rd Floor
Brooklyn, NY 11201
(800) TEACH-NYC
www.nycteachingfellows.org
The Teaching Fellows program is an alternative certification route for

mid-career professionals interested in teaching in New York's public schools. The Fellows program recruits aggressively and holds candidates to rigorous standards. Teaching Fellows receive ongoing professional development, support, and a subsidy to pursue master's degrees.

Recruiting New Teachers, Inc.

385 Concord Avenue, Suite 103
Belmont, MA 02478
(617) 489-6000
www.rnt.org

Established in 1986, RNT is a national nonprofit organization whose mission is to raise esteem for teaching, expand the pool of qualified teachers, and improve the nation's teacher recruitment, development, and diversity policies and practices. RNT pursues its goal through innovative public-service outreach, action-oriented research, and national conferences.

Teachers of Tomorrow

Office of K–16 Initiatives and Access Programs
Teacher Recruitment and Development Unit
Room 1071 EBA
Albany, New York 12234
(518) 474-5315

TOT is a statewide program in New York to attract teachers to the neediest schools. They provide grants of $3,400 renewable up to three years for teachers choosing to teach in the neediest schools.

Teach for America

National Office
315 West 36th Street
New York, NY 10018

(800) 832-1230

www.teachforamerica.org

Teach for America's primary goal is to eliminate educational inequity in this country. To that end, they recruit and train recent college graduates to make two-year commitments to teach in the neediest urban and rural schools. Their recruitment efforts have been remarkably successful, and recent studies indicate TFA teachers are having a positive impact in the schools where they work.

The New Teacher Project

304 Park Avenue South, 11th Floor

New York, NY 10010

Phone: (212) 590-2484, ext. 1031

Fax: (212) 590-2485

www.tntp.org

Founded by a group of Teach for America alumni, TNTP partners with school districts, education schools, and state departments of education to increase the number of outstanding individuals who become public school teachers and create environments for all educators that maximize their impact on student achievement. They have attracted and prepared over 10,000 new, high-quality teachers and launched thirty-nine programs in eighteen states since 1997.

OTHER EDUCATION ADVOCACY, REFORM, AND SUPPORT ORGANIZATIONS

American Association of School Administrators

801 Quincy Street, Suite 700
Arlington, VA 22203-1730
(703) 528-0700
www.aasa.org

For more than 150 years, the AASA has seen its primary mission as that of standing up for public education, advocating for support and resources so schools can continue to be "the cornerstone of the common good." They have supported legislation to improve teacher education programs and funding to support the preparation of teachers in high-need areas.

Coalition of Essential Schools

1814 Franklin Street, Suite 700
Oakland, CA 94612

(510) 433-1451

www.essentialschools.org

In their efforts to create smaller, more effective schools, CES focuses on equity, personalization, and intellectual vibrancy. They have a network of local affiliates and 600 schools, and their principles have spread to thousands more around the country. They have recently partnered with the Bill and Melinda Gates Foundation to create what they call the "next generation of high schools."

Education Trust

1250 H Street NW, Suite 700

Washington, DC 20005

(202) 293-1217

www.edtrust.org

Established in 1990 by the American Association for Higher Education, Ed Trust supports reforms in K–12 education that help schools and colleges meet the needs of the students they serve. Ed Trust works specifically on issues related to the achievement gap that separates low-income students and students of color from other youth. They offer a wide range of publications and data tools to support research in K–16 education.

National Association of Elementary School Principals

1615 Duke Street

Alexandria, VA 22314

(800) 386-2377

www.naesp.org

NAESP supports and advocates on behalf of principals in elementary and middle schools. They believe early education is crucial to children's future and that principals are the key leaders to ensuring the quality of that education.

National Coalition for Parental Involvement in Education

www.ncpie.org

NCPIE advocates for greater involvement of parents and families in their child's education. They do this by conducting activities and providing resources and legislative information to promote greater parental involvement in schools and communities.

National PTA

330 North Wabash Avenue, Suite 2100

Chicago, IL 60611

(800) 307-4782

www.pta.org

The National PTA is primarily a child-advocacy organization. They also seek to encourage greater cooperation among teachers and parents. The organization is a strong supporter for improving teacher quality and reducing class size.

Teacher Union Reform Network

www.gseis.ucla.edu/hosted/turn/turn.html

With members leading local NEA and AFT affiliates, TURN advocates union reforms to promote better learning and higher achievement for students. They seek to end the era of hostile labor relations and to work cooperatively with districts while continuing to protect their members' interests. TURN is affiliated with the Graduate School of Education and Information Studies at the University of California, Los Angeles.

RESEARCH ORGANIZATIONS

Center for American Progress
805 15th Street NW (at H Street NW)
Suite 400
Washington, DC 20005
(202) 682-1611
www.centerforamericanprogress.org
The Center for American Progress is a nonpartisan research and educational institute that works to advance policies to create sustained economic growth and new opportunities for all Americans, including reforms aimed at teacher quality and teacher compensation.

Center for the Study of Teaching and Policy
Consortium for Policy Research in Education
Offices at the University of Pennsylvania, Harvard University, Uni-

versity of Wisconsin–Madison, Stanford University, University of Michigan

www.cpre.org

Since 1985, CPRE has been studying how education reforms in policy, organization, and structure create improvements in the work of schools. In addition to work in the area of teacher compensation, CPRE researchers also study school finance, teacher quality, working conditions, instruction, and accountability, among other areas. CPRE researchers have served as consultants for and studied compensation reform efforts across the country in states including Ohio, Colorado, California, Rhode Island, and Minnesota.

North Carolina Education Alliance

200 West Morgan Street, Suite 200

Raleigh, NC 27601

www.nceducationalliance.org

Created in 1998, the work of the NCEA is focused on students and creating educational reform in North Carolina. The mission of the Alliance is to identify and publicize innovative, effective solutions to educational problems.

The Progressive Policy Institute

600 Pennsylvania Avenue SE, Suite 400

Washington, DC 20003

(202) 547-0001

www.ppionline.org

The Progressive Policy Institute bills themselves as a catalyst for political change and source for "Third Way" thinking, leaving behind traditional left wing/right wing debates. The Institute's work rests on ideals of equal opportunity, mutual responsibility, and self-governing citizens and communities. As part of their 21st Century Schools

Project they have advocated for salary reform that raises pay and reforms old pay systems.

Public Agenda

6 East 39th Street
New York, NY 10016
(212) 686-6610
www.publicagenda.org
Public Agenda publishes a number of extremely useful reports and studies across many areas, focusing on public opinion about issues ranging from education to foreign policy to immigration to religion and civility in American life.

PERIODICALS

Education Next

226 Littauer North Yard
1875 Cambridge Street
Cambridge, MA 02138
www.educationnext.org

Education Next is the educational quarterly published by the Hoover Institution, a think tank operated out of Stanford. The journal strives to present "the facts as best they can be determined, giving voice (without fear or favor) to worthy research, sound ideas, and responsible arguments."

Education Week

Editorial Projects in Education Inc.
6935 Arlington Road, Suite 100
Bethesda, MD 20814-5233
(800) 346-1834
www.edweek.org

"Our primary mission is to help raise the level of awareness and understanding among professionals and the public of important issues in American education. We cover local, state, and national news and issues from preschool through the twelfth grade. We also provide periodic special reports on issues ranging from technology to textbooks, as well as books of special interest to educators. *Education Week* and *Teacher Magazine* continue to raise the level of awareness and understanding among professional educators and the general public, and to contribute significantly to the welfare of American education."

Rethinking Schools
1001 East Keefe Avenue
Milwaukee, WI 53212
(414) 964-9646
www.rethinkingschools.org
"While the scope and influence of *Rethinking Schools* has changed, its basic orientation has not. Most importantly, it remains firmly committed to equity and to the vision that public education is central to the creation of a humane, caring, multiracial democracy. While writing for a broad audience, *Rethinking Schools* emphasizes problems facing urban schools, particularly issues of race. Throughout its history, *Rethinking Schools* has tried to balance classroom practice and educational theory. It is an activist publication, with articles written by and for teachers, parents, and students. Yet it also addresses key policy issues, such as vouchers and marketplace-oriented reforms, funding equity, and school-to-work."

School Reform News
The Heartland Institute
19 South LaSalle Street, Suite 903
Chicago, IL 60603
(312) 377-4000
www.heartland.org

School Reform News is the Heartland Institute's monthly outreach newsletter to school reformers. They are a proponent of school choice and market-based solutions to the problems faced by public education.

NOTES

INTRODUCTION: DO TEACHERS HAVE IT EASY?

1. Ingersoll discusses this in a *USA Today* opinion piece, "High Turnover Plagues Schools," August 15, 2002.
2. American Federation of Teachers, "Survey and Analysis of Teacher Salary Trends, 2002," figure 111.5, p. 40.
3. Richard Vedder, "Comparable Worth," *Education Next* 3:3, Summer 2003.
4. "Status of the American Public Schoolteacher, 2000–2001," National Education Association Research (Washington, D.C.: National Education Association, 2003), table 44.
5. Ibid.
6. Ibid., table 75.
7. Katy Haycock, "Good Teaching Matters . . . A Lot," *Education Trust* (Summer 1998), pp. 3–5.
8. Current Population Survey, and Corcoran, Sean, et al., "Women, the Labor Market, and the Declining Relative Quality of Teachers," 2004.
9. Noel Spring, *The American School: 1642–1993* (New York: McGraw Hill, 2004), p. 105.

ONE: "LOOK DAD, MY BIOLOGY TEACHER IS SELLING STEREOS AT CIRCUIT CITY!"

1. "Status of the American Public Schoolteacher, 2000–2001," National Education Association Research (Washington, D.C.: National Education Association, 2003), table 61.

2. Public Agenda, "A Sense of Calling: Who Teaches and Why," 2000.
3. David L. Henderson and Travis W. Henderson, "Texas Teachers, Moonlighting, and Morale" (paper prepared for the Texas State Teachers Association, April 2002 and April 2004), tables 1 and 5.

Two: THE TEACHERS LIVE IN ANOTHER TOWN

1. Figures taken from the National Association of Homebuilders report on home sales and prices (http://www.nahb.org/page.aspx/category/sectionID=131); F. Howard Nelson and Rachel Drown, "Survey and Analysis of Teacher Salary Trends" (Washington, D.C.: American Federation of Teachers, AFL-CIO, 2002), figures 1.2 and 1.6, table 1.2; 2002 Annual Report, State of New Jersey, Department of Treasury (http://www.state.nj.us/treasury/taxation/pdf/annual/2001/appenda.pdf); Dr. Sandy Baum and Marie O'Malley, "College on Credit: How Borrowers Perceive Their Education Debt," Results of the 2002 National Student Loan Survey (Nellie Mae Corporation, 2002), table 4.

Three: IT'S NOT A BAD SALARY IF YOU'RE SINGLE

1. Mark Lino, "Expenditures on Children by Families, 2003" (U.S. Department of Agriculture, Center for Nutrition Policy and Promotion, 2004), table ES1.
2. F. Howard Nelson and Rachel Drown, "Survey and Analysis of Teacher Salary Trends" (Washington, D.C.: American Federation of Teachers, AFL-CIO, 2002), tables 1.3 and 1.7.

Four: DRIVING THE RUSTBUCKET

1. Harris Poll #57, October 1, 2003.
2. American Federation of Teachers, AFL-CIO.

Six: TEACHING BELL TO BELL

1. "Status of the American Public Schoolteacher, 2000–2001," National Education Association Research (Washington, D.C.: National Education Association, 2003), p. 39.

Eight: SO WHY DO THEY BOTHER?

1. Robert Drago et al., "New Estimates of Working Time for Elementary School Teachers," *Monthly Labor Review* (April 1999), p. 36.

NINE: CRISIS OF FAITH

1. David L. Henderson and Travis W. Henderson, "Texas Teachers, Moonlighting, and Morale" (biannual report since 1980; Huntsville, Texas, 1996).
2. Evren Esen, "Job Satisfaction Poll," Society for Human Resources Management and USAToday.com (December 2002), chart 19.

TEN: THEY LEFT—HERE'S WHY

1. "The Cost of Teacher Turnover," prepared for the Texas State Board of Education Certification by Texas Center for Educational Research, p. 1; SREB "2003 Study of Teacher Supply and Demand in Tennessee, p. 4; see "The Supply and Demand of Elementary School Teachers in the United States," ERIC Digests.
2. Richard Ingersoll, "High Turnover Plagues Schools," *USA Today,* August 15, 2002, p. 13A.
3. For a thorough analysis and explication of this data, see Richard Ingersoll's report for the Center for American Progress, "Why Do High-Poverty Schools Have Difficulty Staffing Their Classrooms with Qualified Teachers?" (www.americanprogress.org)

ELEVEN: "I DIDN'T WANT TO BE POOR"

1. Steve Farkas et al., "A Sense of Calling: Who Teaches and Why," *Public Agenda* (2000).
2. Ibid.
3. Ibid.

TWELVE: SUCCESS IN REFORM

1. Every five years, the raise is $2,000. This feature enables the scale to top out at $65,000 after twenty-four steps.
2. Public Agenda, "A Sense of Calling: Who Teaches and Why," 2000.

CONCLUSION: PAY NOW OR LATER

1. "Fiscal Year 2004 Education Budget Summary and Background Information" (U.S. Department of Education, February 3, 2003), Appendix 1: "Total Expenditures in Education in the U.S." (www.ed.gov/about/overview/budget/budget04/summary/edlite-appendix1.html). This figure includes only state and local funding and does not include federal funds and categorical funds. Numbers like these often beg for international comparisons. Available data compiled by the AFT sug-

gests that U.S. spending is about average relative to other economically advanced nations. The average spending often makes one wonder why U.S. academic performance does not compare favorably with that of European and Asian countries. There is no answer that lies in any simple fact. Education systems in other countries are simply very different from those in the United States; in Europe and Asia, public education is often centralized, and teachers are required to teach fewer classes than teachers in the United States. Though the job of a teacher is more demanding in some ways in the United States, compensation for teachers here is about average compared to other economically advanced nations.

2. Stephen Reder, "The State of Literacy in America: Estimates at State, Local and National Levels, National Institute for Literacy" (www .nifl.gov/reders/reder.htm, February 1998).

3. Bureau of Justice Statistics, U.S. Department of Justice (http://www .ojp.usdoj.gov/bjs).

4. "America's One Million Nonviolent Prisoners," Center of Juvenile and Criminal Justice (www.cjcj.org).

5. Caroline Wolf Harlow, "Education and Correctional Populations: A Bureau of Justice Special Report" (U.S. Department of Justice, January 2003).

6. Lawrence J. Schweinhart, "Benefits, Costs, and Explanation of the High/Scope Perry Preschool Program" (paper presented at the Meeting for Research in Child Development, Tampa, Florida, April 26, 2003), pp. 2–6.

7. Lynn A. Karoly et al, "Investing in Our Children: What We Know and Don't Know About the Costs and Benfits of Early Childhood Interventions" (RAND Corporation, 1998).

8. U.S. Bureau of Justice.

9. Eric A. Hanushek, "The Trade-Off Between Child Quantity and Quality," *Journal of Political Economy* (1992).

10. Boston Public Schools, "Restructuring High School," March 9, 1998, cited in Katy Haycock, "Closing the Achievement Gap," *Educational Leadership* (March 2001 58:6), pp. 6–11.

11. The Education Trust, "Good Teaching Matters: How We Can Close the Achievement Gap," *Thinking K–16* (1998, 3:2), pp. 3–4.

12. Greer Bautz, "Q and A with Richard Murnane and Frank Levy," HGSE News (www.gse.harvard.edu/news/features/murnane06012004 .html).

13. Sean Corcoran, William Evans, and Robert Schwab, "Changing Labor

Market Opportunities for Women and the Quality of Teachers 1957–1992," National Bureau of Economic Research Working Paper No. 9180, 2002. They measure cognitive ability based on rankings on standardized tests in math and verbal skills.

14. Caroline Hoxby and Andrew Leigh, "Pushed Away or Pulled Out? Explaining the Decline in Teacher Aptitude in the United States" (Harvard University, 2003).

INDEX

teacher salaries (*cont.*)
2–3. *See also* families and teacher salaries; home-ownership and teacher salaries; second jobs
teacher turnover, 2, 167–68. *See also* leaving teaching, reasons for
"teaching for understanding" curriculum model, 143–44
Tennessee, 7, 167
Texas, teacher turnover in, 167
Texas Center for Educational Research, 167
Thomas Jefferson High School, Denver, Colorado, 203
Thomas S. Wootton High School, Rockville, Maryland, 78, 309
Torres, Thania, 220
Travelute, Catherine, 118–19, 271, 316

unions: and administrator evaluations, 201–2; and Denver's ProComp system, 9, 197–98, 200–201; and early teacher salaries, 25; and Helena's Professional Compensation Alternative, 9, 235, 238–43, 259; membership in, and social costs of teaching, 89; as scapegoats for teaching-reform failure, 8–9. *See also* National Education Association (NEA); *names of individual unions*
United Federation of Teachers (UFT), 9
University of Pittsburgh Graduate School of Education, 12
University of Wisconsin's Center for Policy Research in Education, 233
U.S. Department of Housing and Urban Development, Teacher Next Door program, 270
USA Employment, 263–64

Vaughn Next Century Learning Center and pay-for-performance plan, 15, 196, 218–33, 256–57; base pay and bonuses, 221–24; Chan and the reinvention of Vaughn, 226–28; and the charter, 226–27; and classroom

atmosphere today, 218–21; and the community, 232–33; early challenges and problems at Vaughn, 218, 224–26, 256; and evaluations, 222–24, 228; and extracurricular activities, 222; funding for, 230–31, 257; and future plans, 232–33; how the program unfolded, 228–30; impact of, 231–33, 257; and new teacher applicants, 231–32; and parent participation, 227; program at a glance, 256–57; and school performance goals, 222; and specific performance objectives, 222–24; and starting salaries, 230, 257; and student achievement, 224, 231, 232; and student/teacher attendance, 222, 224; and teachers' improvement, 231
Vaughn Street School, Los Angeles, California, 225–26
Vedder, Richard, 5–6
VICA (Vocational Industrial Clubs of America), 151
Vickery Middle School, Cumming, Georgia, 175

Wallenberg High School, San Francisco, 28
Waller, Willard, 98
Warren Elementary School, Helena, Montana, 248
Werner, Todd, 173–74, 317
West Charlotte High School, Charlotte-Mecklenburg, North Carolina, 168, 311
Willett, Maggie, 210–11, 214–15, 216
Wissink, Becky, 16, 197, 200–201, 210, 217
Wofford, Jennifer, 20
Woodward, Les, 212
Wootton High School, Montgomery County, Maryland, 62, 115, 162, 309
workdays of teachers, 113–22, 123–39; and extra hours, 6, 113–14, 118; intense psychological environment